Romanticism and Modernity

ROMANTICISM AND MODERNITY

Conceptions of Art, Society and Politics in the Modern World

Editors

Shaswati Mazumdar • Claudia Wenner • Sharmistha Lahiri

ARYAN BOOKS INTERNATIONAL
New Delhi

ROMANTICISM AND MODERNITY

ISBN-81-7305-328-6

First Published in 2007 by:
ARYAN BOOKS INTERNATIONAL
Pooja Apartments, 4B, Ansari Road, New Delhi - 110 002 (India)
Tel.: 23287589, 23255799; Fax: 91-11-23270385
E-mail: aryanbooks@vsnl.com

in association with
DEPARTMENT OF GERMANIC AND ROMANCE STUDIES
University of Delhi, Delhi

Cover Illus.: *Chalk Cliffs on Rügen* by Caspar David Friedrich, 1818.

Computer Typeset and Printed in India at
ABI Prints & Publishing Co., New Delhi

Preface

Romanticism and Modernity brings together a collection of papers presented at the International Conference on the theme of 'The Romantic Response to Modernity' organized by the Department of Germanic and Romance Studies, University of Delhi.

The essays included in the volume provide analysis and interpretation of diverse literary works, artistic trends and philosophical perspectives that exemplify the ambivalent, often contradictory forms taken by the Romantic in different times and places: in different parts of Europe against an uneven trajectory of modernization, in the colonies against the backdrop of emerging nationalist movements, and in more recent times. The issue thus attempts to offer comparative perspectives not explored before.

We would like to thank colleagues and staff at the Department of Germanic and Romance Studies, University of Delhi, for having provided the kind of help necessary when compiling a collection of essays whose contributors reside in different parts of the world. Special thanks go to Javed Akhtar for helping us out with the typing and the formatting of the articles.

Editors

Contents

SHASWATI MAZUMDAR, CLAUDIA WENNER,
SHARMISTHA LAHIRI

Introduction

> Into the same rivers we descend and do not descend, we are and we are not.
>
> (Heraclitus, Fragment 49a)

> It is equally fatal for the mind to have a system and not to have one. One would probably have to decide to combine both.
>
> Friedrich Schlegel, Fragments

I

When we chose the theme "Romanticism and Modernity" for this volume, we were drawn among other things by an interest in the controversy around the relationship between the two concepts, a controversy focusing on the question of whether the Romantic was the antithesis of the modern. This controversy evoked particular interest since Romanticism was born so to say in a context of the onset of modernity, of a social order at once marked by the revolutionary but unfulfilled slogans of "Liberty, Equality, Fraternity" and the extreme disorientation of life engendered by the emerging capitalist society.

A variety of conceptions have been put forward for the counterposing of the two concepts "Romanticism" and "Modernity". The Romantic has been seen to be anti-Enlightenment, irrational, escapist, fleeing from the present into the past, and politically reactionary. The political and social conservatism exhibited by some of them has no doubt contributed to this approach. This conservatism took the form of the glorification of the past, particularly of the Middle Ages, support to reactionary feudal rulers and to chauvinist brands of nationalism. But, of course, this is not true for all the Romantics. For those who have seen the distinction between "Romanticism" and "Modernity" in positive terms, the Romantic seemed to provide a secluded haven against the levelling of identities in a modern, secularised world. The definition of the Romantic as the antithesis of the modern thus seems on the one hand to have some legitimacy but on the other to be contradicted by the Romantics themselves.

The controversy has perhaps been most virulent in Germany where, as one historian ironically remarked, the political ambiguity of the Romantic legacy has been sawn off by Nazi pedigree-hunters concerned to demonstrate that the shortest distance between (the German Romantic poet) Novalis and Hitler (or between Romanticism and Nazism) is a straight line. Such a connection of course explosively configures the idea that Romanticism gives expression to national individuality, an idea that has found takers both amongst ardent nationalists and amongst those who were horrified by the brutalities and terror of a chauvinist nationalism. Yet, while the Romantics were reacting to the problems of a modern social and political order, they defined these problems not in national but in universal terms.

Rethinking on the relationship between Romanticism and Modernity has focused largely on the Romantic aesthetic with its modern notions of language, of the separate imaginative sphere of the work of art, of its autonomy and open-endedness, of self-reflection[1] and irony, of a new consciousness of time and of radical experiments in form that undo or subvert the formal distinctions between genres. These modern notions seem to have found their first systematic articulation in the aesthetic theories of the Romantics. Novalis insisted that "a writer is only one who is enthused by language" [*ein Sprachbegeisterter*]. He rejected a merely representational notion of language: "All the superstition and error of all times and peoples and individuals rests upon the confusion of the *symbol* with what is symbolised – upon making them identical – upon the belief in true complete representation...." For Novalis, the peculiarity of language lies in the fact that "it only concerns itself with itself" and thereby "produces the most splendid and original truths":

> If one could only make people understand that with language it is as with mathematical formulae – They constitute their own world – They only play with themselves, express nothing but their wonderful nature, and this is why they are so expressive – precisely for this reason does the strange game of relations of things reflect itself in them.[2]

How does the shift take place from this open-ended, playful notion of language to one which is organically linked to a nation and finally to the idea of a *Volk* or community defining a nation, an idea that was so successfully used by the Nazis? While looking therefore at the concepts that define the modern aesthetic evolved by the Romantics, one has also to address the question as to how these concepts were metamorphosed into narrow, closed categories.

Based on their understanding of language and responding to a rapidly changing world, the Romantics sought through the conscious use of metaphors to destabilise the fixity of determinate propositions and to open up the finitude of the individual spheres of experience. It is in this metaphoric sense that one might look at the Romantic quest for other worlds, worlds distant in terms of time, space or everyday experience, the worlds of dreams, fairy tales, madness, exotic lands, past ages, worlds that evoke desire, longing, enchantment, but perhaps also fear, or horror. Swinging incessantly between the real and the fantastic, the known and the unknown, the familiar and the unfamiliar, the Romantics hoped to poeticise a world increasingly dominated by the narrow rationality of commercial interests and the provincial morality of the emerging bourgeois social order.[3] Curiously, these poetic metaphors of the unknown or unfamiliar often seem to have gone through a process in which they were removed from their poetic, metaphorical context and deployed as substantive descriptions. One could describe this process as a reification of metaphors.

The interest of the Romantics in the Middle Ages seems to be an area in which such a process of reification can be illustrated. Dissatisfied with the rationally defined, fixed norms of Greek antiquity, Novalis in an essay[4] written in 1799 constructed the metaphor of a golden age, of a Romanticised Middle Ages, of a harmonious Christian world, untouched by the schisms and alienation of the modern age, based on innocent trust, peace and love. Novalis was not interested in historical facts. The ideal projected into the past was a metaphor for envisioning a utopian model for a possible future in which the ideals of the French Revolution, of liberty, equality and fraternity, would find their fulfilment. Novalis saw in the rationality of the Enlightenment a means to distinguish between things, to shackle human beings to their egoistic particularity. In love he saw the potential for liberating them from their particularity and thus from the need to be ruled, since such a need would only exist where egoistic interests had to be controlled. As the historian E.J. Hobsbawm has pointed out: "Middle Ages, folk and noble savage were ideals firmly anchored in the past. Only revolution, the 'springtime of peoples', pointed exclusively to the future, and yet even the most utopian found it comforting to appeal to a precedent for the unprecedented."[5]

Moreover, the ideal of a golden age, of a primitive, pre-modern society was not particularly Romantic. Hobsbawm points out again: "The Primitive existed in every village; but he existed as an even more revolutionary concept in the assumed golden communistic age of the past, and as the free noble savage abroad ... From Rousseau, who held it up as the ideal of free social man, to the socialists, primitive society was a sort of model for utopia. Marx's triple divisions of history – primitive communism, class society, communism, on a higher level – echoes, though it also transforms, this tradition."[6]

In the hands of others including of fellow Romantics, however, and in affirmative response to the emerging German nationalist demands after the turn of the century, Novalis' poetic metaphor of a past golden age as a possible model for a future utopia found itself reified into a substantive description of the Middle Ages as the ideal past, and moreover no longer as a common ideal past, but specifically as the real past of the (Christian?) German nation.

The process of reification of poetic metaphors was one in which some Romantics wittingly or unwittingly contributed. It was also one in which the initial ideals of a free and open world republic were more and more discarded in favour of a community-based, closed concept of the nation. This process was further accelerated by the moving apart of the aesthetic and the political in post-Romantic discourse.

The reification of poetic metaphors lent itself to easy appropriation for purposes of legitimising the subsequent process of establishment of capitalism and the integrally linked colonisation of much of the non-European world. The function of these metaphors as an epistemological means to question the finitude of things and to destabilise "petrified relations"[7] increasingly gave way to their appropriation as narrow, sentimental terms into political and social discourse. Inevitably, this also resulted in the commodification of Romanticism.[8] The ambiguity inherent in the Romantic programme thus also led to a trivialisation of the Romantic aesthetic, although its positive legacy found its way into the profusion of modern artistic, literary and other cultural forms of the twentieth century.

The fact of the reification of Romantic poetic metaphors in political and social discourse may be one possible suggestion in trying to understand how a movement which sought to respond with modern ideas to the challenges of the modern age could come to be seen as the very antithesis of the modern. It needs to be noted, of course, that the emergence, influence and specific trajectories of the Romantic notions of art, society and politics reflected the peculiarities of the respective processes of political and social change in the different countries of Europe. Neither all the Romantics nor all the Romanticisms were alike. But common to the Romantic worldview despite other differences is its sense of the contradictions of the modern era, its critique of the bourgeois social and moral order, and its attempts to evolve a modern aesthetic that could give expression both to the emancipatory claims of the modern age and to the simultaneous experience of disillusionment and disenchantment, of loss, crisis and scepticism.

II SHIFTING CONCEPTIONS IN THE RECEPTION OF ROMANTICISM IN GERMANY

If we talk about Romanticism and modernity, it is interesting that we tend to see them as opposites even before we know which Romanticism and which modernity we are talking about and in which country. This might have to do with our everyday-usage of these words, a usage, however, that seems not so far away from that of scholars. There is a tendency to overlook the specific innovatory elements of this period and to stress nostalgia for the old order and even reactionary features. The German scholar Karl-Heinz Bohrer[9] who supports the thesis that aesthetic modernity - and modernity in general - begins around 1800 with Romantic prose, describes the tradition of its - modernity's - prevention. The vagueness of the term "Romanticism" allowed for its identification with contradictory notions such as historical teleological thinking on the one hand - as it can be found in the early Friedrich Schlegel – and a nature-piousness if not an irrationalism on the other hand, which, as a result of Schellings philosophy of nature, had its effect on the so called *Bildungsbürgertum* (the educated classes) where it appeared as a Romantic quietism responsible for a certain apolitical attitude. With the definition of Romanticism as historicism, and with the nineteenth century being characterised by historicism, Romanticism was seen as the main feature of German intellectual history (*Geistesgeschichte*), although the critical attitude towards Romanticism dominated intellectual and academic discussion far into the last third of the nineteenth century. But the reflexivity of the work of art as well as the notion of the fantastic - both crucial for Romantic consciousness - were persistently ignored for almost a century. Modernity in the sense of an awareness of contingency and of the accidental and the decaying - notions that were discovered by Romantic poetry and emphatically reflected and developed by Baudelaire, was thus prevented in the name of a modernism which meant political and scientific progress and which the systematic criticism of Romanticism held up against the Romantics' supposed obscurantism. But the positivistic-realistic discourse of the nineteenth century critics - mainly the intelligentsia in the period of the revolutionary upsurges between 1815 and 1848 - and the socio-psychological fact of the "Romantic mentality" of the educated classes had little to do with the Romantic poetics of the likes of Friedrich Schlegel, Novalis, Kleist or Brentano. Their poeticising of the world was a new principle of sensing possibilities (*Möglichkeitssinn*) against the reality principle, which had strong influences on modern literature and philosophy as we can see in the works of Musil, the Surrealists or the early Sartre.

In his book *The Destruction of Reason* which appeared in 1954, Georg Lukács takes the two theses mentioned above to support a third one. The equation of Romanticism and irrationalism as well as the thesis of Romanticism dominating the nineteenth century led to Lukács' (and Thomas Mann's) understanding of Romanticism as a predecessor of fascism and thus to an understanding that was very influential, so much in fact, that till today Romanticism is only acceptable in connection with its critical Enlightenment origins. Lukács' main target of attack is the "indefinite" and the "immediate knowledge". But the metaphors of "sudden" intuition referred to by Lukács are so common in modern literature, that they can only be seen as a prefascist mode if all non-realist modern literature is seen as part of a prefascist ideology. The debate between Lukács and Adorno made this very clear.

Eventually, after a long period of negative generalisation of Romanticism, early Romanticism was rehabilitated in the sixties and seventies. This rehabilitation was closely connected with the utopian movement of 1968 (Bohrer's term), although this movement was itself interpreted as a "Romantic relapse".[10] But for the rescuing of philosophical early Romanticism and its enlightenment tradition a price had to be paid: the price was a split off from late Romanticism and a blindness to the aesthetic structures of the fantastic and the imaginative. A second track of research saw early Romantic poetics in analogy to idealistic philosophy. Romanticism and especially early Romanticism was seen as a project serving the philosophy of history. With its literariness having to serve a utopian telos, vast parts of Romantic prose had to be ignored because of their catastrophic and discontinuous structure. It was only in the eighties and nineties that German Studies opened up to new approaches in the discussion of Romanticism, namely to literary theory (psychoanalysis, structural semiotics, discourse analysis and deconstruction). Although it is difficult to label and systematise these recent works of research, one can certainly say that they focus more on the literariness of the Romantic texts and their modes of functioning.

In 1968 the University of Massachusettes, Amherst, organised a conference on the subject *Das Nachleben der Romantik in der modernen deutschen Literatur* (the posthumous life of Romanticism in modern German Literature).[11] What is meant by *Nachleben* is only made clear in Theodore Ziolkowski's contribution on methodological questions: Apart from the fact that the word *Leben* (life) suggests that Romanticism is a living thing or being, the term is not self-explicatory. Ziolkowski defines it as a category which should not be confused with *Nachwirkung*, a term meaning pretty much the same thing, only with a more technical emphasis. By *Nachleben* Ziolkowski means a certain attitude of mind, a certain ideological content, which he calls typological Romanticism. It does not belong to any particular historical time and is defined by a list of criteria such as the belief in poetry and literature as epistemological means, the notion of nature as an organic unity in which the dualism of subject and object is abolished, and the belief that the literature that recognises and seizes this organic unity is a literature of myth and of symbol. *Nachwirken* (after-effects) on the other hand is restricted to the technical devices and aesthetic processes of Romanticism as a historical period. If we are dealing with *Nachwirken* the source can always be identified, says Ziolkowski, and he finds further differentiations such as *Umschreibung* (adaptation) for the modernisation of a subject matter (Ingeborg Bachmanns "Undine goes" would be one example. This is a short text about a mermaid whose figure is taken out of a fairy tale by the German Romantic Motte-Fouqué). Ziolkowski also talks about the *Übernahme* (adoption) of words, quotations, motives, or characters as we find them e.g. in Hesses *Morgenlandfahrt* (Journey to the East) where we meet Anselmus and the Archivarius Lindhurst, two characters from E.T.A. Hoffmann's tale *The Golden Pot* or in Thomas Mann's novel *The Magic Mountain* where Settembrini, one of the characters, talks with Novalis' words. Then there is *Nachahmung* (imitation) concerning the style and tone rather than the subject matter, a device close to parody and fake. And finally there is *Umgestaltung* (rearrangement) when the structure of a particular work of art is revived by means of analogy such as in Hermann Hesse's novel *Steppenwolf* with its two levels of reality, reminding us of E.T.A. Hoffmann's literary fairy tale *The Golden Pot*. Rather schematically Ziolkowski comes to the conclusion that there can be *Nachwirken* without *Nachleben*, such as in Peter Rühmkorf's parodistic poems, or *Nachleben* without *Nachwirken* as in Hermann Broch's novels, or there can be a synthesis of *Nachwirken* plus *Nachleben* as we find it in the so called Neo-Romantics such as Hermann Hesse, the early Hofmannsthal, the early Rilke, the early Thomas Mann. The additional "early" makes one think. For what exactly is Neo-Romanticism? It seems to be a term coined against the preceding epochs of Realism and Naturalism rather than in direct continuity with Romanticism. The trouble with Ziolkowski's differentiations is that they are rather deliberate. Order they create, but only until the next list of criteria comes along. Moreover, his contrasting of technical literary devices and ideological content seems too simplistic an understanding of the correlations of form and subject matter.

The Amherst conference dealt with a comparison of literary Romanticism and Modernism, i.e. with two specific historical periods of time or microepochs. But in order to characterise a microepoch, we must look for distinctions, programmatic differences, separations and exclusions, so that we tend to systematically overlook common features and isolate what is not so isolated after all. Little does it help to try and bring together again that which has been so thoroughly separated. Instead we have to change the paradigm, that is to say, the perspective, and take a broader view, looking for larger contexts and connections. This is what an international and interdisciplinary conference did at the University of Hildesheim in 1996, focusing on Aesthetic Modernity in Europe[12] i.e. on a period of time in which we still live and which began around 1800 with early Romanticism in Germany. The research done on this so called macroepoch is somewhat different from that of microepochs in that it looks at a subject over a longer period of time. Some of its interests are processes of development, such as the development of the notion of aesthetic autonomy since the late eighteenth century, the development of the aesthetics of the fragment from early Romanticism up to Derrida, the evolution of an aesthetics of ugliness since Friedrich Schlegel, or the development of experimental aesthetics from early Romanticism up to the language-experiments of contemporary literature. At the same time macroepoch research analyses the inner connections of synchronical opposites, and this seems a particularly interesting point. At first sight the acceleration of time for example is only the opposite of the longing for the past and for something permanent. But both phenomena can be seen as belonging together, as two contrary responses to the same basic problem of modernity: the faster it goes, the less time it has got - an experience which creates a longing for a different way of experiencing time. Other examples are the correlation of freedom and anxiety, aesthetic autonomy and social responsibility, fantasies of chaos and order, the experience of dissonance and the need for harmony, and the opposites of future-oriented thinking and historicising. One way of thinking already includes the impulse of its antithesis thus leading to a typical modern dynamic.

According to Silvio Vietta and Dirk Kemper, both editors of and contributors to the conference papers, there is a certain agreement about the constituting central function of Romanticism for Aesthetic Modernity. It consists not so much in single phenomena such as autonomy, subjectivity, or a new experience of time, but in the fact that Romanticism, while creating such central concepts and ways of experience, simultaneously reflects and gives form and a voice to the questionability and destructibility of these very concepts. (In a recent postscript to his essay of 1988 Karl Heinz Bohrer warns, however, against overtaxing Romanticism with a teleological approach that sees in it the beginnings of modernity, an entelechy that finds completion in infinity, to be admired as a project in nascent condition.[13])

From Romanticism onwards, aesthetic modernity thus constitutes itself as an epoch of sharp contradictions and of inner conflict and disunity. We are still part of this past, and this is why it is so difficult to define it. Giving up a conception of Romanticism that is purified of its contradictions means that we no longer need to think of modernity as a deRomanticised Romanticism, to use an expression by Hugo Friedrich who in his famous book *The Structure of Modern Poetry* in 1956 was one of the first scholars to call Romantic poetry modern rather than looking for its effects on Modernism. But giving up the notion of a 'Romantic' Romanticism means that we do not need to think of modernity only as a deRomanticised epoch.

III

The issue before us brings together contributions presented on the theme at a seminar organised by the Department of Germanic and Romance Studies in April 1999. These contributions focus on a variety of texts - artistic, philosophical, political - and their authors. They reflect the differences in perspective that any serious engagement with Romanticism inevitably entails. They also highlight differences in how Romanticism is defined, what are seen as its central constituting categories and which of these are felt to have relevance in our own time and place.

The issue begins with three contributions that bring into the discussion an analysis of Romantic responses in the context of colonialism, exemplifying also the importance of such a discussion even outside the parameters of time and place within which Romanticism initially emerged as a phenomenon. The question of the relationship between Romanticism and nationalism, albeit in the colonial context and therefore in opposition to colonialism, necessarily takes a central place.

Namwar Singh discusses the question of where to locate the beginnings of Indian Romanticism and argues emphatically against the widely prevalent view that associates it in the main with the twentieth century Hindi literary movement called 'Nai Kavita'. He suggests that Romanticism in India starts in the nineteenth century with Rabindranath Tagore in opposition to British colonial rule and long before the national struggle for independence had become a movement, though Romanticism itself became a movement at the time of the non-cooperation movement led by Gandhi. He also discusses the differences between Tagore and Gandhi in their mode of defining nationalism. While analysing the social and political context for the emergence of Indian Romanticism in its particular form, he points to its similarities and differences with German Romanticism.[14]

Tapan Basu introduces his piece by distinguishing between the specific forms of ideological ambivalence that were common to the European Romantics and their American counterparts of a few decades later. Common to both groups was a critique of a society in which human relationships were increasingly dominated by business interests. Basu argues that while this critique was marked by political conservatism in the case of the European Romantics, in the American case it took the form of a simultaneous enthusiasm for the possibilities opened up by the world of commerce and industry. Basu then undertakes a comparative reading of two texts, *Walden* by the American Romantic Henry David Thoreau and *Hind Swaraj*, a Critique of British Colonial Rule in India by Mohandas Karamchand Gandhi.

Dilip Loundo gives a comprehensive appraisal of the characteristic features of Romanticism in Brazil and links it up with the socio-historical background and the emerging process of the political transformation of the country. He refers to the works of novelist José de Alencar and poet Castro Alves in this context and identifies three main strains in Brazilian Romanticism: a Romanticisation of the Indian and African matrices of Brazilian identity, valorisation of the natural landscape, and the proposal of a national language. Loundo argues that it was an imperfect Romanticisation of Brazilian cultural identity, being superimposed by its Caucasian links, whereas the experiment with Brazilian Portuguese language was nominal. At any rate, Loundo observes, it was crucial for the development and consolidation of Brazilian cultural identity in the Modernist movement of the 1920s, which found expression in the works of Mario de Andrade and Oswaldo de Andrade.

After the foray into the colonial context, the issue looks at two major figures of the Romantic movement, the Russian poet Alexander Rushkin and the Italian poet Giacomo Leopardi.

In his readings of Alexander Pushkin's poetry, Abhai Maurya brings out the spirit of idealism and the revolutionary text in the verses, and the power and the depth of his sentiments, which celebrated, through poetry, the triumph of human spirit against 'a cruel age' of despotism. Maurya rejects Russian critic D. Blagoi's notion of a threefold division, or the three distinct moments in Pushkin's poetry and ideology, proceeding from one of least consciousness through one of affiliation with his own class of the aristocracy and gentry, and finally to the shifting of loyalties to the petty bourgeois philistines. Maurya argues forcefully, through textual analysis and documentary evidence, that Pushkin remained steadfast in the pursuance of the revolutionary ideal and his loyalty to the Decembrists' cause, which he articulated in the ingenious ways of poetry, addressing the compulsions of the moment in tsarist Russia. Maurya concludes with a parallel reading of the compositions of Derzhavin and Pushkin, sharing the same title, *The Monument*, and underlines Pushkin's deep sense of affiliation to the peoples' cause.

Sharmistha Lahiri posits the question of determining a historical and cultural contextualization of Italian poet Giacomo Leopardi's works within the principal cultural categories of the period, and underlines his independent profile in relation to the ideological specificities of Italian Romanticism. The essay ponders on some of the conceptual nuclei of his poetics, deriving from classical culture, not least theories of eighteenth-century philosophers and trends of European Romantic thought, but not identifiable with any single epistemic field. The author examines a selection of Leopardi's lyrical compositions from his volume of poems in the *Canti* with the purpose of showing how the defining elements of a modern poetic category came to be formed in these texts. The essay contends that Leopardi demonstrates traits of modernity in his anti-conformism vis-à-vis the dominant ideologies of his time, as also in his search for the inner links within the multiform and apparently oppositional structures of reality. Lahiri shows that Leopardi's use of metaphor is totally new. It "evokes" when it "narrates", and creates – as Paul Ricoeur would say – a surplus of meaning in the poem, "to reconstruct reality", in a modernist sense.

The next four pieces look at the influence of Romanticism on writers of a later age in England, Hungary and France.

In her piece on Forster's *Howard's End*, Lalita Subbu traces the elements of continuity and separation that mark the two contiguous movements of Romanticism and Modernity in Forster's work, and considers the choices lying before the Modernist writers who 'are looking back and ahead'. In this context, she addresses issues related to form, theme, theory and ideology, the question of genre transformation - from poetry and philosophy to fiction – in Forster's text. Subbu institutes a parallel between Forster and D.H. Lawrence, both caught between a Romantic nostalgia for the countryside on the one hand, and a radical awareness of a modern consciousness on the other, and compares Lawrence's heroines in *Women in Love* with those of Forster in *Howard's End*, the life of the emotions being valorised in both. While locating Forster's notions on Romantic ideology and modernism, she analyses the related English theoretical concerns on art and aesthetics and brings the contemporary perspectives of Raymond Williams and Roger Fry within the scope of discussion. Subbu argues that in *Howard's End* Forster concedes the limits of a Romantic perspective within the social realities of modernism, and 're-enacts' the Romantic dilemma between his poetic sense of individual happiness and its obstruction by the pressures of modernisation.

Krishnan Unni P. surveys the varying responses of English Romanticism to the challenges of Modernity and identifies the major areas of difference and discontinuity in the notions of time, space, and language, which developed in relation to the evolving questions of selfhood and subjectivity. Through his 'excursus' of the principal concerns of poetry and philosophy, from Wordsworth, Coleridge and Shelley to Virginia Woolf, from Kant and Hegel to Heidegger, to Paul de Man, Raymond Williams, Deleuze and Guattari, the author traces a radical breach from Romantic notions, for example, private space, seclusion, or retrospective past, marking the evolution of a language of conscious and exemplary subjectivity, which would unfold consciousness.

Margit Köves introduces the East European chapter in the story, discussing the question of a dialogue between Romanticism and Modernity. She highlights, in this regard, the creation of the collective subject of the nation in Eastern Europe, as against the emphasis on the individual subject in Romanticism in Western Europe. A variant strain is identified in Hungary, which attempted to reformulate in aesthetics the relationship between the individual, the community, and the universe. Köves examines a collection of texts from Hungarian literature, namely, an acoustic poem by Ákos Szilágyi, the 'grotesque' in the short stories of István Örkény, along with some references to Hungarian 'concept art', alternative theatre, and the films of Miklós Jancsó of the 1960s, to show how literature and art merged boundaries, leading to the break-up and new fusion of genres, similar in aim to the Romantics in the nineteenth century. Köves's study shows how these new art forms transcended the established notions of subject, object, time, experience and reception. While the essay traces the elements in which these new trends corresponded to Romantic sensibilities, it underlines with precision the areas of divergence between the traditional inward-looking subject and the new subject "engaged in an open, sensual world of reality and different levels of consciousness".

In a related vein, Dominique de Gasquet examines the construction of "the ball scene" in various texts of French literature of the nineteenth and twentieth centuries, to explore a new consciousness of time unfolding within the cultural ambit of Romanticism and Modernity. She views "the scene of the ball" as a time-space, the typical Bakhtinian 'chronotope', and analyses two nineteenth century texts, *Spirite* of Théophile Gautier and *La Fanfarlo* of Baudelaire, along with two twentieth century texts, *Le Ravissement de Lol V. Stein* of Marguerite Duras and Yukio Mishima's *Sotoba Komachi*, engaging in a comparative case-study of the changing shades in the representation of time and space. De Gasquet analyses the close interrelationship between dance and literature in these texts, each indicative of the socio-cultural context of the period, and observes that dance escapes real time in Duras, entering into imagination as in a fairy-tale, indicating an aspect of "a modern revolution, of a new consciousness of time".

The social ambivalence inherent in the Romantic vision had specific consequences for emerging Jewish identity. The formation of the historical consciousness of Jewish identity in Germany in the nineteenth century and the interactive process vis-à-vis German Romanticism is brought into focus by Kavita Bhatia. The author considers the situation of social and cultural ferment obtaining in Germany in the eighteenth and nineteenth centuries and studies the question of Jewish identity against the backdrop of the life and salons of Rahel Varnhagen in Berlin, reflecting on the twin impulses of emancipation and assimilation, which characterised the evolution of Jewish cultural consciousness at the turn of the nineteenth century.

Coming to the sphere of European art, Virginia Nieto-Sandoval Millán analyses art movements in the period of Romanticism and identifies two central concepts, 'nature' and 'fear', which formed the leitmotif in artistic expressions across different countries. She notes a pre-eminence of landscapes in the paintings of the eighteenth century, and the replacement of the characteristic classical ruins by Romantic and Gothic architecture in the landscape. The author explains 'Imaginary Prisons' of 1720 by the Italian artist Giovanni Battista Piranesi as a "prelude to Romanticism", with the agonising prisons symbolising the despotism of Neo-classicist art. Millán explores the aesthetic categories in terms such as 'sublime' and 'picturesque' that recur in Romantic portrayal of nature and refers, in this connection, to German painter Caspar David Friedrich's reassertion of the Nordic landscape, British painter Joseph Turner's water colours and the theme of the 'industrial society' in the Great Western Railway, and the 'picturesque' and the sensational in the play of light and shadow in the works of John Constable. While in the nineteenth century nature comes alive in the creations of the Romantic artists, it also appears as a terrifying monster, as Millán underlines, above all in the various paintings of the Spanish artist Francisco Goya, for example, in Los Caprichos. She traces the development of the thematic of fear in other European artists, for instance, in the works of the Swiss painter Henry Fuesli, the creator of an iconography of the irrational, and in the prophetic force emanating in the paintings of the visionary English artist, William Blake.

The two concluding pieces focus on philosophical questions, the first looking at elements akin to the Romantics in the work of the leading Enlightenment philosopher Immanuel Kant and the second on the more contemporary and apparently dissimilar writings of Paul de Man and Jürgen Habermas. On the philosophical underpinnings of Romanticism, Rekha Basu in her essay on 'Kant and the Limits of Rationality', offers a reading of the *Groundwork of the Metaphysics of Morals*, and indicates the dual significance in Kant's rationality, focusing on his division between 'pure' reason and 'practical' reason. Thus, notwithstanding his firm adherence to the Enlightenment ideal, Kant also showed an awareness of the limits of reason, a perception, which was re-appropriated by Romanticism. In Kant's notion of the dynamic moral subject, intrinsically associated with social obligations, Basu detects the element which captured Romantic imagination. She argues that while Kant resolves not to use experience in his position on the metaphysics of morals, he occasionally resorts to explicitly empirical premises and "regresses to experience", leading to traditions post-Kant, and development of ideas which would address themselves to the "antecedent conditions of moral choice", presupposing a moral agent, "which is not truncated but feeling, emoting, and ratiocinating as well".

Continuing the enquiry in the sphere of philosophy, the focus turns on Modernity in the concluding essay by Kathleen Kerr. Here, the author addresses the question of Modernity through a comparative analysis of the postulates of the social theorist and philosopher, Jürgen Habermas, and the literary critic, Paul de Man. Kerr compares Habermas's view of Modernity as "an unfinished project" with Paul de Man's view of it as "a concept at odds with history". Whereas Habermas' concern is with theorising a unifying context, a public sphere capable of continuing the Enlightenment project, de Man's concern is to contextualise resistance to unity, to analyse the disruptive function of literariness ("the use of language that foregrounds the rhetorical over the grammatical and logical function"). The central point in her essay is the theme of doubling in the concept of Modernity – divided between its "rationalising", "evolutionary" and progressive image, and its "course of conflict with history", and the break with the past. In her study, Kerr attempts to overcome the oft-repeated dissimilarities between Habermas's critical theory and de Man's critico-linguistics on the notion of philosophy and its aim, and tries to approach a "potentially productive critical engagement" between their positions on the question of Modernity.

NOTES AND REFERENCES

1. "Reflective thinking won its special systematic importance for Romanticism by virtue of that limitless capacity by which it makes every prior reflection into the object of a subsequent reflection." Walter Benjamin, 'The Concept of Criticism in German Romanticism' in *Selected Writings, 1913-1926*, Vol. 1, eds. Marcus Bullock and Michael W. Jennings. Cambridge (Massachusetts) & London 1996, p. 123.
2. Novalis, *Monologue*, 1798. Paul de Man in an essay on the 'Intentional Structure of the Romantic Image' draws attention to the shifting "importance of the image as a dimension of poetic language" and calls the Romantics "the first modern writers to have put into question, in the language of poetry, the ontological priority of the sensory object". In conclusion he says: "We are only beginning to understand how this oscillation in the status of the image is linked to the crisis that leaves the poetry of today under a steady threat of extinction, although, on the other hand, it remains the depository of hopes that no other activity of the mind seems able to offer" in *The Rhetoric of Romanticism*, New York 1984, pp. 1-17.
3. "As thinkers within the terms of reference laid down by the economists and physicists, the poets were outclassed, but they saw not only more deeply but also sometimes more clearly. Few men saw the social earthquake caused by machine and factory earlier than William Blake in the 1790s ..." E.J. Hobsbawm, *The Age of Revolution 1789-1848*, London 1962, p. 318.
4. Novalis, *Die Christenheit oder Europa*, 1799.
5. E.J. Hobsbawm, *op. cit.*, pp. 322-323.

6. *Ibid.*, p. 322.
7. "These petrified relations must be forced to dance by singing to them their own melody." Karl Marx, *Die Frühschriften*. ed. Siegfried Landshut, Stuttgart 1953, p. 311.
8. "Romanticism too is a commodity here. It appears only as content, not as form." Bertolt Brecht, Anmerkungen zur Oper *Aufstieg und Fall der Stadt Mahagonny* in *Schriften. Über Theater*. Berlin 1977, p. 111.
9. Karl Heinz Bohrer, 'Die Modernität der Romantik. Zur Tradition ihrer Verhinderung' in *Merkur* 3, 1988, pp. 179-198.
10. Cf. Richard Löwenthal, *Romantischer Rückfall*. Stuttgart 1970.
11. Wolfgang Paulsen (ed.), *Das Nachleben der Romantik in der modernen deutschen Literatur: Die Vorträge des zweiten Kolloquiums in Amherst/ Mass*. Heidelberg 1969.
12. Silvio Vietta/Dirk Kemper (eds.), *Ästhetische Moderne in Europa: Grundzüge und Problemzusammenhänge seit der Romantik*. München 1997.
13. Karl-Heinz Bohrer in a postscript in J.Weiss and U. Helduser (ed.), *Die Modernität der Romantik: Zur Wiederkehr des Ungleichen*. Kassel 1999, pp. 79-81. The warning is certainly justified, although not all the examples that Bohrer cites in support of his argument are necessarily self-evident: For instance, he interprets the category of the fantastic as a new style that in principle abandons the category of the subject and its conceptual classification, whereas Vietta sees E.T.A. Hoffmann and his use of the fantastic precisely as a literary experiment in the self-exploration of subjectivity. (Silvio Vietta: "Die Welt als Konstrukt der Einbildungskraft: Deutsche Romantik und Aesthetische Moderne." NZZ 29/30.7.2000, Nr. 175).
14. The piece by Namwar Singh is a translation from the recording of his talk presented at the seminar. We have deliberately maintained the style in which it was delivered.

NAMWAR SINGH

Colonial Romanticism and the Challenges of Modernity

I am happy that the Department of Germanic & Romance Studies has started a debate on Romanticism in the present context. I wish to draw your attention to the fact that the form in which the debate on modernity is taking place in this country, namely a debate on modernity within the framework of postmodernism, - most participants in the debate are people concerned with social issues, intellectuals from the fields of political science, sociology, philosophy - it is surprising that Romanticism has no place in it.

Recently I saw Javed Alam's book *India: Living with Modernity*, a very good book by a Marxist critic. It focuses on Bankim[1] in great detail, Gandhi too is included, but there is no mention of Rabindranath Tagore and no mention of Romanticism in the entire debate on modernity. The fact is that in the mental world of the intellectuals of today, Romanticism has no place in modernity.

I mention this while recalling that I started a journal called *Alochana* in 1966 and the third issue of the journal, which came out in October-December 1966, contained a discussion on the Romantic versus the Modern. 1966, it may be recalled, was a time when student and youth movements had emerged, the Naxalabari movement had begun and in the field of poetry the 'Nai Kavita', in the tradition of the modernist poetry of Eliot and Pound, had more or less come to an end. In that context there was a discussion on the Romantic versus the Modern and I got Ram Vilas Sharma[2] to begin it. I chose Ram Vilas Sharma because he was one of the poets included in the first collection of modernist poetry, *Tarsaptak*, which came out in 1944 and was edited by Agyeya.[3] Ram Vilas Sharma had also been a professor of English and was a Marxist critic. This discussion on "Romanticism versus Modernism" took place in 1966. The participants included Murli Manhorar Prasad Singh, who is present here, and whose contribution was published. Many of those who participated perhaps may not be known, Girja Kumar Mathur who was a poet of *Tarsaptak*, Bharat Bhushan Aggarwal, Srikant Verma. I will not go into the details of what was established in that discussion but only refer to it.

Before that there was a discussion in 1962 in the *New Left Review* (Numbers 16, 17 & 18). This discussion included a piece by Stanley Mitchell,[4] the same Stanley Mitchell who edited a book of writings by Walter Benjamin titled *Understanding Brecht*. In that entire discussion it appears that amongst the English intellectuals too there was a new thinking about and interest in Romanticism.

When the issue of *Alochana* appeared in 1966 there was a new political atmosphere. Non-Congress governments had taken office in the states, the Fourth General Elections had been held, and for the first time a change had taken place. This was the post-Nehru era and the kinds of passions that moved the youth are exemplified to some extent in the Naxalbari movement as also in what was happening in poetry and literature. Two major events should also be remembered: the India-China border conflict and the India-Pakistan war. Nationalism of the aggressive kind that one sees today had just entered the political stage with the inclusion of the Jan Sangh in some of the coalition governments.

This was the political milieu in which what we call Modernism had more or less come to an end in the sphere of literature. In this context we were thinking of alternatives or of our literary heritage, of older traditions. This is why I am happy that once again there is a discussion on Romanticism in the context of the debate on modernity. Is there or can there be something called Romantic Modernism, what is the place of Romanticism in the many versions of Modernism, whether Romanticism can have anything to do with Modernism, that is what I wish to discuss.

In the debate on modernity our intellectuals have brought the nineteenth century and the pre-independence twentieth century into the discussion to quite an extent - Raja Ram Mohan Roy, Bankim, Iqbal,[5] that entire movement, Gandhi. It is surprising that while all this is part of the debate on modernity, the spheres of culture and literature are more or less completely missing. This needs to be underlined since the question arises whether the entire debate on modernity only refers to the European context or whether India too has a place in it.

This modernity is greatly under attack today. There is an anti-modernity wave. Is this wave also linked to an anti-Romanticism or not, this is the question that interests me and is the point of reference for what follows.

It appears today that we seem to assume many things to be in the singular as if the differences between the singular and the plural had been erased. Modernity is treated as a singular concept and so too is Romanticism. We seem to have frozen both the concepts, as if Romanticism were here and modernity there, and all discussions seem to take place in this framework. That they can be plural, that both modernity and Romanticism are in fact plural, is a fact that is entirely overlooked. The question that arises is whether the Romantic is modern, whether it was modern. Is it possible for us to reestablish our links with this heritage and to consider what role it might have in the discussion underway.

In this regard I would like to draw your attention to a third phase of the debate. In 1985 Marshall Berman published his well known book *All That Is Solid Melts Into Air*.[6] The book took a phrase from Marx to focus on modernity and modernism. It was once again the *New Left Review* that drew attention to this book and Perry Anderson then wrote an article called *Modernity and Revolution*.[7] That modernity and revolution can have any relationship to each other is not reflected at all in the debates in India that I have referred to. A very sophisticated, completely abstract philosophical discourse characterises these debates.

The debate on modernity has several aspects that should, but unfortunately do not, find a place in the debates in this country. Perhaps the discussions initiated by the Department of Germanic & Romance Studies will throw some light on the area. I would like to raise certain questions. I would like to underline particularly that whenever the Romantic Movement is referred to in India - in Indian literature there is no one Romanticism, just as in European literature there is no one Romanticism. There is Romanticism in Urdu, Punjabi, Bengali, Hindi, Marathi, or in Malayalam. It is correct that there was one common Indian context which we call colonialism. Some things were certainly common but there were differences related to the local limitations and historical development. But there is one person who represents almost all of Indian Romanticism, who influenced or inspired all of Indian Romanticism, and that is Rabindranath Tagore. I wish particularly to refer to him, his theoretical positions and his literary work.

Why is this necessary? The intellectuals of Bengal are known for their Bengali chauvinism. But they themselves - whether it is Partha Chatterjee or Ashis Nandy, who has also just written a book on Tagore in the context of nationalism, - do not allow Rabindranath Tagore to enter anywhere into the discussions on modernity.

On Bankim there is a complete industry that has developed and a university has been established. Suddenly Bankim has become very popular even for the Bharatiya Janata Party and for those intellectuals too who think of themselves as more sophisticated than the Bharatiya Janata Party. That is why I particularly wish to refer to Rabindranath Tagore. Just as any discussion of Romanticism, of Romanticism at a world level, is incomplete without Shelley and similarly incomplete without Pushkin, it is also incomplete without Rabindranath Tagore.

As far as the two terms "Romanticism" and "modernity" are concerned, the greatest difficulties are associated with the terms "modernity" and "modernism". Perry Anderson's argument was valid when he called modernity the emptiest cultural category. The gothic is clearly defined and so are the baroque, classicism, mannerism; even Romanticism is quite well defined despite all its diversity. In comparison, modernity is the emptiest category into which any meaning can be filled. That is why "modernity" and "modern" are interpreted in whatever way one wants. How were "modern", "modernism", "modernity" understood here? This is what I would like to talk about.

When Rabindranath Tagore started to write poetry, it was still the nineteenth century. Let me clarify that, in the Indian context, Romanticism is commonly considered a twentieth century phenomenon and in Hindi literature Romanticism is associated with the period from 1920 to 1936-38, or the period of the freedom struggle which started in the main with Gandhi's *satyagraha*. To set the historical record straight, if you keep Rabindranath Tagore in mind then Romanticism had already started in India in the last decades of the nineteenth century. Romanticism begins with all the poems of that period by Rabindranath Tagore. The first poem, *Nirjharer Swapna Bhanga*, was written in 1882, a famous poem which appeared in the book *Prabhat Sangeet*[8] - please note, *Prabhat Sangeet* (Morning Songs). Many people think that the sun has just risen when we open our eyes. So, in many Indian languages the sun of Romanticism is considered to have risen around 1920 with the arrival of Gandhi. For Rabindranath Tagore *Prabhat Sangeet* took place in the twentieth century around 1882. At that time Gandhi was nowhere close to India. Lokmanya Tilak was also not around. In *Prabhat Sangeet*, in the poem *Nirjharer Swapna Bhanga*, the call for freedom is heard for the first time in the words "bhang, bhang, bhang kara" (break, break, break the prison).

In Romanticism, in Romantic imagery, there are frequent images of twilight. The open sun cannot be Romantic and even the complete blackness of night cannot be Romantic. Partly dark, partly light, whether it is the twilight of dusk or dawn, this is considered Romantic. Those who know nothing else of Romanticism recognise it by these twilight images. In *Prabhat Sangeet* these twilight images of course appear for the first time. The collection is full of these images and there are so many poems on evening. *Duhsamaye* (dark times) is the name of a well known poem with which it starts. Romanticism is also known for something else. We talk of the flight of imagination, for imagination is central to Romantic images. Imagination and Romanticism are very closely linked. In fact, a book of Rabindranath's poetry bears the title *Kalpana* (imagination). This book came out in the nineteenth century, around 1883 and includes his famous poem 'Sonar Tari' or the golden boat. The boat is also such a Romantic image that is found in Romantic poetry all over the world, as a drunken boat.

I would therefore like to reiterate that while one can discuss whether Romanticism is modern or not, in India Romanticism began in the last decade of the nineteenth century and not at the beginning of the twentieth century or in its second decade. I say the last decade of the nineteenth century because if we look at the England of that time with which we were linked, what was the state of Romanticism in that England? The death of the Romantic poet Wordsworth must have taken place around that time or a little before that. Tennyson was the poet laureate and it was the end, the evening of Romanticism. The era of the great Romantics, which starts with Blake and includes Shelley, Keats, Byron, was over. All of them were dead. Though people said that the sun never sets in the British empire, but that must have been some other sun. When the sun of Romanticism was setting or had set in England, it was rising in India. These two factors need to be kept in mind.

When Romanticism was at an end in England, Tennyson was the poet laureate. His influence was considered to be widespread. Even in India the readers of the *Golden Treasury* had read Tennyson's poem 'In Memoriam'. At such a time a person like Rabindranath Tagore is born in a colony of England and writes a poem like 'bhang, bhang, bhang kara' which reminds one of Shelley. It does not remind us of Tennyson, nor even of the later Wordsworth period. This is one thing that I would like to mention. The other thing that I wish to say in regard to Rabindranath is that he wrote an essay on W.B. Yeats with 'Bangabda' mentioned at the end. Bangabda is the Bengali Year 1310, calculated according to the harvest, and by adding 600 we get the Christian year. The essay entitled 'Kavi Yeats' (the poet Yeats) was therefore written at the beginning of the twentieth century. Rabindranath never wrote any essay on T.S. Eliot, though he had read him and referred to him in several places. People might say that he wrote on Yeats because Yeats got him the Nobel Prize or perhaps also because Yeats wrote a poem on *Gitanjali*. But this is not the reason for his writing an essay on Yeats and not on Eliot. Why did he write on Yeats?

The Eliot-Yeats controversy, about who was the greater of these modern poets, started in India after a long time at the Delhi University. If I remember correctly, Pratipal Chand Rajan, who had become an admirer of Yeats and written a book on him, was a participant

Rabindranath wrote his essay on Yeats at a time when Eliot was considered the greater of the modernist poets. If you look at the essay, it focuses on the issue of Ireland and the Irish freedom struggle in which Marx and Engels were also keenly interested. In India too there was great interest in Ireland during the independence movement. And if one looks at the journals of that time, then one can see how much was written about the heroes of the Irish freedom struggle. Rabindranath wrote that Yeats' poetry was an expression of the mental independence of the Irish, of their fight for independence against England, a country that had subjected Ireland to oppression and servitude. Yeats had used the legends and myths of Ireland - some of them may even be considered superstition - but Yeats had used all this to create a poetry which no other poet in English had done and Rabindranath called this poetry modern. It is modern poetry because in a colony such as Ireland it reflects the aspirations of the Irish people for freedom, for freedom of expression. At a time when the scope for political struggle was narrow, there was a cultural revolt and poetry took its place as the medium of this revolt. Yeats gives expression to the soul of Ireland through his poetry, his art. That is why Rabindranath called him modern. And he said this with great sorrow. About English poetry of the period of the early Yeats, before he wrote the poem 'Tower', Rabindranath wrote: "I have derived great pleasure from old English literature. It not only gave me aesthetic pleasure but also enlightenment. But today I feel the impenetrability of a closed Europe, and particularly in modern English literature." This English literature, he wrote, was narrow-minded, it was conservative. At a time when Eliot's poetry was seen as an expression of revolt and revolution, in Rabindranath's eyes this poetry was conservative, it was narrow-minded, and Eliot was a poet of liberalism. This is the opinion that Rabindranath held at the end of the nineteenth and beginning of the twentieth century about the English poetry which was called modernist. He considered it narrow-minded. In regard to W.B. Yeats he uses the term *swadeshikta* (nationalism), not in the sense of Murli Manohar Joshi but in the sense of Gandhi. For Rabindranath, Yeats expressed the Irish nation and nationalism with its entire traditions from antiquity, with its myths, legends, folklore, its entire culture. It is for this reason that Rabindranath considers him modern.

From here on Rabindranath differentiates between modernism and modernity. Thus, Romanticism in India distinguished between modernism and modernity from the very beginning. In fact, it distinguished between two kinds of modernism - the modernism of the Irish poet W.B. Yeats and the modernism of the America returned English poet T.S. Eliot.

Rabindranath writes that when reading W.B. Yeats he is reminded of his own country, his own independence and his own struggle. I mention this because India at a certain stage saw a relationship between itself and Ireland. Today, when this discussion on Romanticism is being initiated by the Department of Germanic & Romance Studies, I also see a relationship in some respects to German Romanticism.

Properly speaking, Romantic philosophy, or the philosophy that emerged as part of the Romantic movement, found its strongest articulation in Germany. This is found not only in the Schlegel brothers but also in Kant and Hegel, and, if I may say so, some reflection of this Romanticism, even if in a critical form, is also found in Karl Marx. As Marshall Berman's book *All That Is Solid Melts Into Air* demonstrates, modernity is also related to modernisation and if modernisation has anything to do with capitalism then the person who wrote *Das Kapital* and tried to engage with capitalism is surely also in a certain sense a part of that modernity. Romantic philosophy also finds reflection in a poet like Heine, in Schiller and even in Goethe to some extent. But in what way is German Romanticism at the end of the eighteenth and beginning of the nineteenth century related to Romanticism in India?

The Romantic movement began in Germany at a time when the revolution had already taken place in France and Napoleon had defeated Germany. Germany was not a colony but within Europe it was a dark age for Germany. Marx and Engels have also written about it. On the one hand the revolution had taken place in France and on the other hand Germany was in darkness. It is in this context that it was said that the owl of Minerva spreads its wings only in darkness. In this German backwardness the roots of feudalism were still strong and capitalism and the process of industrialisation had not developed to the same extent as in England and France, though this was happening in the Netherlands. In such a backward Germany, as Madame de Staël wrote, "the Germans engaged in politics through aesthetics since they had neither space nor possibility to directly involve themselves in politics". Kant and Hegel were not involved in politics, their preoccupation was aesthetics. Schlegel, Schiller and Goethe too engaged in politics only through aesthetics.

In India too at the end of the nineteenth century and at the beginning of the twentieth century the scope for doing politics was restricted to forming the Indian National Congress, meeting once a year, preparing a petition of demands and submitting it to the Viceroy. No big movement was taking place in India and feudalism was still in place. In fact, after the uprising of 1857, the British, instead of doing away with feudalism, reestablished those very princes who had been in the forefront of the 1857 uprising. The landlord system was reestablished by Lord Cornwallis, the rule of the Nawabs continued in Bengal and a new type of landlord system (*zamindari*) was established. Even after they had defeated all the Indian princely states, one after the other, more than half of India remained feudal. In the form of the princely states and through the new *zamindari* system in the rest of India, the landlord class had more or less reached a pinnacle of power. The situation in this feudal India, where the intelligentsia was weak, was somewhat similar to that of Germany of the eighteenth century, though the French Revolution had taken place in its neighborhood. The state of the German intellectuals of that time may be comparable to that of the Indian intelligentsia amongst whom the majority was from Bengal. This was because with the Bengal Renaissance consciousness had grown more in Bengal than anywhere else.

The biggest irony of the German intellectuals was the fact that they could neither accept the old feudalism nor the French Revolution as an alternative. They could accept neither the bourgeois system nor feudalism. Mixing the bourgeois and the feudal produced a strange new phenomenon. But what was most important was the fact that they could not accept the challenges thrown up by the French Revolution. During this period a special type of German Romanticism was born which started its political struggle through aesthetic struggle. Therefore all its quandaries were similar to those of the early Rabindranath Tagore at the time of writing *Sonar Tari*: *Niruddeshya yatra kothaye aamake niye jabe re - swapna sundari*? (Where will this journey with an unknown destination take me - oh beautiful dream?) The journey had to have an unknown destination because far and wide the end of the colonial domination was not in sight. There was no alternative.

The birth of Romanticism took place at such a juncture which Perry Anderson has also tried to describe through the three arguments in his article. The condition of England during Shelley's age was somewhat different and better than that of Germany. It had a semi-aristocratic, semi-industrialised capitalism and a labour movement that was emerging but was non-resurgent. No big labour movement was to be seen those days. English Romanticism was born in such an atmosphere. German Romanticism was born in conditions worse than this. If you look at other parts of the world, the December Revolution had been crushed in 1812 when Pushkin emerged during Russian Romanticism. It was a time of Czarist rule. In spite of all the campaigns conducted by Peter the Great capitalism had not made much progress in Russia and was far behind that of even Germany. Thus Romanticism is born in a semi-feudal, semi-capitalist context in which the working class is very weak and no organised struggle of the common people has taken place. This is how it started in many countries. In India, while Rabindranath Tagore also starts writing in this context, a new element is added to the movement which separates Indian Romanticism from German and from English Romanticism. And if at all there is any resemblance, then it is with Russian Romanticism, because of the common factor of peasant revolt.

In the debate on modernity we talk about the Bengal Renaissance, we talk about the Indian Renaissance, but in all this development we forget that before India was ruled by the British, from the time before they arrived in India, i.e. from 1770 till 1880, there were so many spontaneous peasant revolts, the last and biggest of which was in Pabna. If we look at the background to those peasant revolts, we see that their climax was reached in Chauri Chaura in 1920 during the non-cooperation movement led by Gandhi. Romanticism may have been started by Rabindranath in the nineteenth century itself, but it became in the true sense a movement, an all India phenomenon - in Hindi, Bengali, Marathi, Gujarati, Malayalam, Assamese, Oriya, in fact in all these languages -, during the non-cooperation movement. By that time it was not merely Romanticism. The non-cooperation movement took place at a time when India was a colony and it was perhaps the first country amongst the colonies where people started such a massive movement. Chauri Chaura, to which peasants came in such large numbers, is the symbol of that protest.

Thus this is the period when the Romantic movement becomes directly political. It was not just an aesthetic substitute as it was in Germany. That is the reason why the Romantic movement had a longer life in India. Starting from 1880 it lasted until 1940. It lasted therefore for sixty years and not just for twenty years. Rabindranath died in 1941. In the period of sixty years from 1880 till 1941 the Romantic movement became political and the political shape it took shows the limits and internal conflicts of Romanticism.

1921 is the year in which the non-cooperation movement was withdrawn. In the same year an extraordinary historical controversy arose. Rabindranath Tagore gave a lecture at the University Institute in Calcutta with the title 'Call of Truth' in English and *Satyer Ahwaan* in Bengali. That was the time when foreign-made clothes were being burnt and they were being burnt at a call from Gandhi. Rabindranath was not in favour of this. Gandhi on the one hand burnt the foreign-made clothes and on the other hand, by selecting the *charkha* (spinning wheel) as a symbol, he started a movement. Rabindranath wrote his article *Satyer Ahwaan* in 1921 and Gandhi gave a reply two months in the October issue of the journal *Young India*. I would like to give you a glimpse of both.

The Rabindranath, whom Gandhi addressed as 'Gurudev', who had already written *Gora* in 1910, who had taken part in the *Swadeshi Andolan* (national movement) during the Banga Bhanga movement[9] (1905), and who played an important and active role in the initial development of the national movement, the Rabindranath who was an activist and had also many written poems - that Rabindranath also writes on nationalism and calls it is a most dangerous thing. And for him it was not a matter limited to books alone. He had himself experienced the national frenzy at the time of the burning of foreign-made clothes. It was against this national frenzy that he wrote the article *Satyer Ahwaan* (Call of Truth). It is a long article and the English translation is also easily available. Rabindranath says in the article:

> Today, at the dawn of the awakening of universal consciousness, if in our national struggle this universal voice is missing, then it will only reveal our poverty. I do not say that we should leave aside the tasks related to the proposed purpose, but when the early morning bird awakens, its awakening is not merely for the purpose of looking for food. Its two untiring wings accept the call of the sky. The joy of seeing the light makes him burst out into song. The consciousness of the universal man of today has called out to our consciousness.

Rabindranath talks about universalism in this article. We should not forget that the act of burning foreign-made clothes represented a latent national arrogance, a kind of chauvinism. Rabindranath sees this chauvinism in the burning fire. And in front of this blazing fire he said that Romanticism has both aspects. If Romanticism is a movement for national freedom, then it also accepts the universalism of the Enlightenment. If you emphasise only one side of Romanticism you will see that all those who talk about Hindutva will become Romantics.

They will be accepted too. Romanticism means a national struggle, a national struggle for freedom. But the Enlightenment, which talked about universalism in the name of reason, is also present in Romanticism. Rabindranath had both these aspects in him. And where he saw distortions in either of them, he thought it necessary to raise his voice. And this Rabindranath did in 1921, - yes, in 1921, when the non-cooperation movement and the boycott were at their peak. This was the poet who had refused the knighthood in 1919. You cannot therefore doubt his intention. You cannot suggest that he did it to please the British. On the one hand he declined the knighthood and on the other hand he objected to the latent chauvinism in Gandhi's call to burn foreign-made clothes. And Rabindranath called it *Satyer Ahwaan*, the 'Call of Truth'. Gandhi could compete with the best of Marxists in polemics. Marxists, of course, have a bad name when it comes to polemics. Gandhi carried on a battle of polemics against Rabindranath. From the entire long article by Rabindranath, Gandhi chose to point only to that bird which flies in the sky early in the morning. It reads as follows in the English translation:

> When there is war, the poet lays down the lyre, the lawyer his law reports, the school boy his books. The poet will sing the true note after the war is over. When the house is on fire, all the inmates go out and each one takes up a bucket to quench the fire. When all about me are dying for want of food, the only occupation permissible for me is to feed the hungry. It is my conviction that India is a house on fire, because its manhood is being daily scorched. It is dying of hunger, because it has no work to buy food with. In burning my foreign clothes I burn my shame. True to his poetical instinct, the poet lives for the morrow and would have us do likewise. He presents to our admiring gaze the beautiful picture of the birds early in the morning singing hymns of praise as they soar into the sky. These birds had their days' food and soared with rested wings in whose veins new blood has flown during the previous night. But I have had the pain of watching birds who for want of strength could not be coaxed into a flutter of their wings. A human bird under the Indian sky gets up weaker than when he pretended to retire. For millions it is an eternal vigilance or an eternal trance. It is an indescribably painful state which has to be experienced to be realised. I have found it impossible to suit suffering patience with a song of Kabir. The hungry millions ask for one poem: invigorating food. They cannot be given it. They must earn it, and they can only earn it by the sweat of their brow. Let Tagore spin like the others. Let him burn his foreign clothes. That is the duty today. God will take care of the morrow. As it is said in the Gita - do right.

That is Gandhi. You can see that in the debate on modernity Rabindranath Tagore condemns on the one hand the danger of a latent nationalism and on the other hand he talks about universalism. And then Gandhi replies on behalf of that hungry bird of India. Both are right. It is difficult to choose given the nature of the dispute. Tagore is right in his own way and Gandhi too is right in his own way. It is not as if Gandhi was only engaging in polemics. And there are two sides to it. In Indian Romanticism, around 1920-21 and thereafter as well, the hungry bird also finds its place. It is there even in the poems of Rabindranath. It is there in his literary works, in his stories. But I can cite an example from Hindi. Suryakant Tripathi 'Nirala'[10] had written a poem around the same time with the title *Badal Raag*, which reads in part as follows:

> *Ruddh kosh hai, kshubdh tosh / angana ang se lipte bhi / aatank ank par kaanp rahe hain. / Dhani, bajr-garjan se baadal / trast nayan-mukh dhaanp rahe hain. / Jeern baahu, hai sheern shareer / tujhe bulata krishak adheer / Ai, viplav ke veer.*[11]

I have mentioned Nirala because Nirala is one of those poets who read Rabindranath in the original Bengali. And Nirala has also written an entire book on Rabindranath. Nirala had a profound respect for Rabindranath, just as Gandhi also had for Rabindranath. In spite of that Nirala wrote an article about the dispute with the title 'Charkha' (spinning wheel), in which he argued that Gandhi was right and that Rabindranath would have to spin the *charkha*. Nirala took the side of Gandhi. That is because he was related to the peasants of Baiswara - those peasants of Awadh who had struggled for their rights, who had fought under the leadership of Baba Ramchandra for their lands during that very period.

Thus colonial Romanticism did not merely represent a fight for national freedom. Indian Romanticism was anti-feudal too. English Romanticism, and this was the term of reference for us, was only anti-feudal and a bourgeois revolutionary movement. India's colonial Romanticism was not only anti-feudal, it was anti-imperialist too. It combined both these aspects and is therefore a Romanticism that is difficult to compare with the Romanticism of any other country.

I cannot say much about Romanticism in other parts of the world, about Romanticism in Poland, in Hungary, and in Italy. When one looks at Romanticism in world literature, however, it is strange that where the French Revolution had taken place, there Romanticism seems to appear in the weakest form compared to Romanticism in other parts of the world. The greater Romanticism was that of Russia, the Romanticism of Pushkin. Which poet did France produce, except for Victor Hugo who wrote some poetry? French Romanticism was basically expressed in the field of fiction. Stendhal, Balzac, and Baudelaire? How Romantic was he, partially? It is a strange irony. The fact is that, all in all, no Shelley was born in France, no Pushkin was born there, nor any Heine.

It is the special feature of Indian Romanticism that it not only had Tagore in Bengali, but in all other Indian languages - you may call them junior Tagores - there were Romantics. Urdu had a poet like Iqbal. All sorts of things are said about Iqbal and many call him the creator of Pakistan. But compared to Bankim, Iqbal was better in this respect. Whatever he might have said against Islam, Iqbal never said anything against Hindutva, whereas Bankim not only propagated Hindutva but also insulted Muslims and Islam. Iqbal used to call Ram the *Imam-e-Hind*.

German Romanticism differs from Indian Romanticism in its emphasis on religion. Schlegel himself considered the religion of Christianity an essential part of Romanticism. A religious element was more dominant in German Romanticism. In comparison, Indian Romanticism, Tagore, Nirala are more secular than what one might expect. I don't say fully secular, but more secular than expected. You may find religion in the works of Bankim in the form of Hindutva. Rabindranath too could have praised Hindutva like Bankim. But he did not do it. Rabindranath's *Gora* is against Hindutva and in honour of Indianness. It is the irony of Hindutva that gets reflected in *Gora*. He says that during his entire life he kept thinking that he was a Hindu only to realise at the end that there was no place for him in Hindutva. That is why, in comparison to German Romanticism, Indian Romanticism is more secular. We did not become victims in that age.

I would like to conclude by saying that a lot has been said about Indian Romanticism, its contradictions and other aspects. It is a strange irony of modernity in India that the intellectual class here, which is well conversant with the English language, has not been able to digest Indian Romanticism right from beginning. Unfortunately, this became the culture of the Indian intelligentsia under the influence of New Criticism. This tradition based itself on Eliot and F.R. Leavis. And in the throes of modernism, the modernism of Eliot and Pound, this tradition saw its first duty in dismissing Indian Romanticism - just as they had buried English Romanticism - and to start a new poetry, the *Nai Kavita*, in the name of experimentation.

The biggest opponent of Rabindranath was Buddhadeva Bose[12] who called himself a modernist. Rabindranath remembered Buddhadeva Bose well in his last novel *Shesher Kabita* in the figure of Amit Ray. Today's intellectuals who take part in debates on modernity and who consider themselves postmodernist, and also followers of Gandhi - intellectuals like Partha. Chatterjee, Ashis Nandy - in the name of accepting Romanticism they not only forget Tagore, this group is also a kind of anti-thesis of Gandhi, it disrespects him, it does not recognise him, the Gandhi who argued with Tagore. They stand in the tradition of the same Buddhadeva. After modernism, overwhelmed by the phenomenon called postmodernism, which has been given to us by post-colonialism, we are forgetting our Romantic heritage, that precious heritage, complicated and full of contradictions, which is rich, plural and closer to the common people. And in the current age of darkness it warns us that even if the philosophy of German Romanticism might have gone from Heidegger to Hitler, the heritage of Indian Romanticism, the heritage of Tagore, cannot give strength to Hindutva, nor join with it. In fact, the greatest opposition to Hindutva today is in the Romantic tradition nearest to us, which is secular, in spite of all its limitations, and revolutionary, which has a vision of the future. Romanticism gives us memories, it also gives us a vision. In the world of today we have almost fallen prey to amnesia and in the postmodernist age we have started regarding utopia too as something outdated. Romanticism gives us a socialist utopia. I say 'socialist' utopia intentionally. It is there in Rabindranath, in the 'Letter from Russia'. The dream of socialism was there in our Romanticism. It was there in Rabindranath and in Nirala too. If we want this socialist dream to stay alive, perhaps we can find it in our own Indian Romanticism.

- *Translated by Shaswati Mazumdar and Madhu Sudan Joshi*

NOTES AND REFERENCES

1. Bankim Chandra Chattopadhyay (1838-1894), Bengali writer, author of the novel *Anandmath* (1882).
2. Ram Vilas Sharma (1912-2000), Hindi poet and critic.
3. Sachchidananda Hirananda Vatsyayan (1911-87), popularly known by his pen-name 'Ajneya' or Agyeya, leading representative of modern Hindi literature, editor of the *Saptak* series which introduced new trends in Hindi poetry known as 'Nai Kavita'.
4. Walter Benjamin, *Understanding Brecht*. trans. Anna Bostock, Introduction by Stanley Mitchell, London: New Left Books, 1973.
5. Muhammad Iqbal (1877-1938), poet (wrote in Urdu and Persian) and philosopher.

6. Marshall Berman, *All That Is Solid Melts into Air: The Experience of Modernity*, New York: Simon and Schuster, 1982.
7. Perry Anderson, 'Modernity and Revolution' in L. Grossberg and C. Nelson (eds.), *Marxism and the Interpretation of Culture*, London: Macmillan Education, 1988.
8. Rabindranath Tagore, *Prabhat Sangeet*, first published in 1883.
9. The British Government wanted to divide Bengal into two parts. The eastern part was proposed to be merged to Assam and the western part was to be added to Bihar. The agitation against this plan was called the Banga Bhanga movement.
10. Suryakant Tripathi 'Nirala' (1896-1961), modern Hindi poet, leading representative of the Chhayawad movement.
11. The coffers are full, but still not satisfied / embraced by beautiful women / they tremble in the lap of terror. / The rich, hearing the thundering of clouds / cover their terrified eyes and faces. / Their arms lifeless, their bodies torn / the peasants call to you eagerly / oh heroes of revolution.
12. Buddhadeva Bose (1908-74), Bengali writer of the 'post-Tagore' generation.

TAPAN BASU

Henry David Thoreau and Mohandas Karamchand Gandhi : Romantics, Rebels or Reactionaries

In her revisionist study of the Romantic Movement in English literature, *Romantics, Rebels and Reactionaries : English Literature and its Background 1760-1830,* Marilyn Butler endeavours to problematise the larger-than life image of the Romantic thinker/artist as a revolutionary iconoclast which, she argues, was more or less always a posthumous manufacture thrust upon the real authors who had lived and produced their works during an indubitably revolutionary period of European history. Unfortunately, remarks Butler,

> ...this equation of one kind of revolution with another is much too simple. The German writers who first called themselves Romantics were not supporters of the French Revolution at all. They were, on the whole, German patriots, who increasingly came to approve of the involvement of the various German states in the war against republican France. Their opposition to eighteenth century classicism might even be read as opposition to a style they associated with France, the home of a revolution that had turned expansive and aggressive. For the first two decades of the nineteenth century, German Romanticism remained Catholic and counter-revolutionary. In both France and England during these decades, it was the classical or antique style that was commonly linked with republicanism. When the Gothic or medieval or avowedly Romantic taste began to gain ground in England after the peace came in 1815, it was at first identified with the *ancien régimes* which had triumphed over France, and with their extreme political conservatism Indeed it was not until the **next** French Revolution began to get under way – until events in France began to build up to the 'July Revolution' of 1830 – that Romantic artists in any country became generally identified with the radical cause in politics.[1]

If Butler's thesis holds good as a statement about the ideological ambivalence of the European Romantics, it is even more pertinent to the case of the Romantics of America. The Romantic Movement in America, stretching through the 1830s to the 1860s, found its most typical expression in the so-called transcendentalist school of thought. The New England transcendentalists, led by Ralph Waldo Emerson (1803-1882), mounted an attack upon the economic, political, cultural and religious ideals which their forefathers, not to mention their contemporaries, had blindly and blandly projected as being the most appropriate for the "most perfect society now existing in the world." [St. Jean de Crevecover's description of *Letters From an American Farmer* (1832)]. Apart from Emerson, the group included such persons of eminence as Theodore Parker, William Ellery Channing, Amos Bronson Alcott, Orestes Brownson, Margaret Fuller, and Henry David Thoreau, the last named indeed so "transcendent" that he resisted official membership in this, or in any other group. Nevertheless, there can be no doubt that Thoreau, in both his thought and his actions, belongs to the transcendentalist denomination. Each of these transcendentalists regarded himself or herself to be a dissenter, or to put it in their own peculiar rhetoric, "a nay sayer" to the contemporary national mainstream. Their expressions of defiance were often eccentric and even extremist, but as much as with the European Romantics, their views also represented, to quote Perry Miller, "the first (and in many respects most eloquent) protest of the American sensibility against what ... was rapidly becoming ... a 'business' civilization."[2]

Unlike the European Romantics, however, they were never quite able to conceal their enthusiasm for the possibilities opened up by commercial and industrial development. Writing rather like a successful business entrepreneur, Emerson opined:

> The division of labour...which is nothing but a large allowance to choose his work according to his faculty - to live by his better hand - fills the State with useful and happy labourers; and they, creating demand by the very temptation of their products, are rapidly and surely rewarded by their good sale : and what a police and ten commandments their work thus becomes. So true is Dr. Johnson's remark that "men are seldom more innocently employed than when they are making money."[3]

It is doubtful that any of the notable European Romantics would have cited Dr. Johnson's observation with so much enthusiasm. And yet, it is in it is in the same essay that Emerson advised his reader: "Hitch your wagon to a star. Let us not fag in paltry works which serve our pot and bag alone."[4] Transcendentalism was, then, an ambivalent negotiation, or attempt at negotiation, between the incongruities of an anti-materialist sentiment and a rhetoric of laissez-faire individualism. As such, it was as Duane E. Smith has pointed out, "a curiously American manifestation of the Romantic Movement."[5]

In the following part of my paper, I shall focus upon one of the key texts of transcendentalism, namely *Walden or a Life in the Woods* (1854) by Henry David Thoreau, to illustrate some of the ideological ambivalences of the school that I have already talked about. Then in the subsequent and final section of the essay, I shall examine the appropriation of Thoreau's ideology in a text called *Hind Swaraj* (1909) by his most celebrated adherent in the twentieth century, Mohandas Karamchand Gandhi (1869-1948).

Thoreau was born in 1817 in Concord, Massachusetts, the son of a pencil-maker. He attended Harvard College where he may have been among the audience of graduating students who heard Emerson deliver his 'American Scholar' address in 1857. After college he returned home and taught school with his brother until 1841 when he joined Emerson's household as a companion and handyman. Though he lived with the Emersons for only two years, and though he came to regard his friendship with the older man as a 'long tragedy', this relationship which began in the mid-1830s and lasted to the end of his life, was central in Thoreau's development. He grew eventually to be more than a disciple, which was hard for Emerson to acknowledge, but his indebtedness to works like Emerson's article on "Nature" and to the personal stimulus and support of Emerson is unquestionable.

In 1845 Thoreau began the adventure which he made exemplary in *Walden*. He settled by Walden Pond on some land belonging to Emerson and passed about two and a half years there, living not as a hermit, for that was not his intention, but essentially as a scholar disengaged from worldly affairs. The time at Walden was an opportunity for communion with nature, but also, and perhaps more importantly, an opportunity for study and a great deal of writing. Thoreau, like Emerson, had kept a journal for many years; at Walden Pond he added to it extensively and mined it for composition of his first book, *A Week on the Concord and Merrimack Rivers*, which was published in 1849. Only after he left Walden did he deliberately undertake a book about his experience there, returning to his journals, adding later observations, revising, compressing and shaping his material into an extremely artful record of a single year. *Walden* was published in 1854; Thoreau wrote no other books. In his later years he lived mainly with his family, visited various parts of New England and Canada, and acquired a certain notoriety for his passionate defence of the abolitionist John Brown. The last two years of his life were marked by declining health and in 1862 he died.

At the core of Thoreau's rejection of his society is profound hostility to the process of exchange, to what he calls the "curse of trade".[6] He pictures a contemporary Concord where everyone is implicated in the market, in market relations and market identities, and he articulates a critique of that milieu as antithetical to freedom, to happiness and to life itself.

His anti-market attitude, deriving from an erstwhile system of social relations when most Americans, white Americans at least, were independent freeholders, harvesting just enough produce to fend for their own needs, is in direct opposition to the market place equations that were increasingly gaining in currency among his contemporaries. Around this period a number of factors combined to provide a runaway boost to industry and commerce in America. Poor transportation facilities, the dearth of capital for investment, and chronic labour shortages had inhibited growth in the early national period. After 1815 improvements in existing land routes and the construction first of canals and then of railroads sharply reduced transport costs and led to the emergence of a national market. Income from exports, particularly cotton and grain, helped to finance these developments, while the proliferation of state banks made credit and money more generally available. Bank notes became the major circulating medium of the market revolution. Population increase was another important prod to the expansion of business. The high native birth rate and the influx of immigrants in the second quarter of the century provided an elastic supply of labour conducive to manufacturing growth. Cities expanded even faster than the population of the country as a whole ensuring large concentrated markets for foodstuffs and consumer goods. Statistics convey some sense of the magnitude of these changes: between 1820 and 1860 the population grew from about 10 million to almost 32 million while the proportion of Americans dwelling in cities rose by 800 per cent; railroad mileage went from zero to over thirty thousand and there was a five fold increase in the number of banks and the value of notes in circulation.

Thoreau however regards such symptoms of marketisation with high suspicion. For him, the market place was not a training ground for self reliance and self-expression, an arena where the man of enterprise can prove his worth, but rather as a site of compromise where the seller has to conciliate potential buyers to gain their custom. The interactions of exchange, in his view, breed not selfhood but servility. Nor, insists Thoreau, does nineteenth century agriculture offer an exemption from the dependencies and debasement of the exchange process. The land has become an investment like any other and the farmer a willing participant in the market place. The husbandmen of Concord, immortalised by Emerson for their stand "by the rude bridge that arched the flood", are now "serfs of the soil" who spend their lives "buying and selling" and have forgotten the meaning of self-sufficiency. Thoreau envisions them, in a celebrated image, "creeping down the road of life", each pushing before him "a barn seventy five feet by forty ... and one hundred acres of land, tillage, mowing, pasture and wood lot".[7]

For Thoreau, commercial agriculture has an impact on the physical world which is just as devastating as its effect on the farmer. In the chapter, "The Ponds", he describes an agricultural entrepreneur named Flint for whom nature exists solely as a commodity. Indeed, on Flint's farm the use value of natural objects has been consumed by their exchange value; their abstract nationality as potential money has completely obliterated their "sensuous" reality (to use a favourite adjective of Karl Marx in this connection) as fruits and vegetables. The result is an impoverishment of the thing, an alteration of its very nature. "I respect not his labours", Thoreau writes of Flint,

> his farm where every thing has its price; who would carry the landscape, who would carry his God, to market, if he could do anything for him; on whose farm nothing grows free, whose fields bear no crops, whose meadows no flowers, whose trees no fruits, but dollars; who loves not the beauty of his fruits, whose fruits are not ripe for him till they are turned to dollars.[8]

As Thoreau's denunciation of Flint makes clear, his quarrel with the market-place centres upon his perception of the exchange process as emptying the world of its concrete reality and not only converting objects into dollars but causing their "it-ness" or being to disappear. A particularly powerful statement of this idea occurs at the beginning of "The Ponds" in the passage where Thoreau assails the marketing of huckleberries. He argues that nature's fruits "do not yield their true flavour" either to the man who raises them commercially or to their urban purchasers. The huckleberry cannot be tasted or even said to exist outside its native habitat: invariably it undergoes a fatal transformation en route from the countryside to the metropolis. What reaches Boston is not the fragrant berry itself but the "mere provender" that the fruit has become in being transported to the customer. Its bloom has been "rubbed off in the market cart" and its "ambrosial and essential part" extinguished by its conversion into an article of trade.[9]

Thoreau believes that along with the degradation of the physical object in exchange there occurs a shriveling of the individual. Men in the market place, according to *Walden*, do not relate as persons but as something less than human; they commit violence against their own natures in their incessant anxiety to induce others to buy their products or their labor. "The finest qualities of our nature", Thoreau says, in a passage paralleling his discussion of the huckleberry, "like the bloom on fruits can be preserved only by the most delicate handling. Yet we do not treat ourselves or one another thus tenderly".[10] The labourer's self, his authentic being has as little chance to survive the exchange process as a genuine huckleberry. To satisfy his employer, he has to suppress his individuality and become a mechanical thing. "Actually, the labouring man has not leisure for a true integrity day by day; he cannot afford to sustain the manliest relations to men; his labour would be depreciated in the market. He has no time to be anything but a machine."[11] The final disappearance of the person, the most extreme form of absence would be death, and Thoreau does in fact equate exchange with deprivation of life. "The cost of a thing", he writes, "is the amount of what I will call life which is required to be exchanged for it, immediately or in the long run."[12]

Michael T. Gilmore, to whose ideas I owe much of the preceding arguments, has commented in his book *American Romanticism and the Market-Place* (1989), that Thoreau's analysis of commodification has certain affinities with the Marxist critique of capitalism. His comments on the erosion of human presence in exchange evoke the notion of reification, a concept developed in the twentieth century by Georg Lukács. Reification refers to the phenomenon whereby a social relation between human beings assumes the character of a relation between things. Because they interact through the commodities they exchange, including the commodity of labour, individuals in the capitalist market-place confront each other not as human beings, but as objectified, non-human entities. They lose sight altogether of the subjective element in their activity. An important corollary to this loss of the person is a confusion of history with nature. By mystifying or obscuring man's involvement in the production of his social reality, reification leads him to apprehend that reality as a "second nature". He perceives the social realm as an immutable and universal order over which he exerts no control. The result is to greatly diminish the possibility of human freedom.

Thoreau reaches a similar conclusion about the decline of liberty under capitalism: he portrays his townspeople as slave-drivers of themselves, and himself in the woods near Walden Pond as a fugitive slave writing his own slave narrative à la Frederick Douglass and other celebrated African-American ex-slaves who had been able to escape to freedom.[13]

But as Michael Meyer has indicated there is more than a hint of self-indulgence in Thoreau's startling analogy between his own situation and that of a fugitive slave like Douglass.[14] The chief discrepancy between their two situations, as presented through their writings, is that while the fugitive slave's purpose is to convince his mostly white readers that he is really no different from them, Thoreau's effort is at alerting his readers, also mostly white, that they can be like him. This crucial difference allows Thoreau considerably more latitude. He can be outrageous, he can exaggerate, he can be whimsical because he is writing essentially for those readers who enjoy the same status privileges as himself. The fugitive slave, on the other hand, is burdened with the task of demonstrating that blacks were fully capable of living conventional respectable lives. It is difficult to imagine any fugitive slave in the middle of the nineteenth century writing a witty, subversive sentence about the work ethic such as this one of Thoreau's: "It is not necessary that a man should earn his living by the sweat of his brow, unless he sweats easier than I do." Thoreau had the liberty to write sentences that continually outmanoeuvreed his readers with his rhetoric because he had to worry only about raised eyebrows rather than raised fists. He knew his task was not to reassure his readers by appealing to their dormant or undeveloped sense of decency but "to leave out all the flattery, and retain all the criticism". Thoreau had nothing to lose because he was convinced that a person was "rich in proportion to the number of things which he can afford to let alone", and public approval was one of them. Acceptance was not a pre-requisite to freedom as it had to be for the fugitive slave.

Yet acceptance, if not public approval, are the rewards that Thoreau craves for too as a writer. "I do not propose to write an ode to dejection, but to brag as lustily as a chaunticleer in the morning, standing on his roost, if only to wake my neighbours up", is the announcement with which he prefaces *Walden*. Thoreau is especially aware of his need to have an appreciative readership since his writing has an avowedly didactic intention.

> I would fain say something, not so much concerning the Chinese and Sandwich Islanders as you who read these pages, who are said to live in New England; something about your condition or circumstances in this world, in this town, what it is, whether it is necessary that it be as bad as it is, whether it cannot be improved as well as not....[15]

It is clear that Thoreau, in spite of his repudiation of his society, wants that his narrative of adjustment should be read and re-read avidly and voraciously by the members of the very society that he has repudiated. This duality in his attitude towards his fellow-Concordians reveals itself right from the outset of his text. As Stanley Cavell has put it "...Thoreau's problem is not to learn what to say to them; that could not be clearer. The problem is to establish his right to declare it."[16]

It is not at all surprising that Thoreau finds it difficult even to put his project into words, since the language, which would be most accessible to Concordians, is the very language he would rather eschew. Thus his statement of intention in chapter 2 is marked by curious tautological exercises on the one hand and lapses into representational modes of the abjured society on the other.

> I went to the woods because I wished to live deliberately, to front only the essential facts of life, and see if I could not learn what it had to teach, and not, when I came to die, discover that I had not lived. I did not wish to live what was not life, living is so dear; nor did I wish to practice resignation, unless it was quite necessary....[17]

Thoreau apprehends, however, that his writing will not satisfy the tastes of the popular readership of the age which, he alleges, have been pandered to and perverted by the "modern cheap and fertile press." As against the pulp production of this press, Thoreau promotes the classic such as Homer's *Iliad*, "the heroic books", which he himself reads and which

> ... even if printed in the character of our mother tongue, will always be in a language dead to degenerate times, and [to understand which] we must always seek the meaning of each word and line, conjecturing a larger sense than common use permits out of what wisdom and valor and generosity we have.[18]

Thereby, Thoreau elevates himself to the position of not only an ideal reader of classics but also an actual writer of one, his own *Walden*, which he fears few readers might willingly want to read.

As Michael T. Gilmore has suggested, Thoreau's diatribe against the "modern press" smacks of a grapes-are-sour attitude at not being able to compete in the market place with its "cheap and fertile" publications. As a writer, Thoreau is not merely enticed by the possibilities of the market place; he is positively excited by them.[19] His paean to commerce, in chapter 4, is most telling in this context.

> What recommends commerce to me is its enterprise and bravery. It does not clasp its hands and pray to Jupiter....[20]

Even more significant is his eulogistic invocation to the railway system, which he identifies as the very epitome of the business civilization.

> When I meet the engine with its train of cars moving off with planetary motion - or rather, like a comet for the beholder knows not if with that velocity and that direction it will ever revisit this system, since its orbit does not look like a returning curve - with its stream cloud like a banner streaming behind in golden and silver wreaths, like many a downy cloud which I have seen high in the heavens, unfolding its light - as if this travelling demi-god, this crowd-compeller would ere long take the sunset sky for the livery of his train; when I hear the iron horse make the hills echo with his snort like thunder, shaking the earth with his feet, and breathing fire and smoke from his nostrils, (what kind of winged horse or fiery dragon they will put into the new Mythology I don't know), it seems as if the earth had got a race now worthy to inhabit it. If all were as it seems, and men made the elements their servants for noble ends! If the cloud that hangs over the engine were the perspiration of heroic deeds, or as beneficent as that which floats over the farmer's field, then the elements and Nature herself would cheerfully accompany men on their errands and be their escort.[21]

His scepticism of the machine completely outdone by his wonderment, he is ready to absorb the railways into a re-defined landscape of nature.

Contrast this with Gandhi's view of the railways as expressed in *Hind Swaraj*:

> It must be manifest...that but for the railways, the English could not have such a hold on India as they have. The railways, too, have spread the bubonic plague. Without them, masses could not move from place to place. They are the carriers of plague germs. Formerly we had natural segregation. Railways have also increased the frequency of famines, because, owing to facility of means of locomotion, people sell out their grain, and it is sent to the dearest markets. People become careless and so the pressure of famine increases. They accentuate the evil nature of man. Bad men fulfil their evil designs with greater rapidity. The holy places of India have become unholy. Formerly, people went to these places with very great difficulty. Generally, therefore, only the real devotees visited such places. Nowadays, rogues visit them in order to practise their roguery.[22]

Thoreau's influence upon Gandhi's thought is well known. *Indian Opinion*. The South African newspaper published by Gandhi from Durban between 1903 and 1914, in whose Gujarati columns *Hind Swaraj* was initially brought out in serial instalments, records in several of its issues Gandhi's intellectual debt to Thoreau. Readers of *Indian Opinion* were frequently reminded of Thoreau's essay on "Civil Disobedience". Thoreau had opposed the enslavement of man; Indians, being enslaved themselves, needed encouragement in their struggle. The Indian community in South Africa was engaged in openly defying some of the racist laws framed by the South African government, and the resistances of Tolstoy, Thoreau, Jesus, and Socrates seemed vital confirmations to Gandhi. On November 9, 1907 *Indian Opinion* announced an essay contest on "The Ethics of Passive Resistance". The terms of the competition stated that the essay should contain an examination "of Thoreau's classic, 'On the Duty of Civil Disobedience,' Tolstoi's works - more especially' 'The Kingdom of Heaven is Within You', and also the application of the 'Apology' of Socrates to the question". Those who entered the essay competition had access to "Civil Disobedience" as it had been reprinted in pamphlet form for sale at 3 pence and issued in time to be used by contestants not familiar with the essay. Nor was Thoreau ignored by Gandhi during the years after *Satyagraha* was first tried out in South Africa; for several years after 1908 passive resistance was offered on a minor scale, and Gandhi himself did not court arrest. Two years after *Indian Opinion* had printed extracts from "Civil Disobedience", it printed selections from Mazzini with the comment:

> We believe that when the first stage of passive resistance was at its height, the extracts we gave from Thoreau's essay 'On the Duty of Civil Disobedience' were very greatly appreciated by Indian passive resisters.

Gandhi himself was still reading Thoreau; by 1909 he considered that "railways, machineries, and the corresponding increase of indulgent habits are the true badge of slavery of the Indian people, as they are of Europeans".[23]

What then accounts for the rather divergent viewpoints of Gandhi and Thoreau on the issue of modern (read post-Enlightenment Western) civilization of which both regard railways to be a primary metonym? To answer this question it is imperative that we examine the argument of *Hind Swaraj* as a whole.

Written in dialogue form, *Hind Swaraj* is ostensibly a reproduction of Gandhi's conversations with "misguided" patriots in London, whom he places in a group as the Reader while he himself appears as the Editor. It may be recalled, incidentally, that he was at this time about forty years old.

Here, in this short work, is the first clear landmark in the evaluation of Gandhi's philosophy. He begins with a laudatory estimate of the Indian National Congress and pays high tribute to the "drain of wealth theorists of colonialism", Dadabhai Nauroji and Gopal Krishna Gokhale. Then he passes on to the dramatic theme of the Partition of Bengal effected by Lord Curzon in spite of the emotion-charged, desperate protest of the entire people. "That day may be considered to be the day of the partition of the British Empire...."[24] As the Partition overrode all prayers and petitions, a new spirit was born in Bengal, he noted. The *Swadeshi* movement sprang into life. And the spirit of revolt was asweep from the Punjab to the Cape Comorin.

All this material of history is only a backdrop for what Gandhi has to say. His startling observations begin in chapter 4. The Editor presupposes that the British have quit India. What happens then? The Reader gives the answer that India will then become a great country like Japan with its own army and navy and all the trappings of splendour, its strident voice ringing through the world. The Editor's reply is ironic. "It means this: we want English rule without the Englishman."[25] The Reader, unperturbed, insists that it is proper for India to copy the British institutions. And the Editor's final comment is loaded with sorrow, "What you call Swaraj is not truly Swaraj."[26]

From the next chapter, the book begins to gain in steam. With firebrand, if utterly gender-insensitive rhetoric, Gandhi gives the analogy of the "Mother of Parliaments" which he characterises as a "sterile woman" and a "prostitute".[27] As for the British voters, they are described as being gullible and fickle, and their democratic choices highly suspect. The present state of England, however, according to Gandhi, is not due to any fault of the people. "It is due essentially to the modern civilization... it is a civilization only in the name."[28]

But what, in Gandhi's opinion, is the meaning of civilization?

Civilization in the West, as Gandhi sees it, means nothing but the trappings of material affluence. Better housing. Better clothing. Better eating. Machines in lieu of manual labour. Terrific speed of transport and communication. Ever newer luxuries. Revolvers replacing spears. New diseases too. "This civilization is such that one has only to be patient and it will be self-destroyed."[29]

Gandhi's agenda, in contradistinction to Thoreau's agenda, is not to make an incisive criticism of a dehumanised consumer culture. His agenda, instead, is to revive memories of a vanquished national culture, "unquestionably the best",[30] as a counter to this victorious alien culture. For Gandhi, India's hoary civilization transcends history,

> ... and that is her glory. It is a charge against India that her people are so uncivilized, ignorant and stolid, that it is not possible to induce them to adopt any changes. It is a charge really against our merit. What we have tasted and found true on the anvil of experience, we dare not change. Many thrust their advice upon India, and she remains steady. This is her beauty, it is the sheet-anchor of our hope.[31]

India's culture becomes, in fact, through this paradoxical construction, the world's one and only master-culture.

> If this definition be correct, then India, as so many writers have shown, has nothing to learn from anybody else, and this is as it should be....
>
> And where this cursed modern civilization has not reached, India remains as it was before. The English do not rule over them, nor will ever rule over them....[32]

Whereas Thoreau's ideological ambivalence vis-à-vis modern civilization prevents him from outlining any alternate framework to it, Gandhi's ideological single-mindedness translates itself into a nativist tirade which is also dangerously chauvinist as well as sectarian at the core.

> I do not wish to suggest that because we were one nation we had no differences.... What do you think could have been the intention of those far-seeing ancestors of ours who established Shevetbindu Rameshwar in the South, Juggernant in the South-East, and Hardwar in the North as places of pilgrimage? You will admit they were no fools. They knew that worship of God could have been performed just as well at home. They taught us that those whose hearts were aglow with righteousness had the Ganges in their own homes. But they saw that India was one undivided land so made by nature. They, therefore, argued that it must be one nation...[33]

I leave the iconography of the passage to speak for itself.

NOTES AND REFERENCES

1. Marilyn Butler, *Romantics, Rebels and Reactionaries: English Literature and its Background 1760-1830,* London: OUP, 1981, pp. 4-5.
2. Perry Miller, 'New England's Transcendentalism : Nature or Imported?' in *Critical Essays on American Transcendentalism*, ed. Phillip F. Gura and Joel Myerson, Boston: K. Hall and Co. 1982, p. 390.
3. Edward Waldo Emerson Cd., *The Complete Works of Ralph Waldo Emerson VII,* Boston: Houghton Mifflin, 1903-1904, pp. 26-27.
4. *Ibid.*, p. 33.

5. Duane E. Smith, 'Romanticism in America: The Transcendentalists', in *Critical Essays on* ***American Transcendentalism***, ed. Phillip F. Gura and Joel Myerson, Boston: G.K. Hall & Co. 1982, p. 484.
6. Henry David Thoreau, *Walden and Civil Disobedience*, ed. with an introduction by Michael Meyer, New York: Viking Penguin, 1986, p. 113.
7. *Ibid.*, p. 47.
8. *Ibid.*, p. 244.
9. *Ibid.*, p. 220.
10. *Ibid.*, p. 48.
11. *Ibid.*, p. 48.
12. *Ibid.*, p. 73.
13. *Ibid.*, p. 49.
14. Michael Meyer, 'Introduction' to *Walden and Civil Disobedience by Henry David Thoreau,* New York: Viking Penguin, 1986 pp. 28-29.
15. Henry Davil Thoreau, *op. cit.*, p. 46.
16. Stanley Cavell, *The Sense of Waldon*, New York: Viking Penguin, 1972, p. 11.
17. Henry Davil Thoreau, *op. cit.*, p. 135.
18. *Ibid.*, p. 145.
19. Michael T. Gilmore, *American Romanticism and the Market-Place,* Chicago: University of Chicago Press, 1985.
20. Henry Davil Thoreau, *op. cit.*, p. 164.
21. *Ibid.*, pp. 161-162.
22. Mohandas Karamchand Gandhi, *Hind Swaraj and Other writings,* ed. with an Introduction by Anthony J. Parel, New Delhi: Foundation Books, 1997, p. 47.
23. *Indian Opinion*, February 20, 1909, pp. 89-90.
24. Mohandas Karamchand Gandhi, *op. cit.*, p. 19.
25. *Ibid.*, p. 28.
26. *Ibid.*, p. 29.
27. *Ibid.*, p. 30.
28. *Ibid.*, p. 33.
29. *Ibid.*, p. 37.
30. *Ibid.*, p. 72.
31. *Ibid.*, pp. 66-67.
32. *Ibid.*, pp. 67-70.
33. *Ibid.*, pp. 48-49.

DILIP LOUNDO

Romanticism and the Roots of Brazilian Nationalism

Perhaps more than any other literary current in modern world literature, Romanticism has a congenital articulation in particular circumstances and backgrounds. In fact, while undertaking the critique of classical and neo-classical tendencies, Romanticism divested itself from universalities and put emphasis on individual and collective personae as subjects of reactive processes in situations of crisis. Thus, without forgoing the European genetic context, it seems that Romanticism is better defined as an aesthetic expression of a general human perplexity before specific social transformations and transitions.

This being so, while investigating the causes, nature and prospects of Romanticism in Brazil, one has to characterise, at the outset, the local context of insertion. On the one hand, it's no denying the fact that Brazil - and perhaps the majority of Latin American formations - is a cultural by-product of European expansion and, as a consequence, the intellectual events that took place in the Old Continent received a natural and immediate diffusion in the New World. But, on the other, it is equally true that the development of a set of local interests and, moreover, the compulsory exchanges that followed between the colonialists and other ethnic groups, lent the whole historical process a rather peculiar character. This circumstance has been described by the critics as the peripheral factor, understood as a distinctive element of post-colonial cultural situations in Latin America.

The transitional event that forms the background for the expansion of Romanticism in Brazil, is the process of political autonomy which docked at the declaration of independence from Portugal in 1822 under a monarchic regime. The historical convergence between Romanticism and freedom struggle is a distinctive mark in Latin American formations. In Europe, Romanticism emerged mostly in times of economic (industrial revolution) and socio-political (French revolution) transformations. In Brazil, it emerged amidst a fundamental political change which, by its very nature, ruled out the immediate possibility of a socio-economic follow-up. The political exclusivity was deeply rooted in a peculiar cultural dynamics. While in Europe transformations took place within consolidated cultures, in Brazil they were part of an incomplete process of cultural genesis. On the one hand, as a new cultural entity, Brazil emerged as a synthesis of European, African and native Indian (Amerindian) ethnicities. The de-culturation and subsequent fusion of those ethnic matrices brought about the formation of a *mestizo* culture characterised by a tendency to homogenisation. But, on the other hand, this emerging formation was politically born with a fundamental structural deficiency: it presented a dissociation between a mass of *mestizo* and Negro slave population, in one extreme, and a dominating economic elite alienated from the grass-roots and culturally identified with Europe, in the other. It is to be noted that, different from other Latin American situations, Brazilian elites were predominantly composed of *mestizos* rather than *creoles*. Such a structural deficiency was generated by two basic colonial institutions which remained very much alive in the post-independence period, placing Brazil in the periphery of the international geopolitical scenario: (i) the slavery system and (ii) the export-oriented economy.

The hypertrophy of a political sphere that limits and monopolises a transitional process through the agency of externally oriented economic elites, constitutes the ground on which Romanticism flourished in Brazil. As a necessary corollary to the diplomatic efforts, Brazilian elites realised the urgent need to justify Brazil's separate political existence on the grounds of a distinct cultural identity - a condition *sine qua non* for the nation's recognition and survival. Thus, the chronological precedence of political autonomy to cultural maturity was indicative of Brazil's ironical situation: those who were urged to present a distinct image of the nation, were precisely those imperfectly aware of its fundamentals, for they themselves were intimately identified with the Old Continent. And, yet, they had an imperative task of affirming, at any cost, a difference from the Portuguese. The confluence of these contradictory aspects led to the construction of artificial identities – a task in which Romanticism showed its architectural capabilities. It performed efficiently the role of stating negatively Brazil's cultural identity, i.e., affirming what Brazil was not; but, at the same time, failed to evolve positive and substantive representations of such identity.

The organic relationship between the political sphere and the literary circles is nowhere so conspicuous in Brazilian history as it happens in the case of Romanticism. In fact, the movement was officially launched in 1836 with the publication of the book *Poetical Sighs and Longings* (*Suspiros Poéticos e Saudades*) by Gonçalves de Magalhães (1811-1882), a well known associate of the Brazilian monarch D. Pedro II. While taking over the literary circles, Romanticism revealed its two basic articulations. First, as a means of presenting an image of Brazil, Romanticism was the source of (proto-)nationalist ideologies that proved equally effective internally (viz., as an ideology of domination which exploited subaltern imaginaries) and externally (viz., as an alleged identity distinct from that of the colonialists). Second, as a creator of an image of Brazil relatively dissociated from the country's cultural roots and thoroughly dependent on political compulsions, Romanticism was defective in aesthetic innovations. This resulted in relatively modest literary creations, basically characterised by thematic novelties (African and Indian motifs) subsumed by formal and ideological emulations (European academicism). But for a few authors, the movement would have had merely an historical relevance as the official ideology of imperial Brazil (1822-1889).

The exercise of unveiling the cultural and aesthetical limitations of Romanticism, does not in any way diminish the relevance of the movement in the history of Brazilian literature. In fact, for an emerging culture, an ideology of freedom even if productive of partial apprehensions of one's identity, is bound to have a positive impact. In fact, nationalisms before the nation's maturity, inasmuch as they attempt as pioneers to formulate the question of the nation, may have a positive, stimulating and even didactic impact by stirring up, in the middle and long run, genuine and authentic processes of self-reflection. Accordingly, contemporary critics tend to look at the defective symbols produced by Romanticism, not as absolute imperfections but as steps towards a definitive self-awareness of one's Brazilian-ness – a major pre-requisite for achieving aesthetical excellence.

Despite relevant confessional expressions, the theme of Brazil's identity was dominant throughout the period that goes from the '30s till the '80s of the nineteenth century. It was the nodal point to where the best aesthetical realisations of the movement converged. In overall terms, one could say that the merits of Romanticism in Brazil lay in its capacity to put forward some of the major issues and levels under which the question of the nation should be posited henceforth. They were: (i) a distinctive cultural environment, which brought to centre stage themes related to the marginalised ethnic matrices of Brazilian culture, viz., the Indian and the Negro population; (ii) a distinctive natural scenario, which described and presented the exoticism and uniqueness of tropical landscape; (iii) the distinctive development of the Portuguese language, which endorsed the canonical independence of Brazilian Portuguese; and finally (iv) a prospective design, which put emphasis on the fact that no cultural answer could be found in the past or, in other words, that for a new culture like Brazil the past was but the colonial system and the Portuguese culture, to be transcended. An instinct of nationality commanded, therefore, the development of Romanticism in Brazil. This is the reason why despite its shortcomings, the movement can legitimately be considered the first manifestation of a national literature in the country.

To appreciate the concrete responses, ideological contents and literary merits of Romanticism in Brazil, it would be appropriate to make a quick incursion into the realm of literary production in Brazil during the second half of the nineteenth century. The two most important representatives of the period – a unanimity among the critics - are José de Alencar (novel, 1829-1877) and Castro Alves (poetry, 1847-1871). A typical representative of the movement, José de Alencar had a direct participation in the political process as a member of the Parliament. A personal altercation with the Emperor over a political issue led to the estrangement of relations between the two, but did not shake Alencar's personal faith on the monarchy and the slavery system, on which his silence was so conspicuous. Castro Alves, on the other hand, displayed a different political articulation. As a critic of controversial imperial policies, he joined the national campaign that lobbied for the end of slavery, which would ultimately succeed in 1888, just one year before the establishment of the Republic (1889). Both José de Alencar and Castro Alves produced national myths associated with the marginalised matrices of Brazilian culture. Their ideologies became known in literary criticism, as the themes of Indianism (Indian) and Negrism (Negro) respectively: the first was conveyed by the prose of Alencar and the second by the poetry of Castro Alves.

Indianism was the fashion theme of the Romantic period and the subject-matter of several other writers besides José de Alencar. It is characterised by the exaltation of the native population of Brazil - a multitude of ethnic groups subsumed under the abstract concept of "Indian". In comparison to his contemporaries, Alencar was able to find a rare balance between a nationalist orientation and a suitable aesthetical form. His books were published in form of episodes in daily newspapers, and found a wide range of public among the emerging sections of urban population. His most well-known works are precisely those belonging to the so-called Indianist trilogy which includes *Guarani*, *Iracema* and *Ubirajara* (all named after the main Indian characters). It is important to note that Brazilian Indianism differs from its homonym in the Hispano-American world, among other reasons, because it is almost void of the ethnic element: not only the Indian is never a writer himself, but also there is no real attempt to describe his ethnic peculiarities. Since those conscious efforts are absent, it does not seem to me to be correct to judge those narratives as misrepresentations. In fact, the absence of an ethnic element was itself that which allowed the free constructions of those narratives. An absence, I should say, that reflected a tragic realism: the Indian tribes of Brazil had been the victims of a massive process of elimination that took place either by physical destruction, miscegenation or cultural assimilation. This being so, we are in an altogether different context from that of Rousseau's *bon sauvage*: Alencar does not create idealisations of a 'national' past. There are instead conscious efforts to create subjectively, i.e. Romantically, mythical idealisations by resorting to local motifs. The character of an 'Indian' fits that purpose exactly because it is able to convey a myth of origin as a fundamental nationalist myth, i.e., a myth that repeats itself cyclically, contemporary to its creation and relatively free from the challenge posed by historical or ethnographic evidences (particularly in urban conglomerates).

On the other hand, the basic source for José de Alencar's Romantic and idealistic construction can be found in the self-styled (European) Caucasian qualities of nobility, courage and chivalry. In his own words, Peri - *Guarani*'s main character and hero - is "an European gentleman in the body of a savage". This Caucasianisation of 'local' characters follows the lessons of French Romantic René Chateaubriand (1768-1848) - whom Alencar admired for treating the Indians like characters of Homer – and is not confined to the Indian element. Even a more realistic symbol of Brazilian cultural identity - the *mestizo* - is equally submitted to this 'whitening' process of Caucasianisation, in which his *mestizo*-ness finds itself reduced to nothing more than a racial combination. This is well conveyed by the character of Moacir, the son of a white warrior and an Indian woman called Iracema, in the novel named after the latter. Thus, the real point of contention in José Alencar's fictional narrative is not the fact that he de-ethnicises the Indian and *mestizo* (when understood as a physical mixture of Indian, African and European matrices) characters: the real processes had done the same. The basic problem lies on the superimposition on them of a white, Caucasian quality. This posture is very much akin to the racist procedures in vogue during that period. But at the same time, his narrative possesses a quantum of national reality - that minimum which was acceptable to the elites. The co-existence between the elites and the 'Indians' - even if mythological - amounted to an unconscious recognition of the latter's intrinsic participation in the process of formation of Brazilian culture.

The poetry of Castro Alves represents an interesting variant of the basic trend to idealise national matrices. His *negrism* presents a sharp difference from the later Caribbean and African movement known as *negritude*. Not only does the Negro not have a literary voice of his own, but also the author never deals with any particular African ethnicity as an historical victim. His subject is the de-ethnicised black slave of coffee and sugar-cane plantations - the abstract 'African', born, nourished and abused in America. The psychological specificity of the fictional Negro follows the same pattern of José de Alencar: the same exaltation of a European ethics and morality, the same 'whitening' process of Caucasianisation. And yet he operates an important and absolutely necessary inversion of predominant feelings. The morality of the slave could not be classified as heroic in the sense of chivalry. It was however heroic in the Christian sense of goodness, of courage and, mainly, of a humanistic capacity to endure and resist suffering amidst a situation of cruel exploitation, as the beautiful and pungent poem of Castro Alves *The Ship of the Slaves* (*Navio Negreiro*) exuberantly shows.

The 'reverse' psychology of Castro Alves' characters seems to come as a recognition of the fact that the Negro represented a reality empirically closer than the Indian did. The Negro was a contemporary 'available' both in rural and urban centres, both as a slave of every coffee and sugar-cane plantation and as a growing contingent of marginalised labour in the major cities. As a consequence, the process of mythification could not be as discretionary as in José de Alencar. Castro Alves' poetry had to remain 'controlled' by the overwhelming testimonies of 'African slaves'. This explains, to a certain extent, the solidarity and commitment lent by some Romantic writers like Castro Alves to the liberal cause of abolition of slavery. And yet the African slave, though real, was no longer the ethnic African. And he was, besides, the focus of a discretionary treatment that tended to veil his existence under the superimposition of Christian qualities such as forbearance and sacrifice - the other face of an ideal human heroism. Accordingly, this process of superimposition did not cease after the abolition of slavery: the heroism to resist a situation of social inferiority was replaced by the heroism to resist a much harder – and, perhaps, insurmountable - condition of racial inferiority. The Romantic ideal of Caucasianisation not only persisted, but also received a considerable boost during the ensuing decades. But, finally, just as in the case of José de Alencar, one cannot deny a quantum of national reality imbibed in the poetry of Castro Alves - that minimum which was acceptable to the elites. The co-existence between the elites and the 'Africans' - even if mythological - amounted to an unconscious recognition of the latter's victimisation as a form of genuine participation in the process of formation of Brazilian culture.

One of the most important overtures of Romanticism to empirical and descriptive assessment is found in its valorisation of the natural environment. In José de Alencar, the tropical landscape emerges as the natural habitat of the mythical Indian. He is the lord of all fields, all regions - the mirror in which the landlord elites projected their desire to become so native to those lands as the ethnic Indians presumably were in the past. The beautiful description of bucolic scenes of the interior of Brazil not only complemented the process of idealisation of the Indian – a spark of consciousness and order within the nature - but also and foremost, presented a 'national scenario' abounding in realistic and naturalist elements. The description renders the reader a pantheistic contemplation of all natural forms - their mutual accord and vitality. The sensual and pictorial portraits of Brazilian geographical diversity cause a quasi-religious impact and amazement – the eternal mystery of God and its creation. It is a practical lesson of natural ethnography, botany, zoology - all this vivified by an impressionist appreciation that constantly reveals the analogical links between nature and the states of mind. It is, finally, a conscious attempt to signal a definitive departure from the European landscape. The realm of virgin plains, forests, mountains, and unique fauna and flora impresses for the exotic, the picturesque and the fantastic.

A final point of paramount importance in the development of Romanticism in Brazilian literature relates to the very instrument of aesthetical creation, i.e., the Portuguese language. José de Alencar was, perhaps, the first writer to consciously sustain the need to adjust the literary language to the Portuguese spoken in Brazil, which had largely departed from some of the Lusitanian canons. Many representatives in the Romantic circles felt tempted to take that suggestion to its ultimate consequences by suggesting that an independent and separate Brazilian language was on its way, basically on account of a realistic cultural difference which were clearly noticeable between Brazil and Portugal. The 'separatists' – as the group became known – constituted a fair example of how the idealist spirit fuelled by nationalist feelings was ready to sacrifice basic scientific principles. The concept of a Brazilian language was shown to be, in course of time, nothing but a Romantic myth. Not only did it not exist at the ground level, i.e., in its spoken form, but also it did not inspire major changes in the literary field, not even those which realistically accounted for the gap between both the forms. Conservatism prevailed and the writers of the period continued to follow the Lusitanian norms. The few innovations introduced were restricted to lexical curiosities, many of them deliberately included in order to create an aesthetical impact. That is particularly true in the case of the utilisation of words of African and Indian origin. Their 'disproportionate' utilisation suited the Romantic exercise of adding exotic flavour to the narrative. In the ultimate analysis, however, the Romantic cry for a Brazilian language was the first major expression of the intuitive feeling that the autonomous development of the Brazilian Portuguese since the sixteenth century was a natural consequence of the development of a new culture in the tropics. Even admitting that the Brazilian Portuguese could not and need not claim any separate status, it had however earned the right to an independent formulation of linguistic canons and lexicons which demanded a fair literary expression.

In sum, the three basic aspects analysed above – viz., (i) the ideology of Indianism / Negrism, (ii) the valorisation of the natural landscape, and (iv) the proposal of a national language – show that the Romantic search for a national cultural identity was ambiguous and often contradictory. Brazilians were no longer Portuguese, and yet they were like Europeans or white Caucasians adjusted to the tropics. Their territory was no longer Europe, but it was still the locus of an ethics of chivalry. And there was a Brazilian language that innovated in nothing but a few lexical peculiarities.

Though the answers were ambiguous, the questions were rightly formulated for the simple reason that they were based on an instinct of nationality. The evolution of Brazilian literature from Romanticism until the emergence of the modernist movement in 1922 - passing through Realism, Parnasianism and Symbolism - was substantively marked by a continuous influx of additional steps forward. The resolution given by the modernism signalled the country's definitive attainment of cultural and literary independence. Mário de Andrade (1893-1945), the greatest personality of the movement, paid tribute to the Romantic period for initiating the process and creating the basic conditions for the subsequent pursues. The modernist initial steps took the form of a de-construction of many of the Romantic responses, lending a new semantics to the same empirical references: the noble Indian became the cannibal, the 'eater of men'. It was celebrated in Oswaldo de Andrade (1890-1954)'s *Anthropophagous Manifesto* as a symbol of a new routine of incorporation of external inputs, free from both emulation and xenophobia. The Negro martyr became the crafty, shrewd and the son of the Devil - the hero without any character of Mário de Andrade's famous novel *Macunaíma*. But most important, the Brazilian *mestizo* - to where the critical assessment of the Negro and Indian elements ultimately converged - became the realistic and optimist symbol of Brazilian synthetic and relatively homogeneous culture. The word *mestizo* itself became the less and less appropriate for a new entity which emerged as a positive reversion of a painful process of de-culturalisation and de-ethnicisation of all matrices (the proto-Brazilians), viz., the Indians, the Africans and, obviously, the Europeans.

REFERENCES

José de Alencar. *O guarani*, Rio de Janeiro: Edições de Ouro, n/d.

——. *Iracema*, Rio de Janeiro: Edições de Ouro, n/d.

——. 'Pós-Escrito' in *O Português do Brasil*, São Paulo: Edusp, 1978.

Castro Alves. 'O Navio Negreiro' in *Obra Completa*, Rio de Janeiro: Nova Aguillar, 1997.

Mário de Andrade. *Macunaíma*, Belo Horizonte: Itatiaia, 1986.

——. 'O Movimento Modernista', in *Aspetos da Literatura Brasileira*, São Paulo: Livraria Martins, 1974.

Oswaldo de Andrade. 'Manifesto Antropófago' in *Obras Completas-6*, Rio de Janeiro: Civilização Brasileira, 1972.

Alfredo Bosi. *História Concisa da Literatura Brasileira*, São Paulo: Cultrix, 1999.

Darcy Ribeiro. *O Povo Brasileiro*, São Paulo: Companhia das Letras, 1995.

Roberto Schwartz. *Misplaced Ideas: Essays on Brazilian Culture*, London: Verso, 1992.

Thomas Skidmore. *O Preto no Branco: Raça e Nacioalidade no Pensamento Brasileiro*, Rio de Janeiro: Paz e Terra, 1976.

Luís Viana Filho. *A vida de José de Alencar*, Rio de Janeiro: José Olympio, 1979.

ABHAI MAURYA

Alexander Pushkin – A Revolutionary Romantic or a Prudent Realist?

This paper discusses the problems of Romanticism both on the aesthetic and the ideological planes. Pushkin himself had been deeply exercised over the aesthetic and theoretical dimensions of the conception of Romanticism. In his writings on literature, his correspondence with his contemporaries and his random notes he had commented on this question recurrently.

Writing to A. A. Bestuzhev on November 30, 1825 about his work *Caucasian Prisoner* and other works, Pushkin affirms,

> I have written a tragedy and am very pleased with it, but am very afraid of sending it out in the world – our timid palate will not accept true Romanticism. By Romanticism we understand Lamartine. Read what I may of Romanticism, I still cannot get to the right thing; even Küchelbecker is wrong.[1]

Küchelbecker looked for national individuality in Romantic poetry and criticised his contemporaries for being too imitative of foreign writers and scholars: Zhukovsky, considered the father of Russian Romanticism, of Schiller and Pushkin of Byron.

It is true that Pushkin was under the spell of Byron as a poet and a crusader for liberty of enslaved peoples. He admired the "sombre, heroic, forceful, Byronic poetry".[2] But his understanding of Romanticism was different. In the realm of Russian literature at that time, in Pushkin's own assessment, by the term 'Romanticism' reviewers implied "works bearing the stamp of melancholy and reverie" and they "unceremoniously set on one plane Dante and Lamartine, and autocratically divide European literature into Classical and Romantic, conceding to the first the languages of the Latin south and attributing to the second the Germanic tribes of the north, so that Dante..., Ariosto, Lope de Vega, Calderón and Cervantes, find themselves in the classical phalanx ..."[3].

In Pushkin's opinion the majority of Russian critics and theorists had borrowed the French conception of Romanticism lock stock and barrel. In his miscellaneous notes Pushkin writes, "French critics have their own conception of Romanticism. They class as Romantic all those works, which bear the mark of melancholy and reverie. Some of them term neologism and errors of grammar Romanticism."[4]

In Pushkin's opinion Romanticism should have meant a revolt against classicism leading to bold experiments and innovations both in the form and the content of literary works. Writing on his tragedy *Boris Godunov*, Pushkin states, "I imagined that we had indeed tired of the decorum and perfection of classical antiquity and of the pale, monotonous copies of its imitators, that our jaded taste demanded other, stronger sensations and was seeking them in the turbid but boiling sources of a new, native poetry." Pushkin further adds, "I confess that in literature I am a sceptic (to say no worse) ... Should the literary conscience be superstitiously subject to conventions and forms?"[5]

Pushkin was convinced that in France it was "Romanticism, which will regenerate poetry, which is at present dead".[6]

True to this understanding of Romanticism Pushkin wrote a "truly Romantic tragedy" *Boris Godunov*, in which he discarded the two classical unities – of time and space –, barely retained the third unity, i. e. that of action. He radically transformed the style of French classical tragedies and replaced the respected alexandrine by blank verse; he did not divide the tragedy into acts and, finally, inserted even a prose text in between the long poetic stretches. Such a bold innovation, understandably, attracted harsh criticism from conservative literary mandarins like Lobanov, who, while speaking at the Russian Academy of Sciences in 1836, said, "Romanticism – a word, which – though as yet vague – has magic in it – has become for many a *cover for complete arbitrariness and literary extravagance*."[7]

Here we are not in a position to dwell at length on whether Pushkin's conception of Romanticism in literature is adequate or not. Suffice it to say that it did correspond to the main element, which is accepted by all the theorists to be the quintessence of Romanticism, i.e. Romanticism seeks to transform the existing stale literary processes by infusing fresh, vibrant and invigorating emotional and ideological tonality into them. Pushkin did not theorise much on the issue as it had been historically a complex issue, understood differently by different scholars in different historical epochs – it was "liberalism" to A. N. Vesyolovsky, "idealism" to I. I. Zamotin, "individualism" and "subjectivism" to V. V. Sipovsky, P. S. Kogan and G. A. Gukovsky, "renunciation of the real ground reality" to P. N. Sakulin, "dream" to B. S. Meilakh, "affirmation of an ideal" to N. K. Gey, "absolute character of ideals coupled with the realisation of impossibility to achieve them in the given reality" to A. M. Gurevich, "intuitive understanding of reality" to A. N. Sokolov, "running away from contemporary issues and juxtaposition of present times with the past" to V. V. Vanslav. The list is by no means exhaustive.

In the present context it is neither possible nor required to go into a comprehensive definition of Romanticism. We would only add that the cult of individuality, fantasisation, pangs of loneliness, craving for freedom, total lack of rationalisation and cold-blooded calculation, flight from routine and mundane life to unknown horizons – soaring into the skies, to high mountain peaks, plunging into open seas and forests, spontaneity of thought and actions, particularly rebellious ones, and subversion of the existing order of things are some of the essential dimensions of Romanticism.

In other words a Romantic is a rebel both in life and literature. However, a Romantic is only a rebel against and not a rebel for creating an alternative system or structure in place of the one he wants to subvert. He simply is not aware of what he wants to build in place of the one he wants to demolish. Thus, from a Romantic a revolutionary is only one step away. In this sense it could be safely concluded that Pushkin remained a Romantic till the very end of his creative life. At times he was constrained to blend it with prudent realism by the circumstances in which he had been placed. A cursory perusal of his literary pursuits would substantiate our point beyond any shred of doubt.

From his Lycee days Pushkin found himself in the vortex of nonconformist friends like Pushchin, Küchelbecker, the future Decembrists. These comrades were already involved in secret revolutionary activities, but they did not involve Pushkin in the subversive actions because of his impulsiveness.

Pushkin, however, fully shared the revolutionary ideas of his friends. At eighteen Pushkin wrote his famous poem *Freedom* (1817) in which he overtly and covertly contrived to cock a snook at despotism. In this poem he openly declares:

> I want to sing a song of Freedom
> And jolt the vice embedded on thrones.

Then he goes on to describe the tyranny, the slavery under which people had been reeling all around:

> As far as I cast my glance
> Everywhere I see the whipping of people in fetters,
> ...
> Everywhere the naked dance of slavery.

It is in this background that Pushkin gives a clarion call both to tyrants and to their victims:

> Tyrants of the world! Come to your senses!
> And you the fallen slaves!
> Pick up courage,
> Awaken, rise in rebellion!
>
> (*trans. mine*)

It was nothing less than a feat of valour in those days of strict censorship and ruthless suppression in Russia to have written *Freedom*, a poem permeated with the notes of open challenge thrown to despotism, be it that of Napoleon or that of Alexander I.

In 1818 Pushkin writes the poem *To Chaadaev*, in which he openly expresses his disillusionment with the rule of Alexander I. He is convinced that the star of freedom will certainly rise in Russia:

> Dear friend, have faith: the wakeful skies
> Presage a dawn of wonder – Russia
> Shall from her age-old sleep arise,
> And despotism impatient crushing,
> Upon its ruins our names incise!
>
> (*trans. by Irina Zheleznova*)

Soon after this in 1819 Pushkin writes another rebellious poem *Village*, in which having described the natural beauty of the countryside in the first part, he embarks on debunking the tyranny being perpetrated by ruthless landlords on hapless peasants:

> But a sombre thought is casting a morose shadow on my mind:
> Not paying any heed to tears, not hearing any bemoaning,
> The cruel barons here are laws unto themselves.
> . . . .
> They have mercilessly usurped
> The labour, the property, and the time of poor peasants.
> Here the slavery personified
> Is dragging out a miserable existence
> Bent on plough burrows of ruthless lords.
> . . . .
> Here the innocent girls grow up
> To blossom for the whims and fancies of wicked lords.
> The poem concludes with a rhetorical question:
> O Friends! shall I see some day people without fetters?
> Shall I see the end of slavery, the creation of tsar's megalomania?

> Will the wonderful dawn of enlightened freedom
> Spread its glittering light over my motherland?
>
> (*trans. mine*)

No wonder that Pushkin's revolutionary poems spread far and wide in the whole of Russia. Very soon they were on everyone's lips: "There was not at that time a literate ensign in the army who did not know them by heart. Generally speaking, Pushkin became the voice of his generation ..., a truly national poet, such as Russia had never had,"[8] wrote the Decembrist Ivan Yakushkin.

Naturally, the inevitable had to happen. The emperor was furious and he told the Director of the Lycee, "Pushkin will have to be exiled to Siberia: he has flooded Russia with scandalous verses; all the young men know them by heart."[9]

Fortunately, on the intervention of some friends Siberia was substituted by the Caucasus and Pushkin was exiled to Ekaterinoslav to work under General Inzov. These were the days when Byron had become a shining star, participating in the war of Greek independence. He achieved apotheosis upon his death in this war.

While staying in the Caucasus Pushkin began learning English, using Byron's poems as textbooks, from his friends and muses of that time, the Raevsky girls. Here he wrote his first Byronic poem "The day's lamp has gone out ...." Thus, during this sojourn in the Romantic Caucasus Pushkin was completely under the spell cast by Byron.

The spellbinding scenic beauty by which Pushkin found himself surrounded reinforced the sway of the Byronic mood. The crystalline beauty of the snow clad peaks of the Caucasian mountains, dominated by Elbruz, gleaming majestically against the azure sky deepened his Romantic fervour. Pushkin was also mesmerised by the life style of the primitive Circassian tribes, who in their austere and uncomplicated life often displayed undiluted loyalty and bravery. The local colour and customs became natural adjuncts to his Byronic Romantic mood. The virtues of unspoilt peasant life contrasted in their majesty with the vices of over-civilised urbanity. Pushkin consolidated his Romantic ardour by studying the mores of the Circassians and gypsies. All this became an ideal setting for creating the first long Romantic poem *The Prisoner of the Caucasus* – the story of the self-sacrificing, unrequited love of a Circassian girl for a Russian prisoner, freed by her. The love of this pristine beauty breaks against the drained out emotions of the prisoner and the girl has no option but to drown herself in a fast flowing Caucasian brook after filing through the chains of the prisoner. The Russian protagonist looks back on the girl plunging in the river, but does not dive in to save her.

The poem is replete with thumbnail sketches of the Circassians, bristling with weapons, making a last ditch effort to defend their mountain fastness against the plundering Cossacks.

This Romantic mood of Pushkin gets a further boost through his encounters with the revolutionaries – the future Decembrists like Yakushkin, General Orlov, and above all, with Pestel, the most dynamic and energetic of all the revolutionaries. It is probably in dedication to Pestel that he wrote the splendid short poem "The Dagger", in which he warned tyrants of the Nemesis that awaited them if they continued with their tyranny. The poem, naturally, could not have been published in his lifetime and it circulated far and wide in manuscript.

In moments of frivolous naughtiness he wrote the blasphemous "Gavriiliada", a poem which Pushkin did not own up to having written at all. Nevertheless, he had a serious skirmish with the establishment, particularly with the church for the blasphemous content of the poem. This trouble was further confounded by the interception of a letter he had written to a friend in which he admitted of "taking lessons in pure Atheism" from a deaf English philosopher, who was "the only intelligent Atheist"[10] he had met. Pushkin's captor at that time, Count Vorontsov had got tired of his bohemianism and he used this act of open iconoclasm to send him out of Odessa. But before that Pushkin had begun writing his best known Romantic poem *The Gypsies.*

Pushkin was ordered into exile to his ancestral estate at the village Mikhailovskoe, not far from Petersburg, where he was to live under police surveillance.

On his arrival at Mikhailovskoe he completed his last Romantic poem *To the Sea*, a farewell to the Black Sea as well as to Byron who had died in 1824:

Another genius has left us,
Another master of our thoughts.
Leaving the world his laurel-wreath ...
The earth has emptied ...

Having thus bid farewell to "the Romantic beauties, the demonic companion, the crags and cliffs"[11] Pushkin settled down to a life of rural seclusion.

In this background it is important to cite the view propounded by a very authoritative Russian literary scholar D. Blagoi, who in his monograph *Sociology of Pushkin's Creative Writings* stated: "In the evolution of the class consciousness of Pushkin one can discern three main phases, which coincide with the spanning of the general philosophical and political world-view of the poet as well as with the main mile-stones in his creative development ....

The first period – the phase of least class consciousness, obtaining in Pushkin's world-view – is linked with the Lycee and the initial years of post-Lycee life of the poet (from 1817 to 1823 approximately)."[12]

Blagoi terms the second stage, i.e. the period spanning from 1823 to 1830, as the phase of Pushkin's identification with the class of aristocracy and gentry. The third and the last phase, according to Blagoi, is marked by the realisation on Pushkin's part that the aristocracy was doomed to perish. Hence he shifted his loyalty and commitment to the class of 'meshchanstvo' which could be roughly translated as petty-bourgeoisie, a class of philistines.

What is noteworthy is that Blagoi builds up his thesis in extremely categorical terms, in black and white hues without taking into consideration the complicated circumstances in which Pushkin had been placed. Even the erratic temperament, with which most creative personalities, particularly the poets of Romantic bent are imbued, did not receive adequate credence and consideration.

Beginning from his days in exile at Mikhailovskoe Pushkin got embroiled in more staid works like Evgeny Onegin and others. But even at the end of the first stage, as defined by Blagoi, Pushkin's view vis-à-vis the aristocracy, the peasantry and the autocracy are crystal clear. In his notes on Russian History written in 1822 while in exile at Kishinev Pushkin states "... Only a fearful cataclysm could destroy the deep-rooted slavery which exists in Russia; and nowadays our political freedom is inseparable from the emancipation of the peasants."[13]

It is true that when Pushkin shifted to Mikhailovskoe he had matured in age and thoughts. But he had neither abandoned his democratism, nor had he walked over to the aristocracy lock stock and barrel. What, in all probability, had happened was that Pushkin had learnt to be more careful, wiser in expressing himself publicly in the conditions of strict censorship and police surveillance in exile. Another method he had begun evolving was that of putting on a mask with a view to camouflage his mission while working under the Damocles' sword of ever imminent danger, a device which he was to perfect a great deal in the later stages of his life.

Blagoi also forgets that it was on December 14, 1825 that the Decembrist uprising took place in which his closest friends were involved. Indeed, the events of 14th December jolted Pushkin badly as he was deeply anxious both about his own fate and that of his close comrades.

His poems were found in manuscript form almost with all the rebels and they quoted profusely from them at the trial. All of them admitted that they were deeply influenced by the revolutionary ardour of Pushkin's poems and that Pushkin was their poet laureate, their "poet of freedom". Tsarist authorities even sent investigators to check on Pushkin's sources, but they found nothing. Indeed, Pushkin had to destroy every shred of paper that could be used as evidence against him and his comrades. He burnt even his very valuable work – his memoirs, which was ready in almost final form.

But Blagoi should have given some credit to Pushkin's bold reply to the Tsar when Pushkin was invited to his personal court after the failure of the December uprising as to where would he have been had he been in Petersburg on 14th December. Pushkin was laconic and precise in his response: at the senate square along with his friends in rebellion. No, Pushkin had not changed his strategy, his basic aesthetic and ethic positions. He had changed only his tactics. And that was the need of the hour. Blagoi is needlessly bent on converting Pushkin into a lackey of the gentry, an ardent supporter of his class, the aristocracy.

Even when Pushkin had to keep silent, even when he had to put on a mask, even when he had to indulge in double-speak, Pushkin remained true to his salt, to his original convictions. The truth, however, is that Pushkin did not really fall silent fully. It is in 1825 that Pushkin writes his Romantic tragedy Boris Godunov. In 1826 Pushkin writes his extremely significant poem "The Prophet" in which it is as if God calls upon a poet:

> Arise, O sage! ...
>
> . . . .
>
> Stride over the earth, a prophet, searing
> The hearts of men with righteous words.

In 1827 Pushkin, even in the face of sure peril in case of being betrayed, sends his famous poetic message to his comrades, the Decembrists, who were languishing in the Siberian ravines:

> Deep in Siberian mines, let naught
> Subdue your proud and patient spirit.
> Your crushing toil and lofty thought
> Shall not be wasted – do not fear it.
>
> . . . .
>
> The prison walls will crash ... Content
> At door will freedom wait to meet you;

Your brothers, hastening to greet you,
To you the sword will gladly present.

(*trans. by Irina Zheleznova*)

In the second half of the 1820s and in the early 1830s Pushkin created masterpieces of politically loaded poems, plays and stories, notwithstanding the fact that the Tsar Nikolai I had assumed the role of his first and foremost censor. In 1830 Pushkin writes *Tales of Belkin* in which for the first time in the whole of Russian literature he brilliantly portrayed the characters of what in Russian literary criticism came to be known as little men. These protagonists hardly belong to Pushkin's own class – the aristocracy, to whom, according to Blagoi, Pushkin should have sung panegyrics. But the great author with an immense power of empathy created powerful and endearing characters of an innkeeper, a coffin maker, peasant girls, gentlemen, sensitive young women and so on.

In 1833 Pushkin writes his long poem *The Bronze Horseman* in which he "held a mirror up to the despots and Nicholas I flinched at the reflection".[14]

In the last years of his life, though married and having enormous additional family responsibilities, Pushkin did not convert himself to meshchanstvo. On the contrary he remained true to his ideals, his times, family obligations and the hopelessness of the cause he stood for notwithstanding. The poet, however, chose to use discretion. From an infantile Romantic he had matured into a prudent realist with a fair smattering of Romantic streaks still flowing underneath the surface. Indeed, he used ingenious methods to pursue the same goal for which he stood in his youthful pre-Decembrist days.

Radishchev and his book *Journey from Petersburg to Moscow* (1790) had been a taboo with the Tsar and his hangmen; even a word could not have been uttered or written on this topic in those times. The aim of the autocracy was plain and simple – the revolutionary writer and his book, in which there was an open call to people to overthrow despotism through people's revolution, should be wiped out from people's memory completely.

But Pushkin had other ideas. He did not want that the feat of valour accomplished by Radishchev should be thrown into the dustbin of history so easily. Nor did he want to allow him to be forgotten by the people and the powers that be. However, he invented ingenious ways of keeping Radishchev's brave ideas ablaze. In 1834 he embarked upon writing a polemical work ostensibly to counter Radishchev's 'mad' ideas in the form of *Journey from Moscow to Petersburg*. By starting the 'journey' in the opposite direction to that of Radishchev's, Pushkin appeared to refute the former chapter by chapter and point by point. But what did he end up doing?

Pushkin engages in polemics with Radishchev only on peripheral issues, maybe for diverting the attention of the censors and the tsarist hangmen. For instance, he leaves Radishchev's idea of peoples' revolution totally undisputed; he bypasses Radishchev's "An Ode to Freedom" without uttering a word. Indeed, Pushkin mentions in passing all the vital problems and issues posed by Radishchev, and instead of refuting them he facilely passes on to the discussion of other innocuous questions. He does it with regard to issues like forcible conscription of Russian peasants, the only bread-earners of families, into the tsarist army, on the sale of peasants, the serfs, in auction, on censorship and so on. In fact, on some of the problems Pushkin is constrained to concede defeat to Radishchev. On the question of forced recruitment of peasants after quoting Radishchev, Pushkin concludes: "The picture is terrible because it is true. I shall not drown myself like Radishchev in his exaggerated but sincere daydreaming ... with which this time I am in agreement willy-nilly."

The same is true of the description of tyranny perpetrated by the local tyrants, the landlords and their cohorts on peasants, be that in the form of exploitation by them of serfs or deflowering of innocent peasant girls by landlords and so on. On some occasions, agreeing with Radishchev, Pushkin adds his own gory details to the horrible picture already created by his predecessor.

A.S. Makogonenko is right in his conclusion that Pushkin's "decision of writing a rejoinder to Radishchev's book" meant at the same time a "conscious decision to include into the ambit of contemporary burning issues the ideas of Radishchev, his experience, his historical generalisations about Russian and West-European social and political reality".[15]

Having discussed Pushkin's *Journey from Moscow to Petersburg* in depth Makogonenko states that Pushkin could not successfully accomplish his mission of giving "an extraordinary rebuttal to Radishchev's positions" because "there was no point of dispute between the two of them ... Pushkin's narrator had to ... fall in line with Radishchev 'willy-nilly'."[16]

If that was so, why did Pushkin launch into polemics with Radishchev? The answer is that Pushkin was indulging only in tactical shadowboxing. He had some other hidden agenda, different from the one that had been announced. By resorting to tactical silences, gaps, retreats and even scandalous agreements with Radishchev's position Pushkin wanted to revive the discussion on Radishchev; he wanted to keep the Damocles' sword of peoples' revolution hanging on the despots of the day.

Precisely with the same objective in view Pushkin returned to Radishchev in 1836, this time in the form of an article titled "Alexander Radishchev", meant for publication in the third issue of *Sovremennik* of which he was an editor at that time. However, the article was proscribed by order of the Minister of Education, S.S. Uvarov, who wrote: "The article in itself is not a bad one and could, with a few alterations, be passed. On the other hand I find it both inconvenient and absolutely unnecessary to revive the memory of a writer and a book, which have been completely and rightly forgotten."[17]

Pushkin's article is written in such a manner that censorship could consider it to be an anti-Radishchev piece and pass it. That is why Pushkin was constrained to describe his book as "a mediocre work" and his action of publishing the book illegally an "act of a mad man". Surely Radishchev's action was bound to wreak havoc with his own life. His misadventure had no chance of success. To that extent Pushkin's epithets against Radishchev are fully justified. But reading between the lines one finds mind-boggling hidden messages, grudgingly granting Radishchev the right to be considered an honourable man. Pushkin writes that Radishchev was a "criminal (he had been so declared by the tsarist authorities - added) of extraordinary spirit; a political fanatic, erring without doubt but acting with amazing selflessness and displaying an almost chivalric conscientiousness".[18]

Obviously the first part of this formulation is meant for the consumption of the censor, while the truth lies in the second. At times one gets the feeling that Pushkin had run Radishchev down too much. But the purpose, which he was pursuing, required this approach and the aim was clear: Pushkin wanted that the book *Journey from Petersburg to Moscow* be revived and allowed to be read by people, who should be the final judge of Radishchev's work : "... it suffices for the reader to open the book at random to convince him of the truth of what we have said."[19] Precisely that was what Pushkin had at the back of his mind: let the book be allowed to be read! No meshchanin, no philistine, no petty bourgeois would dare do it.

1835 was the year of the tenth anniversary of the Decembrist uprising. Russia's best sons were still languishing in Siberia or in the Caucasus. The air in that year was laden with rumours about impending amnesty that was about to be granted to the Decembrists. Some softening of punishment did take place in the form that prison terms had been reduced. But people wanted all the Decembrists amnestied forthwith. Pushkin was most anxious about the prospect. But it was not happening. His heart bled. He again resorted to the allegoric method with a view to squeeze out the amnesty from the stonehearted Tsar Nikolai I. He took an extraordinary step. He decided to show to Nikolai I the mirror of Peter the Great by writing the poem *Feast of Peter the First in 1835*.

Pushkin portrays festive celebrations of a merry feast being organised in the "Tsar's Palace" and expresses his utter amusement and astonishment over the nature of the occasion that had led to the festivities. The poet unleashes a shower of rhetorical questions, trying to figure out the secret of such a rapturous and tumultuous merriment:

> Why is the great Tsar taking to such festivities
> In the city of Petersburg?
> ...
> Has the Russian sword or flag
> Won new laurels?
> Have the sombre Swedes been vanquished?
> Is the terrible foe begging for peace?
> ...
> Is the anniversary of Poltava victory
> Being celebrated as a national day?
> Or has the queen Ekaterina given birth to a son?
> ...
> No! He is celebrating the making of peace with his subjects;
> Forgiving the crime of enemies of yore, his heart is brimming with joy,
> He is sharing one common mug full of beer with them,
> And kissing them in their forehead,
> His heart is leaping out and face is alit with brilliance;
> He is celebrating the mercy shown, the amnesty granted,
> Like the victory over an enemy!

The message to Nikolai I is loud and clear that he should follow the example of his great grandfather, renounce vindictiveness, forgive the 'mistake' of his 'misguided' but selfless subjects, rid them of the stigma of being 'state criminals' and return them home as they had already suffered ten years of slogging in the "Siberian mines". Pushkin even proposed the form of this magnanimity to be shown by Nikolai I – making peace with his subjects. However, Pushkin had not much illusion that the Tsar would be moved as he was incapable of "rising up to the level of his ancestors".[20]

Makogonenko has very correctly understood the real objective of writing the poem *The Feast of Peter the First in the year 1835*: "The publication of the poem had a paradoxical aim behind it: to create an impact on the reader not by the text but what had been invested in the poem in figurative form, by the sub-text – by throwing a challenge to the monarch. The published text as if conveyed to the people – you see, Nikolai I could have followed such a glorious precedent, certainly could have.... But he would not do it. Everything happened as Pushkin had presumed – Nikolai I did not make peace with the Decembrists.

The publication of the poem in the *Sovremennik* created an effect of an indictment of the emperor, though not uttered in as many words – he is not endowed with as large a heart as Peter I and the wisdom which a head of state should have possessed. His actions are propelled by cruel vindictiveness: some of the Decembrists he does not free from penal servitude, while others, who are winning laurels for Russia (the ones who had been exiled to the Caucasus and who now had been fighting in the ranks of the Russian army in the Russo-Turkish war – added), he has exposed to the hail of bullets.... The emperor continues to hound, persecute and humiliate the best people of Russia."

Makogonenko finally concludes: "Having published the poem ten years after the Decembrist uprising had taken place, Pushkin had tried to underline his spiritual, ideological proximity or closeness with his 'comrades and brothers'; he had endeavoured to take stock of his relationship with those whom the government had branded as state criminals."[21]

In 1835 Pushkin launched on another adventure with absolutely identical intentions. However, this time he wanted to bring into focus those of the Decembrists who had been "exposed to the hail of bullets" in the Russo-Turkish war. Pushkin decided to publish his travelogue *Journey to Arzrum*, which, indeed, he had written in 1829 in the hot pursuit of his dangerous journey to the battlefields, the action theatre of Russo-Turkish war that was being fought at that time on the Turkish territory.

Two important questions naturally arise in this context. Firstly, why did he undertake this journey that was fraught with peril and that too after he had been refused permission to do so by the tsarist authorities? Secondly, why did he publish the travelogue in 1835 after having kept it shelved in cold storage for six long years?

The journey undertaken to Arzrum was prompted by several factors. First and foremost was the fact that he knew quite well that apart from being in Siberia several prominent Decembrists were doing active war service in the army of General Paskevich engaged in war with Turkey. Naturally, he wanted to meet his friend-Decembrists, even if he had to go to them without the Tsar's permission. Secondly, Pushkin was getting suffocated in the surroundings of the high society life of 'peaceful' Petersburg. Just after three years of the abortive uprising Pushkin was once again being overwhelmed by Romantic yearnings and urges that could have uplifted him from the mundane life and landed him in some new, fresh, vibrant and dare-devil type of situations. Obviously nothing could have been more tantalising for realising such intentions than the journey through the rugged beauty of the steppes, Kalym territory, Caucasian rivers and mountains, through Georgia, Vladikavkaz, Ossetia, Terek, Darial Pass, snow-clad mountains, waterfalls, Tfilisi, Armenia, fountains of mineral waters, Ararat mountain and finally through the battle lines in Turkey. This journey sometimes on carts, sometimes on ponies and other times on foot through almost a virgin route, infested with dangerous tribal robbers and bandits, was fraught with immense danger to the life of the traveller. But Pushkin braved it all thanks to the Romantic hues and spirit in which he had got coloured once again, inspired by the loftiness of the mission he had embarked upon.

V. Shaduri, an eminent Pushkin scholar, is quite justified when he concludes, "With all his heart and mind, in all his thoughts and dreams, Pushkin was with them (the Decembrist brothers-comrades – added). Because he was getting choked in the capital in the atmosphere of police tyranny and was feeling oppressive loneliness, he was keen on rushing out to the Caucasus come what may. Firstly, it was his insurmountable spiritual requirement, and, secondly, a journey to Arzrum, a meeting with the Decembrists, was part of the creative plans and ideas of the poet at that time."[22]

Precisely that was the third reason for Pushkin to desperately want to go to Arzrum. He wanted to include the Decembrist theme in the next part of his novel in verse *Evgeny Onegin*. The Decembrist movement was also to be a part of other creative works of Pushkin as at that time he was fed up with fiddling with small problems and beating about the bush. What he required was fresh, vibrant and bubbling stuff. So, he was back to his youthful effervescent Romantic mood rather than drowning himself in any philistine superficiality.

However, the question as to why did he keep the manuscript buried for six long years and dig it out in 1835 still persists. We have already discussed the real motivation for publishing the *Feast of Peter the First in*

1835. Apart from some additional factors the fundamental reasons for publishing the *Journey from Moscow to Petersburg* in 1835 were almost identical with those that led to the publication of the *Feast*. Indeed Pushkin had tried to publish his travelogue in 1830. Some extracts of it appeared in the *Literary Gazeta* of 5th February, 1830. But in March, 1830 an arch-reactionary critic Bulgarin, with whom Pushkin had been having a running battle for all his creative life, went hammer and tongs against Pushkin in his journal *Severnaya pchela*: "And so, our hopes have been dashed. We had thought that the author of Ruslana and Lyudmila had rushed to the Caucasus in order to replenish himself with lofty poetic sentiments, to enrich himself with new impressions and then convey to posterity the feats of valour of contemporary Russian heroes in sweet and soothing songs. We had thought that the great events, taking place in the East, that had stunned the world and had evoked respect for Russia among all the enlightened nations would have given a spur to the genius of poets. But, alas, that was not to be. We were mistaken."[23]

Consequent upon such vituperation, Pushkin was publicly accused of not praising the Tsar Nikolai I, not singing panegyrics in his address and not defending his Eastern policies. Indeed, the chief of the secret services or censorship Beckendorff filed a report on this issue with the Tsar: "Bulgarin's pen, which has always displayed unflinching loyalty to the authorities, has subjected the fact to scathing criticism that the journey beyond the Caucasus mountains and the great events, immortalising the recent years of our history, have not given a better flight to Pushkin's genius."[24] Makogonenko brilliantly sums up the entire issue: "In the conditions when they expected and demanded "sweet songs" from Pushkin, in which he should have immortalised the policies of Nikolai I there was no point even to think of publishing his travelogue. After all Decembrists would have become the heroes of these writings."[25]

In 1835 Pushkin wanted to do everything he could to win amnesty for his friends-Decembrists. So, along with *Feast of Peter the First* he decided to publish *Journey to Arzrum* also. In the *Journey* for the first time in Russian literature he created moving episodes in which the exiled Decembrists, the stigmatised "state criminals" are shown to be engaged in dangerous battles with the Turkish army, they are depicted as displaying exemplary courage, bravery and patriotism: General Burtsov falls to a heroic death, General Pushchin is seriously wounded, most other Decembrists are shown to be accomplishing rare feats of valour. By writing on this topic and publishing it Pushkin practically removed the ban on mentioning the Decembrists publicly, particularly by projecting them in a positive light.

V. Aivazyan conveyed this view very succinctly as far back as in 1952: "By restoring the truth (as to whom Russia should be grateful for the victory in the Russo-Turkish war – added) Pushkin once again expressed his loyalty to the ideas of liberation."[26]

V. Shaduri drew a similar conclusion several years later. He observed that *Journey to Arzrum* "is the only published work of this period in which the author managed to say something or the other about the Decembrists". Notwithstanding the ban on mentioning anything in the press about the Decembrists, "Pushkin succeeded in introducing the theme of heroism displayed by the Decembrists, narrate about them in a camouflaged form, which was quite transparent to initiated readers. In the last chapters of the *Journey*, devoted to military events, almost on every page we come across the Decembrists, who had played a decisive role in the military campaign of 1829".[27]

We would conclude our discussion on the topic by briefly dwelling on his last significant poetic work created in 1836 just five months before his death, i.e. *Monument*. It is amazing that Pushkin at the age of thirty seven, as if foreseeing his imminent end, wrote this poem in which he takes stock of his entire creative writing and offers gratitude to his people in extremely eloquent and powerful words for being proud of him, for loving him so much:

> People will cherish my memory for long,
> For enkindling kind feelings by my lyrics,
> And that in my cruel age I sang of Freedom
> And that I begged for mercy for the victims of injustice.
>
> (*trans. mine*)

It is worth noting that it is in 1836 that Pushkin is singing of Freedom/Liberty and not in 1817. This is not the manifestation of the disease of "infantilism" as Blagoi would have us believe. What is more, Pushkin is not mincing words. He is calling a spade a spade, terming his times as "cruel age".

The poem was found to be so volatile that when the monument was built to Pushkin at the time when the poet Zhukovsky was alive, he was constrained to substitute Pushkin's first two lines as cited above in the inscription on the monument by:

> People will cherish my memory for long,
> That I was useful to them thanks to the beauty of my vibrant poems.

Not that Pushkin had become desperate (he was in the prime of his life at thirty seven). Indeed, for bypassing the censorship he hit upon an incredibly ingenious plan. He moulded his poem exactly on the pattern of Derzhavin's poem *The Monument* with a view to creating an illusion that he was merely paying a tribute to the memory of the great Russian poet with a friendly response to his poem.

Pushkin deliberately moulded his *Monument* in a way that it structurally resembled Derzhavin's poem to the maximum possible extent. Both poems consist of five stanzas. So much so that Pushkin repeated the first lines of each stanza in ditto. But what did he achieve by resorting to this 'blatant act of imitating' a well-known Russian poet? Let us take the two poems stanza by stanza:

Derzhavin:
I have raised a monument to myself which is wonderful, eternal,
It is stronger than the metals and higher than the pyramids;
Neither a tempest, nor a lightening thunder would smash it
The fleeting time will not shatter it.

Pushkin:.
I have raised a monument to myself not made with hands,
The pathway to it trodden by people shall not overgrow with grass.
And holding its proud head high
It soars higher than the Alexander's Column.

Derzhavin's monument is "wonderful and eternal" because it is stronger than the metals and higher than the world famous pyramids of Egypt, whereas Pushkin has no claim to compare himself with the 'wonders of the world'. The strength of his monument lies in the fact that people will not forget him, the pathway of people visiting his monument will never overgrow with grass.

Secondly, Derzhavin's monument is "eternal" because no elemental fury can destroy it, while Pushkin's monument will never perish because its contribution, its moral value is higher than the column of the monument of Alexander I, which, at that time was the highest tower in the world. Clearly Pushkin here has the audacity to place a poet on a higher pedestal than that of the kings and tsars. This in those days was quite a provocative claim, to say the least. It must have been a particular affront to the despots in the background of the cruel and repressive regime of Nikolai I.

In the second stanza Derzhavin claims that he would be eternal and his fame will ever soar because large chunks of his being will escape degeneration and will live even after death as long as the world will honour the Slav people.

Pushkin says that he will not vanish in his entirety because his heart will ever throb and palpitate in his poems. He would continue to enjoy fame as long as one single kind heart exists in the world.

In the third stanza Derzhavin boasts that he will be well known far and wide, from White Sea to the Black Sea and numerous people will remember him as somebody who become famous overnight.

Pushkin announces that his name will be on the lips of different peoples – proud progeny of Slavs, Finns, Tungus and Kalmyk peoples, underlining thereby his affinity with living people rather than seas, vast planes and valleys. Pushkin's aspiration is for staying close to the heart of concrete people rather than to the abstract phenomena like seas, oceans, rivers, mountains and so on.

In the fourth stanza Derzhavin boasts of a unique achievement because he was the first to sing panegyrics to the Tsarina Felitsa, to tell the truth smilingly to the Tsar in his heart to heart talk with him about God.

Pushkin underscores that he will be remembered by people because he sang songs of Freedom and sought mercy for the victim of oppression, a cruel age surrounding him notwithstanding.

In the fifth stanza Derzhavin calls upon his Muse to pay back in the same coin to those people who deride it and to build an aura around its face lit by eternal dawn.

Pushkin calls upon his Muse to listen only to the voice of God, not to crave for laurels and not to be too much overjoyed or perturbed by the cacophony of praise or derision heaped upon it from whatever quarter. Pushkin particularly strikes a note of caution that his Muse should not legitimise the ignorant and conceited class of rulers, in Pushkin words, "the black blockheads of high society" or "aristocratic fools", by entering into discussion with them because that would be tantamount to stooping to their level.

There should not be any shred of doubt about where Pushkin's sympathies lay, for whom he cared and what was dearest to his heart on the eve of his death. Surely Pushkin had turned neither a lackey of aristocracy, nor of autocracy nor a petty philistine worm. Till the end of his life he soared high in the skies like a falcon, he did not creep or cringe before the powers that be, despite all odds and the hostile ruling class that surrounded him, seeking to choke him, his lyre, his song, his voice. No wonder that despotism engineered his murder in an orchestrated duel because, to quote two lines by a Russian poet written on the death of Pablo Neruda:

Tyrants poets do not understand,
If they do, they rush them to hang.

NOTES AND REFERENCES

1. A.S. Pushkin, 'Letter to A.A. Bestuzhev, 30 November 1825' in Tatiana Wolff, *Pushkin on Literature*, London: The Athlone Press, p. 164.
2. A.S. Pushkin, 'Letter to A.A. Delvig, 23 Marc 1821', *op. cit.*, p. 40.
3. A.S. Pushkin, *On Boris Godunov*, *op. cit.*, p. 222.
4. A.S. Pushkin, 'Miscellaneous Notes', *op. cit.*, p. 277.
5. *Op. cit.* as in No. 3, p. 221.
6. A.S. Pushkin, Draft of the *Letter to Prince P.A. Vyazemsky*, 4 November 1823, *op. cit.*, p. 76.
7. A.S. Pushkin, *The Opinions of M. E. Lobanov on the Spirit of Literature, both abroad and at home*, *op. cit.*, p. 397.
8. Tatiana Wolff, Pushkin: *Childhood, Boyhood and Youth*, *op. cit.*, p. 11.
9. *Ibid.*
10. A.S. Pushkin, *Letter to V. K. Kuchelbecker,* April/May, 1824, *op. cit.*, p. 88
11. Tatiana Wolff, *Pushkin: South – with Byron*, *op. cit.*, p. 36.
12. *Op. cit.* as in No. 8, p. 9.
13. A.S. Pushkin, *Notes on Eighteenth-Century Russian History*, *op. cit.*, p. 44.
14. Tatiana Wolff, *The New Pushkin*, *op. cit.*, p. 198.
15. G.P. Makogonenko, *Tvorchestvo A.S. Pushkina v 1830-ye gody (1833-1836)* (*Writings of A.S. Pushkin in 1830s (1833-1836)*, Leningrad: 'Khudozhestvennaya literatura', 1982, p. 257.
16. *Op. cit.* as in No. 22, p. 267.
17. Quoted in the book: Tatiana Wolff, *op. cit.*, p. 391 Quoted in the book: Tatiana Wolff, *op. cit.*, p. 391.
18. A.S. Pushkin, *Alexander Radishchev*, Tatiana Wolff, *op. cit.*, p. 388.
19. *Op. cit.*, p. 390.
20. G.P. Makogonenko, *op. cit.*, p. 337.
21. *Ibid.*
22. V. Shaduri, *Dekaberskaya literatura i gruzinskaya obshchestvennost'*, Tbilisi, 1958, p. 390.
23. D. Bulgarin, *Severnaya pchela*, No. 35, March 22, 1830.
24. *Starina i novizna*, IV, pp. 7-8.
25. G.P. Makogonenko, *op. cit.*, p. 313.
26. K.V. Aizyan, 'O Puteshectviye v Arzrum Pushkina' in *Trudy pervoi I vtoroi vsesoyuznoi pushkinskoi konferentsy*, M.-L., 1952, pp. 184-185.
27. V. Shaduri, *op. cit.*, p. 387.

SHARMISTHA LAHIRI

The Poetry of Giacomo Leopardi: Between Romanticism and Modernity – Readings on the *Canti*

> I do not know if my sentiments are born of illness; I do know that whether ill or in health, I trample on the cowardice of men, reject every consolation and puerile deception, and have the courage to bear the denial of every hope, to look without fear at the desolation of life, not dissembling from me any part of human unhappiness, and accept the consequences of a philosophy, painful but true.
>
> Giacomo Leopardi,[1] *Dialogue of Tristan and a Friend*, in *Operette morali*[2]

Efforts to situate Leopardi's texts within a particular cultural category or a determined aesthetic trend present problems, owing not little to the fluid contours and the highly individualized style of his poetry. The question of assimilation of romantic thought in the construction of his poetics in this sense is intriguing for it offers an instance where the authorial intentions seem to be at variance with the semantic autonomy of the text. In his critique of romantic poetry Leopardi opposed the theoretical postulates of Romanticism and defended the classicist tradition as a counterpoint, whereas in the textual dynamics his poetry yielded suggestions with unmistakable implications of romantic sensibilities. His poetics has been variously defined in terms of neo-classicist, romantic and even 'classico-romantic' categories, while being linked also to eighteenth century metaphysical thought and sensistic materialism. It is obvious that the difficulties faced towards a historical and cultural contextualization of his works derive to a large measure from the multiplicity of strands present in the text. Our effort hopes to provide readings from his texts in the *Canti* to probe if his poetry can be seen in the light of a link between the almost contiguous zones of Romanticism and Modernity in European culture. In this context, we examine two of his celebrated Idylls: *The Infinite* (*L'infinito*, 1819.) and *To Silvia* (*A Silvia*, 1828), each corresponding to a distinctive phase in his poetry, and conclude with textual references to one of the final compositions, *Wild Broom or The Flower of the Desert* (*La ginestra*, 1836), his last testimony to the world, one might say. The *Canti*, compiled by the poet himself, emerges as a macrotext in which the individual lyrics are threaded together not in the chronological order of composition but as successive moments in the story of his soul, reminiscent of the tradition of Petrarch's *Canzoniere*. This does not minimize to any extent the import of Leopardi's departure from the same lyrical tradition in terms of formal structure and conventions of versification, which can be seen, for example, in the way he introduced free verses or his poetry broke up what Fubini calls the "architectural symmetry" typical of Petrarch's *canzone*.[3] His text shows a conscious manipulation of aesthetic options that modelled in his verses a unique blend of innovativeness and continuity, setting a paradigm shift in Italian lyrics. We preface our reading of his poetry with a brief reference to his ideas on literature gleaned from his thoughts recorded in the notes in *Zibaldone*, in his letters, in his "Discourse..." on romantic poetry, and other prose texts. Together with the series of allegorical dialogues in satire in the *Operette morali*, these prose tracts trace the stages in the evolution of his poetics and constitute the theoretical background of ideas that his poetry expressed through images in the *Canti*.

In his early notes in *Zibaldone*, while indicating his basic preferences in poetic choices, Leopardi emphasized two qualities that to his mind characterized the essence of lyric poetry: spontaneous inspiration and brevity, attributes characteristic of the ancient Greek Idylls of third and second centuries BC, which give a distinct indication of his poetics in the *Canti*, especially his early Idylls.[4] He wrote that lyric poetry was to be understood not as imitation but the "free and direct expression of whatsoever aspect genuine and heartfelt in man".[5] It is a statement that can be placed within the ideological affiliations of Romanticism, whereas the other quality he mentioned, that of brevity ("poetry lies essentially in an impetus...writing poetry, by nature, should be short. And such was and is all primitive poetry, the most poetic and true poetry of all"[6]), underlined his preference for authentic emotion and simplicity in poetry as against elaborate exercises in erudition and philosophy, not to mention an innate dislike of verbosity and rhetoric. In line with his intellectual formation, a deep appreciation of classical philosophy informed the central notions that structured his poetry-philosophy. To begin with, a cornerstone of Leopardi's early poetics was built on the concept of antinomy between Nature and Reason that he elaborated in *Zibaldone* in relation to the scope and nature of poetry. Inspired by the ideal of essential poetry in the primitive Greek lyrics mentioned above, he defined 'true poetry' as intuitive deriving from 'pure nature' and sensory perceptions, in direct contrast with the poetry of reflections, derived from thought. He extended the same logic of binary opposition between Nature and Reason to explain the distinction that separated beauty from truth, and poetry from philosophy. It can clearly be seen in his early writings where beauty and poetry pervaded the space of Nature and Reason appeared as the place of 'truth', which made poetry arid and dissolved dreams, destroying joy ("As in all sciences, truth is the object of philosophy, so true poetry cannot exist where philosophy reigns"[7]). Thus to the modern poet, continuously threatened by the "arid truth" (*arido vero*), illusion remained the last space for poetry ("reason is enemy of nature...man can be as less or with as much difficulty become great, as much he is dominated by reason: for few can become great [in art or poetry perhaps no one] without being propelled by illusion"[8]). Leopardi's position relented a little in his "Discourse of an Italian over Romantic Poetry" (1818) as we shall see, while on the related idea of separation between poetry and philosophy it attenuated considerably in a later phase, when he came to identify the mark of greatness in a poet only in one who possessed in equal measure the attributes of both the poet and the philosopher.[9] This explains the contradiction that Leopardi, as a rationalist, rejected the metaphysical elements in Plato's philosophy as "bizarre and untenable", but immensely admired him for the *Dialogues*, in which Plato appeared as the emblematic figure of the poet-philosopher.[10] On another plane, nonetheless, his intellectual leanings showed underpinnings of eighteenth century thought and a deep grounding in the rationalist materialism of the philosophy of Enlightenment. The perfection of form in nature found in his early Idylls was in effect demonstrably close to the concept of the 'ideal state of nature' of Rousseau, and as its corollary, to the poetry of Romanticism: it was an Eden that was corrupted progressively by civilization. Unlike Rousseau, however, Leopardi termed man's unhappiness as perennial, existing even in the first man, and traced its root in his cognitive rational faculty, being oppositional in essence to 'pure nature' that prevailed with the ancients. Thus before long, his initial concept of nature had changed into one of total disenchantment and he contested Rousseau's theory, challenging the idea that there ever was a 'state of nature in which man had attained happiness in fulfillment of his "natural pleasures".[11] In literature the idea had its ramification in the concept that man, ordained to be unhappy by the laws of nature, could forget the tragedy of his fate only through *illusion* and *imagination*, a persuasion that obviously militated against the theory of realism and objectivity in literary texts. This brings into fore the equivocal nature of relationship that Leopardi shared with Romanticism, - it was a spiritual affiliation he chose to deny, but which co-existed in him, with his classicist taste and innate rationalist disposition. Such discordance, though, can perhaps be partly explained by the specific features of the Romantic Movement in Italy. Italian Romanticism, in a trend distinct from the movement elsewhere in Europe, was not born in opposition to rationalism and the culture of Enlightenment, and displayed features that led critics to question whether Romanticism ever existed in Italy.[12] It gained ground moving in pace with the national movement of unification and was characterized by a strong ideological component. Rather than on individual will, it focused on the people as a 'collective', to be brought together to foster the growth of a national consciousness, and literature proved to be a powerful tool in this task, awakening in people the memory of a common past of social, political, cultural and moral ideals.[13] Thus elements of history, nationalism and popular if not populist sentiments characterized romantic literature in Italy, which proliferated in prose genre and popularized fiction, especially the historical novel. The space of literature located to be of Italian Romanticism was thus clearly not the one inhabited by Leopardi. Privileging 'the individual', he considered lyric poetry as "the most noble and poetic of all genres", the genre "true for every man, even the uneducated, trying to rebuild or console the self with a song".[14] Excluding all possibilities of action in history, he reflected on ontological issues in a universal perspective and dwelt on philosophical queries linked to existence and its temporaneity that were closer in line with elements of European (here intended as transalpine) Romanticism. On the other hand, his rationalism was too ingrained to allow him to share a common base with the metaphysical strain in European Romanticism, found, for example, in German romantic thought, in the ideas of Schlegel and Schopenhauer. In effect, Leopardi's divergent stand in relation to the position of the Italian romantics stemmed principally from a different literary ideology, spelt out clearly on the issues of form and content, not least the concept of reading. In his "Discourse..." he opposed Italian Romanticism on the criterion of 'utility' as a guiding principle in poetry, especially when programmed with a social and political end; for him the task of poetry was rather to inspire imagination and create illusions, and essentially to give "delight".[15] Nor did he participate in the religious spirit that animated romantic literature in Italy, viewing with cynicism the renewed affirmation of Catholic faith in the cultural polity. Making no secret of his indifference to religion, he had only contempt for its consolatory role in the society. As to a common plane somewhat, while sentiment ("re-proposed as *the pathetic*" by the romantics) acquired a new emphasis in the poetics of Romanticism, Leopardi saw it as a "necessity" in modern poetry, albeit "painful", being more of a compromise with philosophy, but enjoined it in terms of its perennial presence in literature, as the foundation of lyric poetry. On the concept of 'sentiment' his reformulations in the "Discourse..." thus brought him a little closer to the aesthetics of Romanticism, but differences were still fundamental in nature. With his classicist taste and a vocation for logic, order and measure, he abhorred an excessive play of sentiments, not to mention the penchant for the aberrant or 'the macabre', abounding in romantic literature. This also explains his criticism of Byron's poetry, appearing in the "Discourse..." in a polemic rejoinder to the views of critic Ludovico Di Breme in praise of romantic poetry. Taking his distance as much from the neo-classicist model of imitation of classical literature as from the illuminist canons of 'critical intelligence' and ideology, Leopardi opted for creative imagination as the highest expression of individual consciousness.

Intrinsic to Leopardian poetics is then the concept of *illusion*, which he develops in direct correlation to a theory of *pleasure* ("pleasure is nothing but an abandoning and forgetting of life...for life, by nature, is pain"[16]). It is built on the premise of an act of transport through poetry with prospects of reprieve for the aesthetic subject, even if momentary, from the angst of existence. Reiterating an idea found in ancient Greek literature it locates in the 'blazing spirit and fury of the poet' traces of the 'divine' that sublimates the contingent and translates 'fury' into poetic stupor. In his letter to the Milanese journal *Biblioteca italiana*, in rebuttal of Mme De Staël's criticism of the sterile imitation of classical literature in Italian works,[17] Leopardi expounded clearly his position with regard to the role of the poet:

> We do not defend either the abuse or the use of 'the fables of the ancients', we do not want the poet *to imitate any other poet but nature*, ...We want that the poet contemplates, imagines and finds, we want him to be ablaze with the *divine fury* of mind, to have impetus, and to have greatness and force *of affections* and thoughts...[18]

While *imitation of nature* and *force of affections* were ideas considered pivotal to Romanticism, the poetic subject in Leopardi, inspired to *contemplate, imagine and find*, subsumes the role of a philosopher who *contemplated* and with his creative imagination *found* a new meaning for reality. Such a notion of the Muses invests pure poetic intuition with an element of the sacral evoking the powers of revelation that constitutes the essence of poetry. In his early poetry Leopardi viewed real world as a metaphor of constraints and constrictions in which illusion offered the possibility of liberation and the only space of *pleasure* conceded by Nature ("illusions *belong substantially to the system of nature and the order of things*, and as such are *necessary and essential to the happiness and perfection of man*"[19]). To Leopardi, it was only with an acute awareness of the dark opacity of life that one acceded, through the act of poetry, to sudden moments of illumination in which the humdrum quotidian dissolved, showing a different configuration of the world. It created an idea of the liberating force of poetry that erupted as an epiphany, bringing changes in perceptions. Through poetic intuition then one could access the 'other order of meanings' that appeared as though in a "double vision" in relation to the world and the objects. Leopardi indicates as much in *Zibaldone* and states, "to a sensitive and imaginative man", the world and the objects "appear as double". He explains it thus:

> He will see with his eyes a tower... he will hear with his ears a sound of bell; and at the same time in his imagination he will see another tower... he will hear another sound. In the second kind lie the entire beauty and the pleasing nature of things. [20]

The poet with his imagination is then made privy to an alternative reality in which things reveal themselves in their true nature. A century later, Montale would re-evoke the suggestion, in a metaphysical line, in his image of the *maglia rotta* (the tiny ruptures in the manifested world), through which the poet could spy into hidden truths, which appeared at best as 'little flashes" ("barlumi") in a sudden event of "miracle".[21]

Leopardi thus viewed poetry as potentially transformative in relation to the contingent reality. His early lyrics *The Infinite (L'infinito)*, *The Evening of the Festive Day (La sera del dì di festa}*, *To the Moon (Alla luna)*, *Solitary Life (La vita solitaria)*, *The Dream (Il sogno)*, the first four of which are Idylls, composed between 1819 and 1822, lend image to the related ideas elaborated in *Zibaldone*, on the essence of poetry. He explains in *Zibaldone*:

> certain ideas and images of things *supremely vague, fantastic, chimerical*, impossible...those which sublimate you more, draw you out of your

> own self and the real world, delight us totally because they recall our memories of childhood, and the *pleasure* that is produced consist totally and principally...in *remembrance.*[22]

The central themes of 'illusion' and 'indefinite' ("things supremely vague, fantastic, chimerical") around which Leopardi's lyrics develop in this phase predicate on 'remembrance'. He called the Idylls of this period his 'historical Idylls' because of the intimate memory of early experiences evoked and relived in these compositions, in the precise unity of space and time ("Idylls expressing situations, affections, and historical experiences of my mind"[23]). We offer a reading of *The Infinite* to note the structural interplay of these concepts in the poetics of the *Canti*:

> It *was* always dear *to me* this *solitary* hill, / and this hedgerow here that closes out *my view*, / from so much of the ultimate horizon. / But *sitting* here, and *watching* here, *in thought*, / *I create* interminable spaces, / *greater than human* silences, and deepest / quiet, where the *heart barely fails to terrify*. / When *I hear* the wind, blowing among the leaves, / *I go on to compare* that infinite silence / with *this voice*, and *I remember* the eternal and the dead seasons, / and the present, and its *sound, so that in this immensity / my thoughts are drowned, and shipwreck seems sweet / to me* in this sea.[24]

Nature in *The Infinite* is represented in the perfection of form, in an idealized reflection of the transcendent. Here subjectivity gains as the self ("dear to me", "my view", "I create", "I hear", "I go on to compare", "I remember", "my thoughts", "seems sweet to me") obtains a new validation in its interaction with Nature, deified as the omnipotent. The infinite of the universe lends depth to imagination and validates the finite at the moment of its interchange with Nature. The three spheres of the sky ("the ultimate horizon"), the earth ("this solitary hill", "the hedgerow", "these leaves", "the wind blowing among these leaves"), and the sea ("where my thoughts are drowned and shipwreck seems sweet..."), complete the perfection that lies in Nature, viewed in the sublime height of the sky, in the breadth of the wide expanse of the earth and in the mysterious depth of the sea. The concept of the infinite finds its imagery correlative in the unending sweep of the sky, in the circularity of earth's spread, and in the continuum of the ocean. The structure attains perfection when the dynamic element of time conjoins past and present in a cyclical movement, while the static element fills up the motionless stillness of *infinite silence*. It completes the symmetry with the inclusion of the human element in the vertical movement of the poet's eye enclosing in its orbit the three spheres, descending right from the sky to the solitary hill, across the hedgerow and down into the depth of the sea. In the ambit of Leopardian imagination only thoughts are endowed with motion ("sitting here and watching here") and the eye as the metaphor of light mediates between the self and the external world, which is viewed and interpreted as it is illumined. With contemplation the view is appropriated and interiorized, constituting an experience in subjectivity, "a thing of himself for the subject", as Pirandello puts it, "a world of things of his own".[25]

Disagreeing with the romantic critics who decried the lack of colour and the details of landscape in Leopardi's Idylls, Pirandello writes:

> Leopardi was more interested in 'human' things than in the things of external nature; he was interested in things, that is, in this special sense, as keys to the peculiar amalgam of external and internal realities that make up our experience, things in the sense suggested by the Father's speech in *Six Characters in Search of an Author* (1921), when he says, 'We all have a world of things, each a world of things of his own'.[26]

In other words, with the experience itself, feelings attach to the object and make it an event. Here an event of coincidence occurs between external and internal realities.

The distance between the subject and the object is obliterated with the space of the lyrical-'I' expanding to include that of the object and identifying completely with it. In his analysis of the critical thought of the English romantics M.H. Abrams notes the same characteristic in the English romantic poets in relation to Nature, and observes while referring to Coleridge: "When the romantic poet contemplated a landscape, the distinction between 'I' and 'non-I' tended to dissolve." He quotes Coleridge who stated to being habituated since childhood to "de-realize", tending - to put it in his own words - "through a kind of transfusion and transgression of my conscience, to identify with the object".[27]

Similarly, in *The Infinite*, the lyrical-'I', which identifies completely with Nature, is seen enclosed within the perfect whole of the universe. The eye as the immediate sensory link with the outside world is soon replaced by the mind's eye or imagination in the moment in which the object merges with the subject. Thus the semantic accent on vision, for example, in the related lexicon *view* (v.2) or the verb *watching* (v.4), with which the lyric begins, is meant to focus on the immediacy of the visible objects (*the hills* and *the ultimate horizon* beyond) only in the initial verses, while for the rest of the composition the descriptive details of the landscape are substituted by concepts, which typically contaminate the genre with elements of reflections. *Feelings* thus evoked extend to unlock memories of sentiments through revisitations of the past: for example, "in thought I create" (vv.4-5), "the heart barely fails to terrify" (v.7), "I go on to compare" (v.9), "I remember" (v.10)," my thoughts are drowned" (v.12), "shipwreck seems sweet in this sea" (v.12).

Tuning into elements of sonorous perception, so essential in Leopardi, and underlining the sound of silence, are expressions with a number of auditory verbs and substantives: "greater than human silences" (v.6), "deepest quiet" (vv.6-7), "I hear the wind blowing among the leaves" (v.8), "the infinite silence" (v.9), "this voice" (v.10), "the present and its sound" (vv.10-11). The Idyll has a solitary verb in the past tense: *was* (v.1), which appears only once, in the beginning, while the rest of the lyric is dominated by the present tense. As in Wordsworth, it creates a sphere of 'dual consciousness', verifying in the moment of regression into memory two streams of consciousness formed in the parallel incidence of the experiences, once in the past and again in the present, - the past is validated and reinforced with the knowledge of the present. Again, the observation "sitting here and watching here" (v.4), conveying an idea of immobility (separated from the suggestion of movement implicit in the poetic eye) underscores the static element in the scheme of things with allusion to the unchangeable state of human destiny. The eternal present is highlighted by insistence on the demonstrative pronouns, the adverbs of place and the use of the present continuous: "this solitary hill and this hedgerow here" (vv.1-2), "but sitting here and watching here" (v.3), "this voice" (v.10), "this immensity" (v.11), "this sea" (v.13). By this technique the element of the immediate is accentuated and transmitted to the reader who realizes through the very act of reading the simultaneity of his being participative in the same sensations expressed in the poem. While *sitting here* and assimilating the melody in the verses, one can hear the *blowing of wind among the leaves* and visualize the *solitary hill* and *the hedgerow* that obstructs the view from so much of the *ultimate horizon*. The 'here and now' of the present passes on to the reader the possibility of connecting momentarily, through the act of poetry, to an integral link with life, experiences which in other modern poets, such as Coleridge or Rilke, are projected as the exclusive privilege of the poet and guarded in a heavily individualized discourse of interiority. With Leopardi, instead, the reader is invited to glean into the parallel space of illusion where the poet emerges and shares with him a moment of elation no less intense than Rilke's celebratory "high figures of heart's leaps".[28] He had a deep faith in the potency of poetry as an instrument of resistance against the malaise of existence. In a strategy of linking the opposites

Leopardi makes reality align with illusion: the hedgerow, which represents an element of concrete reality functions as a barrier in relation to the reach of human vision. Leopardi writes in *Zibaldone* in 1820:

> At times the mind will desire and in effect *desires a restricted view, confined in a certain way*, as in romantic situations. The reason is the same: that is, *the desire of the infinite*, because then in place of the view imagination works and reality is taken over by fantasy. The mind imagines what it cannot see, what that tree, that hedgerow, that tower hide to him, and he goes wandering in an imaginary space, imagining things he could not have, had his vision extended everywhere, because the real would then have cancelled out imagination.[29]

As a cardinal element in Leopardi's poetics this idea finds concrete shape in his imaging of the *Infinite* and the other Idylls. With the real world blocked from vision the self locates itself in memory at the happy site of childhood, entering into a world of illusion where in the infinite cycle of time and space, past and present coincide: "I remember the eternal and the dead seasons, / and the present, and its sound" (vv.10-11). A modernist element of nihilism is evident in the final verse, in the image of drowning in memory: "and shipwreck seems sweet / to me in this sea".

In its associative imagery of water and submersion, together with that of a primordial darkness, we read the metaphor of the maternal womb (besides a symbolic reading of an initiatory rite in the ritualistic immersion, underwater symbology of the mother figure is implicit in the memory of the first signs of biological life generated in the sea), and the return to a state of union with the mother. In the descent into the state of the pre-natal and the pre-rational emanates the suggestion of the subject's psychological emersion at the level of the sub-conscious, restituting to the self an unmediated condition of integrity. In the images of the self, submerged in the embedded levels of consciousness, Leopardi appears to anticipate elements of twentieth-century Symbolist poetry.

Closely aligned to the concept of the infinite is the lexicon of *immensity* read in v.11 ("so that in this immensity..."), a term suggestive of vastness and unfathomable mystery. The overpowering emotion raised by *interminable spaces*, *superhuman silence* and the *deepest quiet* where beyond the orbit of human gaze extends the infinite universe, evokes an idea of the sublime transcendent similar in spirit to the pervasive awe of Nature expressed in the poetry of European Romanticism. Most important, the key motif of the *infinite* in Leopardi is metaphorized with its semantic extension into the concept of the *indefinite*. Leopardi writes:

> In my theory of pleasure where it demonstrates how objects seen in half or with certain obstructions...arouse in us *indefinite* ideas, it explains why the light of the sun or the moon fascinates us more at a place where they are not visible...or are hazy or impeded.[30]

It is the nebulous element in the indefinite, suggestive of the incomprehensible and the immeasurable that expands into the space of dream and imagination. An indefinite view or an indistinct sound, hazy and distant, evading perception in clear lines, is endowed with a magical potency to operate a momentary displacement of the real world into the category of an alternative dimension. In other words, here *distance* represents the concept of a dematerialized nature of reality in which the poet is invited to participate. Leopardi writes in *Zibaldone* that "a line of trees...a voice or a distant or fading sound, a thunder or a roar of cannon heard in the midst of fields" or "the song of a farmer which is heard through the valleys in the countryside" are distant sights and sounds that suggest indeterminate sensations, truly 'infinite', soliciting one's memory to relive the delectable fantasies of childhood and move in the sphere of imprecise sentiments.[31] He narrates through little quotidian details synchronized in the unity of time and space, whereby images accumulate, expand and suddenly become sonorous. As he recollects in *The Evening of the Holiday*:

> Now I remember, in my young days...deep in the night, / a song I hear in the street, /died, little by little, far off, / crushing my heart, as now. [32]

The poet recounts the familiar sounds of his childhood again in *The Village Saturday* (*Il sabato del villaggio*):

> Now the bells are witness / to the coming holiday: / you would say the heart might take comfort from the sound. [33]

The sound of *bells* chiming far away, the *happy din* of little boys floating up the *tiny square*, or the haunting tune of the whistle of a farmhand (who "returns for his simple meal, / dreams of his days of rest") slowly fading into the night, are comforting *sound* images that evoke traces of childhood memories as well as the call of an arcane world of mystery, touched by the humble quotidian:

> When the other lights are quenched, all round, / and everything else is silent, / I hear the hammer ringing, / I hear the carpenter sawing:

> he's still awake / in the lamplight, in his shut workshop / hurrying and straining, / to finish his task before dawn.[34]

Similarly, the moon is hauntingly beautiful in its hazy and *misty* image when gazed at by eyes veiled with tears, in his lyrics *To the Moon*:

> Filled with mistiness, / trembling, with all those tears that welled up in my eyes, so / troubled was my life, and is, and does not change / o moon, my delight.[35]

If the verse "troubled was my life and is, and does not change" indicates the deep unhappiness in him, the poet finds solace in remembrance and his suffering attenuates through chronicling and enumeration:

> And yet it does help me, to record my sadness and tell / it, year by year /
> ...this remembrance of things past, even if it / is sad, and the pain lasts! [36]

In his early Idylls the Leopardian subject is experiential and connects with Nature directly through his sensory perceptions, through visual and auditory faculties, unmediated by rational thought. Critics have traced this minutest analysis of impressions pleasing to the eyes and ears to sensistic theories, but the force of poetry and imagination in these impressions is obtained through the faculty of memory that opens a dimension in fantasy and sentiments typical of Romantic poetry.[37] After a prolonged gap of 'poetic silence', years devoted predominantly to elaborations in prose, his major poetry appeared again in 1828, in longer compositions, reflective and intense in Idylls such as *To Silvia* (*A Silvia*), *The Village Saturday* (*Il Sabato del villaggio), the Solitary Bird* (*Il passero solitario),* while raising speculative queries in poems like *The Night song of a Wandering Shepherd in Asia* (*Il canto notturno di un pastore errante in Asia*), in the years between 1828-30. As already noted, Leopardi factors into his poetic imagery the elements of barrier that block normal vision or sound and open an alternative dimension in the poetry-narrative. A diminished reality is rendered powerless to rein in impulses of creative imagination. If in the *Infinite* it is the hedgerow that obstructs vision, in *Silvia* it is the enclosure of the paternal mansion that restricts access to the object of his imagination. In his lyrics addressed *To Silvia* the girl who dies at the threshold of youth, the poet, in remembrance, sees himself standing in the balcony of the family library and watching Silvia in fleeting images, through the window of her room in the humble lodgings across the square: "hands intent on household chores", or "rapidly passing over the loom", a flash of her sidelong glance or the smiling eyes, the sound of her *perpetual singing* and his *delight*. Silvia never makes a full, frontal appearance in the poem, but has her presence suggested through fragmentary images in synecdoche. The material barrier of the walls that stands between a direct encounter allows but those little apertures through the balcony or the window to set free the flow of imagination (*il caro immaginar*) and the magic intensifies with the accumulation of a series of congenial images spreading across the distant landscape ("the serene sky, / the gold-lit gardens and paths"). The intervening space between two enclosures acts as the intermediary between two separate dimensions of reality: the "paternal house" (*paterno ostello*) representing the space of authority, immobility and constraints indicates the image of referential realities, whereas the freely flowing lines of Silvia represent the alternative space of creative imagination, the figure of the Muses invested with the dynamism of images in creation, inspiration of poetry. The balcony and the window are thus posited as little apertures that are transformative in relation to the opaque concreteness of the world of referential realities.

The metonymic narration is forwarded by contiguity of sequences, but while it proceeds with analogies and generates polyvalence of signification, employing synecdoche and synaesthesia, it gradually operates a displacement of focus and extends the narration into the metaphoric mode of poetry.

The data of reality, in the story of Silvia, for example, is traced in domestic sequences from the days of her early youth to the time of her premature death ("Attacked, and conquered by secret disease/ you died, my tenderest one, and did not see / your years flower"), closely followed in the background by nostalgic images of the sweet hopes of youth, meant to end with the cold hand of death. The poet addresses in memory this poignant figure remembered from the days of his early youth in his well-known lyrics *To Silvia*:

> Silvia, do you remember those moments in / your mortal life when beauty still shone / in your sidelong laughing eyes and you, *light and / thoughtful*, leapt beyond girlhood's limits? / The quiet rooms and the streets / around you, sounded / to your *endless singing*, / ... It was the scented May. And that's how / you spent your day. / I would leave *my intoxicating studies* / And from the *balcony of my father's house* / strain to catch the sound of your voice / and your hand, quick, / running over the loom. / I'd look at the serene sky / *the gold- lit gardens and paths*: / this side the mountains, that side the far-off sea / And human tongue cannot say what I felt then. / What

> *sweet thoughts*, / what hopes, what hearts, O Silvia mia! / How it appeared to us then, / all human life and fate! / When I recall that *hope* / such feelings pain me, harsh, disconsolate, I brood on my own destiny. / *Oh Nature, Nature / Why do you not give now what you promised then? Why/ do you so deceive your children?* / Attacked, and conquered, by secret disease, / you died, my tenderest one, and did not see / your years flower, or feel your heart move, / by sweet praise of your black hair / your shy, loving looks. /... My *sweet hopes* died also / little by little: to me too /Fate has denied those years. Oh, / how you have passed me by, / Is this the world, the dreams, / the loves, events, delights,/ we spoke about so much together? / ...And from the *distance / with your hand*, you pointed / towards *death's coldness* and the *silent grave*. [38]

It is a sign of modernism that Leopardi's poetry has the dual function of the metonymic and the metaphoric structured into his poetry-narrative. The lyrics are modern in the blending of poetry and narration, and in constructing a textual strategy that accommodates continuities in reflections in a poetic text without stylistic discrepancies. His compositions recaptured the essence of the classical Greek Idylls to perfection, as Bachtin would say, in the element of 'cronotopos', a typical characteristic of the genre,[39] ("It was the scented May, and that's how/ you spent your day" or "from the balcony of my father's house/ strain to catch the sound of your voice, / and your hand, quick / running over the loom"), as the familiar landscape and the bucolic images are revalidated in memory with the enumeration of place and time. Yet, in a way common with the romantic writers elsewhere, Leopardi is also responsible for the transformation if not the superseding of a literary genre, turning Idylls into poetry of reflections; he controverts the simple domestic images, building a mythical undertone of the indefinite into the text. The eruption of the solemn occurs through the employment of an occasional out of category word (*peregrini* or peregrines, as he called them), innocuous words and expressions that operate a shift in the poetry, elevating the discourse and adding an evocative dimension to the lyric. The same, for example, could be seen in the addition of the contrastive adjective *thoughtful* to *light* as it turns into oxymoron the expression "light and thoughtful" and nuances the otherwise carefree, quotidian image of *Silvia*, (implying perhaps a brooding premonition of the impending doom); or the expression "human tongue" in the verse "human tongue can not say / what I felt then", which carries hints of the supernatural, lifting the sentiment above the ordinary. Further, in the verse "the serene sky, the gold-lit gardens and paths, this side the mountains, that side the far-off sea", the descriptive tone detailing concrete things etches out the alternative spaces evoked through the hazy aura of the distant ('sky', 'mountain', 'far-off sea') and the indistinct ('gold-lit gardens and paths') wherein it situates the *indefinite*. The synchronicity of love and death in the classical trope of *Eros and Thanatos* heightens ecstasy and pathos, implying the ultimate denial of hope and the annihilation of life force in both. The poetic narration replete with the elements of space and time extends into a metaphoric elevation with a single expression that again turns it from descriptive to evocative: "from the distance/ you pointed towards death's coldness and the silent grave." The element of the oneiric, introduced earlier in the verse "human tongue can not say", slowly builds up as a premonition of things to come and finally manifests with the appearance of the "hand that from distance" shows the silence of the tomb, bridging the "distance" that separates the living from the dead and predicting an early death for the poet. The transient nature of youth, laughter and spring ("scented May"), all of which end up in "death's coldness and the silent grave", could not more poignantly be expressed.

As the conflicting imagery of the opposites accumulates ("life" / the cruel "fate"; "hope"/"pain"; "sweet thoughts"/ "harsh, disconsolate, I brood"), the tension is finally resolved by the unifying line of poetic reflections on the possibility of happiness only in a state of illusion, for in the nature of things, youth and laughter constitute only an illusory state of hope. In the figure of Silvia it is easy to identify the metaphor of hope and the personification of the tender dreams of early youth ("the dear companion of my young days"), destined to die as one reached maturity and faced the world of reality.

The metaphor is explicated in the subject-object identification between the poet and his female protagonist as co-sharers of the same destiny. In the textual correlation, the speaking subject appropriates the status of the interlocutor and annuls the separateness of the object ("My sweet hopes died also/ ...to me too/ fate has denied those years") from the self. The deceit practiced by Nature ("Oh Nature, Nature, / why do you not give now/ what you promised then? Why / do you so deceive your children?") is stark, as the contradictions between promise and fulfilment get sharper in focus. Nature, as per his earlier Rousseauian concept, represented the site of the primary state of happiness in *The Infinite*. The cracks in that image appear already visible in *Silvia*, showing a gradual transformation of his poetry, from the "idyllic" to the "reflective", which would finally reach out in its ultimate force to the world in the last phase of his life, between 1833 and 1836, pensive and speculative in *Moonset* (*Il tramonto della luna*), and fiery in denouncement in the final composition *Wild Broom*.

Leopardi's earlier notion of aesthetics had represented an essential link between his theory of literature and concept of reading. He was not prepared to eliminate distinctions between popular literature of the common category and a higher category for the discerning reader.[40] In according distinction to a refined category of literature, to be promoted separately from the category of the popular literature of realism, he had privileged the space for pleasure and imagination in the individual literary experience and had proposed a personalized concept of reading. It thus appeared striking when his later statements began to indicate a change in his position, leaning towards the opposing pole of socialization and the real world, not seeking happiness any more in illusion and poetry of "affections", "eloquence" and individual delight ("I do not seek anything outside the truth, which I have in the past hated and detested...I am getting increasing comfort to find out and touch upon the misery of men and things..."[41]), and culminating in his verses in *To Himself*:

> The last illusion has died / I thought eternal. Died. I feel in truth, / not only hope, but desire/ for dear illusion has vanished.[42]

In a significant transition, Leopardi's poetry began to strike a different note of passion from the mid 1820's, coming out of the charmed circle of Idylls, solitude and isolated contemplation of Nature, to address the world of men and reality and participate in the existential issues that plagued fellow beings, tested in the crucible of his own authentic experience.

As his initial fascination with Nature changed, he continued to connect with it through his musings and interrogations but not in passive adulation. It is clear that in the beginning he shared in common with the English romantic poets like Wordsworth, Shelley or Coleridge an intense relationship with landscape and Nature, in an intimate interaction of joy, hope, stupefaction and fear. In *The Infinite*, while contemplating the vastness of the universe and its supernatural silence "where the heart barely fails to terrify", Leopardi sensed the same feeling of awe, which Shelley described as the "tempestuous loveliness of terror" in his *Ode To The West Wind*, 1819.[43] Also the sense of coincidence between life and death, and the uncontrollable power of Nature ("death has met life, life in death ... the blood is frozen - but unconquered Nature/ Seems struggling to the last...", in Shelley's Fragment on *Medusa*[44]), the correspondence between the destructive and regenerative cycles of Nature - symbolized in the motifs of winter and spring - as also the themes of love and death, so compulsive in the English poets, are equally powerful in Leopardi. Divergence is struck when he proceeds towards a negative projection of Nature in a gradual move away from an awe-struck interchange to the demonization of Nature, projected as the destroyer. Unlike Wordsworth of *The Tintern Abbey* (*Lyrical Ballads),* Leopardi does not view Nature as reconstructive. Nor does engagement with Nature in his poetry appear in the form of worship or communion as in the English poet, but is more like interrogation, if not accusation.

In an anthropomorphic construction Leopardi sees in Nature the image of a mother "who bear(s) and nourish(es) to kill",[45] and devours the children, to perpetuate the cycle of regeneration, in order to continue survival. ("Nature, by the necessity of the law of destruction and reproduction, and to preserve the present state of the universe, is essentially, regularly and perpetually the persecutor and the mortal enemy of all individuals..."[46]).

In the period between 1833 and 1837, as his flesh withers in painful illness ("I am just a trunk that feels and pains"[47]), his engagement with poetry culminates in a powerful vindication of his spirit, rising with a new vigour and forceful language. It acquires a progressively accentuated note of irony and dissent against the dominant ideologies of his age in compositions of satire like *Palinode to Marchese Gino Capponi* (*Palinodia al Marchese Gino Capponi*, 1835), *The Newly Faithful* (*I nuovi credenti* 1833), or *Paralipomeni della Batracomiomachia* (a parodical sequel to Homer's work, 1833), manifesting, as Walter Binni highlights, a forceful energy of heroic defiance and courageous intervention, remarkable for example in *Wild Broom* and *Moonset* in the *Canti*, in the satires mentioned, and in the allegorical *Dialogue of Tristan and a Friend* in *Operette morali*, in the last phase of his works, between 1833 and 1836. [48] In these works Binni individuates the new poetics of Leopardi, robust and hard-hitting in the strength of convictions, subtly ironic in denouncing the false pretences and the hypocrisy of the world and compassionate in solidarity for the suffering fellow beings.[49] In *Wild Broom*, writing from atop the slopes of the volcanic Mount Vesuvius, overlooking the ruins of the once prosperous and industrious city of Pompeii, he has only scorn for the harbingers of progress:

> The magnificent and progressive fate / of the human race / is depicted in this place. / Proud foolish century, look, / and see yourself reflected.[50]

Mocking at the false sense of hope spread by religion, and reiteration of faith in the role of the Redentor, he continues:

> ...O children of Mankind... / ...you believe / that you've been appointed the master / and end of all things: and how often / you

> like to talk about the creators / of all things universal, who descended /... and happily spoke to you, often: / and that, renewing these ridiculous dreams / you still insult the wise.../[51]

Elements of the Gothic seem to emerge at last in Leopardi in his spectral depiction of the city of Pompeii "hurled to the heights of heaven / from the womb of thunder". The ancient city devastated by molten lava ("where snakes twist, and couple / in the sun, and the rabbits return to their cavernous burrows: / were once happy, prosperous farms"), is described in dark shades of black and red that evoke a chromatic suggestion of horror and death: it is inhabited by the 'sinister' black and viscid creatures of the dark ("bat and its brood", "where snakes twist") and the violent red of *the deathly lava* spills out like blood, "staining the region round". The wings of doom and destruction that spread over the city carry a sign of the 'ominous' in the pall of gloom:

> And, like night's secret horror, / through the empty theatres, / the twisted temples, the shattered / houses, where the bat hides its brood, / like a sinister brand / that circles darkly through silent palaces, / the glow of the deathly lava runs, / reddening the shadows / from far away, staining the region round.[52]

Leopardi employs the classical theme of metamorphosis in his final image of Nature, which is presented in an act of *anthropomutation*, transforming from woman to mother to stepmother:

> but...blame / on *Her* who is truly guilty, who is the *mother* / of men in bearing them, their *stepmother* in malice.[53]

In the fight against the real 'enemy' (Nature) man has to unite in brotherhood, sharing a common fate of vicissitude:

> and consider / the human race / to be united, and ranked against her, / ...judge all men allies.../ And think / it as foolish to take up arms against men.[54]

Finally, an insignificant sub-species of the biosphere erupts in the desolate landscape, the image of the subaltern, symbolized in the figure of the humble desert flower, bearing a supreme lesson forged in solidarity and compassion for mankind. The little *Wild Broom or the flower of the desert* that grows on the slopes of the volcano might have its head bent in the face of certain death, but continues to spread its fragrance around, not cowered by the might of the terminator:

> yet a head that's not bent in vain / in cowardly supplication / before a future oppressor: not lifted in insane pride towards the stars,/

...and you'll have been so much wiser / ...than man, since you / have never believed your frail species, / can be made immortal by yourself, or fate.[55]

Here poetic imagination is set free from anthropocentric enclosures, allowing it to soar into a panic image of the universe where man does not appear to be superior to the other species in facing the ultimate destiny of annihilation. Leopardi's subject is dialogic but not anthropocentric. It addresses a wide range of interlocutors (*the country girl, the farm-hand, the carpenter, the blacksmith, the shepherd in Asia, the sheep, the solitary sparrow, the desert flower*), reflecting a conscious reckoning of the plurality of forces in play in the existential order, while not ignoring from its view of life-system the voice of the plant and the animal world.

The prior knowledge of doom, a bane of his rational faculty, is a gift of nature that makes man only unhappy as opposed to the other beings in the creation. The whole discourse of man's *progress and magnificent destiny* is reduced to ridicule when confronted with the might of 'unconquerable' Nature and the indifference with which it unleashes calamities to end civilizations. In setting limits to the reach of human potentials and the powers of human intervention to counter Nature, in contesting the logic of viewing man at the centre of the universe on a plane superior to the rest of the creation, Leopardi repudiates some of the basic assumptions of the philosophy of Humanism:

I don't consider a man /a great-hearted creature, but stupid, / who, born to die, nurtured in pain, / says he is made for joy, / and fills pages with the stench / of pride, promising / an exalted destiny on earth, / and a new happiness, / unknown to heaven / much less this world, to people / whom a surging wave, a breath / of malignant air, a subterranean tremor, / destroys so utterly that they / scarcely leave a memory behind.[56]

Leopardi's poetry ran counter to the great myth created by Enlightenment around "rationalism" as means to human progress and happiness. He perceived in man's rational faculty an instrument of demystification totally contrary to his desire of happiness. Critics, for example, Carlo Ferrucci, have noted in these elaborations the presence of elements anticipating the trends of German philosophical thought of the twentieth century.[57] We cannot forget though that Leopardi (especially in his later poetry) valorized in rationality the cognitive instrument of knowledge, an enabling faculty, which taught man to see the truth and accept his fate courageously without the hypocrisy of hope or religious succour.

The oppositional force in Leopardi's poetry emanates from his dialectical approach in relation to the dichotomies in the standardized concepts and the subversion is evident in the grouping together of conflicting semantic categories, such as love and disappointment, life and death, joy and pain, hope and despair, infinite and limit, or reality and illusion. His poetic strategy consists in proceeding with an analysis of contrasts by analogy of affinities, which is followed up by the assimilation of opposites. In fact, in Leopardi's concept the dichotomy between life and death did not exist since he found that life formulated its meaning in a figure of oxymoron with death. In a letter of 19 November 1819, he wrote to Milanese writer Pietro Giordani, his friend and guide of the early years: "I do not see any difference between death and my life where I am denied even the consolation of pain." At a superficial reading the line would appear to be the stereotype of a romantic desolation, yet at another level the sentence, read in conjunction with the crowd of similar observations in *Zibaldone*, would render its deeper implication, lying in a rational view of the coincidence of life and death, which were interdependent terms in Leopardi's lexicon.[58] If death corresponds to the moment in which deliverance from suffering commences, life appears to be a succession of moments of death, each ending irrevocably till reaching the point of final annihilation. Thus, for creatures "born to die and nurtured in pain", it is birth that puts into motion the process of death. Resolution of contrasts in his poetry continues through a similar play of antinomies. The portrayal of the theme of 'love and death' in his lyrics is poignant not because it numbs in pessimism, it owes its appeal instead to the intense sentiment of life that is evoked. In his lyrics he often addresses young women who died young and resembled his own being, faced with a tragic destiny and impending death. In a related context, Timpanaro points out the elements of hedonism in Leopardi's poetics, intimately connected with love and death, much removed from the kind of pessimism typically associated with the romantic poets.[59]

Hedonism in Leopardi finds figurative expression in the iconographical imagery of his poetry, appearing repeatedly in the figures of beautiful women who are shown transfixed in their dying gaze, either in a last gesture of the hand or frozen in the memory of their voice, glance and smile (e.g., *Bas-Relief on an Ancient Tomb; on a Lovely Lady's Image*).[60]

Indeed, there is a procession of faces immortalized in death, reviving the memory of feminine figures from his past - *Silvia*, *Nerina* (*Memories*), *Aspasia, First Love* - women who did not reciprocate his feelings. In his lyrics dedicated to these figures, Leopardi, in a technique of 'mise en abyme', projects a specular reflection of the larger canvas of his fate in the story of his female addressee. Neuro Bonifazi finds in Leopardi's representation of the feminine a conscious formulation that constructs a metaphor of the self, suggested among others, for example, in his self-identification with the tender, sensitive but physically unattractive, classical figure of *Sappho* in the eponymous composition.[61] To us it appears that in identifying himself with the dead women he effects a transposition of the self at the site of another, and unify in a shared fate of suffering. The subject-object divide is obliterated through dialogical openings, projecting out emotionally towards the other through 'compassion' (com+ passion = suffering with), the word traced in its etymological root. Basing his hypothesis on Leopardi's unhappy experiences with women, Bonifazi relates the genesis of Leopardian poetics to personal impulses associated with a feeling of guilt: "Through compassion he atones for the guilt of envy, hatred and other vengeful instincts harboured within and emerges victorious with the joy of liberation from guilt".[62] Without wanting to stretch the hypothesis too far on the element of guilt and the biographical factor, we can perhaps accept that pain and suffering are collateral conditions of joy and liberation in Leopardi's poetry, though not necessarily linked to catharsis. It accentuates the element of human solidarity and the spirit of participation, quite separate from the plaint of sentimental effusion that so often characterized the tales of love and death in the literature of Romanticism.

In Leopardi, the antinomy between joy and pain is resolved primarily by the logic of his radical subjectivity that, to put it in Heideggerian terms, prioritizes the essence of Being, situated in separation from history, from the site of Becoming. Being is located in the ontological sphere of 'feeling' and the sentiments of joy and pain (*sentimento* > *sentire* = to feel) coincide in the semantic accentuation of "feeling" as the most vibrant attestation to life. Referring to "the sweet strings" that trembled in the lyrics of Petrarch, "the unhappy lover", and comparing it with the "boredom that drowns us" in the modern world, he writes:

> Oh you blessed ones, to whom life was tears! ... for us, by the cradle and above the tomb, sits motionless nullity.[63]

The feeling of pain and anguish is here projected as positive, viewed against the all-pervading 'nothingness of existence' (*il nulla*) and the pall of 'ennui' that spreads over the modern world. In his opinion death would be acceptable and even sweet, if life were lived to the full, but boredom was the living death, worse than desperation ("Even the suffering which is born of boredom and purposelessness of things is more tolerable than boredom itself"; "Everything is *a nothing* in this world, even my desperation is *a nothing*... poor me! Even this suffering of mine is pointless, *a nothing*"[64]). The sense of futility and the all-encompassing void (*il nulla* or *le neant* of Sartre), typical features that assail the modern mind, not least the terror and desolation of *ennui* which is "worse than sorrow", would be themes around which much of Modernist literature would grow to ponder upon in the twentieth century.

Leopardi died in Naples in 1837 at the age of thirty-nine. He suffered from solitude, crippling illness and deep disappointments in love. Ahead of his age in ideas, he was plagued by lack of comprehension on the part of his contemporaries whose response to him was often in ridicule, if not contempt. The significance of his lucid prose in the allegorical dialogues of *Operette morali* was to receive due recognition only with re-readings in recent times, while during his lifetime it remained largely ignored. In fact, it would be easy to trace the genesis of Leopardian poetics and his so-called 'endemic pessimism' in his deep-seated personal unhappiness. Yet, as Leopardi himself reiterated, that would amount to an unjust trivialization of his thoughts since he strove determinedly towards transforming the intensity of his emotions into a powerful instrument of poetry in a way that the contingent blurred into the absolute.

He transcended the narrow confines of his existential sorrow to emerge on a wider plane of rational inquiry, engaging in a continuing process of introspection, observation and reflections, in the pursuit of a universal message. Galled by the reductive nature of his critics' reviews, which put down the roots of his poetry-philosophy essentially to his conditions of health, he wrote to Luigi De Sinner, in a letter dated 24 May 1832:

> Before I die I protest against this invention of weakness and vulgarity in my regard, and I appeal to my readers to concentrate rather on demolishing my observations and line of reasoning than blaming my illnesses.[65]

Beset with existential ills but undeterred, Leopardi succeeded in re-appropriating the self in a unique literary identity. In view of his rich individuality it is difficult to locate him at any of the single cultural-ideological formations of his time or attempt a historicizing classification of his poetry that would not appear arbitrary. We may review here some of the cultural categories traditionally ascribed to his poetry. Opinion often associated Leopardi with Neo-classicism in view of his preference for the classical form, emphasizing in this regard his choices in literary iconography, evoking ancient memory through images of sepulchral sculptures and figures of mythology, (e.g., *Bas-Relief On An Ancient Tomb; On a Lovely Lady's Image*),[66] a feature that he shared in common with some other poets of Romanticism (the description of the *West Wind* or the *Medusa* in Shelley, for example, cited by J. McGann in the text quoted above). Yet, in a separate note, the figurative in Leopardi is distinctive in its minimalist appeal. In a notably modern feature, a technique of iconic augmentation applied in his poetry, achieving a heightened degree of expressivity in short and simple verses. In a recent article Gennaro Savarese refers to the figurative in Leopardi as the "visual thought" - a term used by Arnheim cited by Savarese - viewed for example, in the lacerated image of Mother Italy in the composition *To Italy* (*All'Italia*), one of the few instances of patriotic poetry in Leopardi.[67] With focalization on the essence, his poetry delineates the figurative in short sketches, "etched out in few strokes, surrounded by absence", as Paul Ricoeur would put it, which highlights the essential sketch and intensifies signification, as in Impressionist art.[68]

Leopardi's adherence to classical ideals was consequently related more to the essence and was of a personal kind not identifiable with the formal norms of neo-classicist literature.In *Zibaldone*, in his notes written between 1820 and 1830, he criticized much of neo-classicist literature as badly executed, being 'imitative' and of 'superficial erudition'. In fact, he established his distance from the culture of Neo-classicism and monumental literature in the choice of the title itself (*Canti* /songs), associating it with the musicality of the simple, imaginative and oral traditions of the ancient Greek lyrics.[69] An erudite scholar of classical philology and philosophy, Leopardi recognized the rich patrimony that the ancients had left in the sphere of culture and social polity of the western world ("The present progress of civilization is a rebirth again; it still consists, largely, in recuperating the past"[70]), an essential inheritance in terms of principles and ideals that needed to be preserved and nurtured to enrich the foundations of modern culture. It is in this sense that one needed to read his opposition to Romanticism and understand the 'world-view' that lay behind his approach to the poetic text. While defending the use of mythology as the expression of man's original fantasy and creative imagination, what he advocated was "not a blind imitation of motifs and style and language of the classics", but for writing literature with the sensitivity of the classics, "the timeless appeal and natural grace of the idyllic, the titanic, the perennial strength of virtue..."[71]

Leopardi's personalized concept of classicism would validate Ricoeur's notion of the "dialectic of distanciation and appropriation" proposed in reference to past cultures. Referring to the problem of the loss of tradition faced by classical philology in relation to the "reception of historically transmitted cultural heritages", Ricoeur explains:

> Then we have to retrieve its meaning through and beyond estrangement. Henceforth the appropriation of the past proceeds along an endless struggle with distanciation. Interpretation, philosophically understood, is nothing else than an attempt to make estrangement and distanciation productive.[72]

Thus it is in the context of the dialectic of distanciation and appropriation that the relationship between writing and reading accedes to its fullest significance.[73] In the compositions in which he uses themes from classical literature, most significantly in *Sappho's Last Song* (*L'ultimo canto di Saffo*,), *Marcus Junius Brutus*, (*Bruto minore*,), *To Spring or Of the Ancient Myths* (*Alla primavera* o *delle favole antiche*,) and *Fragment* XXXVII (*Odi Melisso*,), classical figures are reinvented to lend a symbolical dimension to the queries raised in the text. While using images, expressions and figures from the past Leopardi infuses new life into the outworn lexicon and revalidates themes with modern concepts, putting forth the rationale of suicide, for example, in both *Brutus* and *Sappho*, problematising the issue of virtue in war in *Brutus* and projecting a psychoanalytic reading of the subconscious death wish, even suggestive of matricide, in the dream sequence of the fall of the moon, in the Fragment XXXVII, on *Alcetus and Melissus*. Here emblematic figures and distant legends are *re-presented* from a modern viewpoint and contemporaneized, while the signification is metaphorized through assimilation. Essentially modern too is his poetic idiom, innovative and simple. Shorn of every element of 'the lugubrious', it could express depth of feelings without the traditional props of elaborate rhetoric or rhyme, and was far removed from the ornate neo-classical style. In an age when literature in Italy oscillated between the bucolic pastoral of the Arcadia and the lyrical melodrama of Metastasio, often stretched to tedium in verbosity and ample rhetoric, Leopardi brought back into Italian poetry the elegance of classical measure and clarity, the grace of simple vocabulary and an idiom that touched the pure essence of poetry.[74]

To sum up, while Leopardi's poetry is informed by romantic sensibilities it finds articulation in a way characteristic of modernity.

To our mind, the modern sensibility in Leopardi is manifest in his belief in discovering the inner links between things, which are diverse:

> Literature, Leopardi writes, connects us to life; binds and nurtures it: in fact the role of the true poet is to show and discover links between things, and he dons the role of the *philosopher* in this faculty of 'discovering' and recognizing the links connecting the particular elements, and comes to generalizations.[75]

Poetry and philosophy are indeed in symbiosis in his text, a seamless concomitance functioning on the plane of imagination which, as Antonio Prete points out, blends the two without producing any incongruity in the text, as "the poetizing thought" (*Il pensiero poetante*).[76]

In the textual economy of poetry-philosophy the surplus of meaning created by symbols in the manner of poetic discourse allows the ordering of the imaginary dimensions of an alternative reality. To explain the point we use Ricoeur's model of interpretation of modern poetry through the language of metaphors. Ricoeur points out that metaphor, through the process of analogy, assimilation and substitution, offers "a new information" or "tells us something new about reality".[77] On this point it is insightful what Leopardi noted in the margin in the manuscript of *Sappho*: "the poet, mainly the lyric poet, who is not bold in his metaphors and is afraid of the insolitary, will not also say anything new."

Leopardi narrates but evokes too. He structures his poetry through a series of antithetical constructions, which creates a force of contrariness and an iconoclastic tension in his poetry. The oppositional dynamics generated in the text in this deliberate induction of confusion by means of, what Gilbert Ryle (cited by Ricoeur) calls a "calculated error" or a "category mistake, is then forwarded by a proliferation of tension metaphors, i.e., metaphors which cause "a new, hitherto unnoticed relation of meaning to spring up between the terms that previous system of classification had ignored or not allowed."[78] Through the language of metaphor the modern poet, as Anthony Cascardi uses an expression of Sartre, "detotalized the totalizing world".[79] If Leopardi's lyrical imagination finds its catalytic moment in and through an act of obstruction, the same obtains as a mechanism for the subversion of reality. The poetry-narrative proceeds with the accumulation and assimilation of conflicting elements, images and concepts in antinomy thrown together in an atypical collage of opposites, each diminished in 'separateness', undermining in the process the notional value of the existing categories in the established order. Proceeding from the semantic level, the metaphorical tension in his poetry proliferates at the level of the signifier through an enigmatic series of asymmetrical images, which are aligned in opposition to the manifest phenomenon and controvert it. As already noted, the key principle in his poetic formulations is 'pleasure' (*piacere*), which he identifies with the desire of man for the infinite and the 'indefinite', to be attained in illusion and imagination, through the attenuation of the phenomenological world. To achieve it, while poetic imagination is paradoxically forwarded by an element of concrete reality, it in its turn functions as obstruction and obfuscates reality. In this sense the poet indicates a new convention of signification by a re-description of the reality.

The subversive element implicit in the questioning of the existing rational order and the polyvalence of signification adds up to a deliberate overrunning of the formal boundaries of separate epistemological structures, pointing to the link between disparate things, a central feature of modern consciousness. It is revealing to read in this regard Leopardi's views in analysis of the "faculty and the vein of similitude" which, as he pointed out, a "true poet" like Homer possessed. He stated:

> ...the mind gripped by enthusiasm, in the heat of any kind of passion... discovers the liveliest similarities among things...shows connections which he had never thought of, gives him, in short, an admirable faculty to approach and compare the object of things very different in themselves.[80]

In his total lack of interest in religion, in his poetry rooted in authentic experience and existential interrogations, in his yearning for the imprecise, the uncertain, and the indeterminate, and no less in his rejection of the ideology of utilitarianism or his lack of faith in the technological advances of his age, Leopardi appears as a precursor of the Modernist trend of early twentieth century. Swimming against tide in terms of the ideological turn in early nineteenth century culture, he raised queries against facile talks of progress and positivistic solutions (that promised *a magnificent destiny for men*!), and displayed total apathy towards the renewed spirit of religious fervour (of the *newly faithful* as he called them) in the society. We read in his rejection of a totalized single vision of reality, especially in his later poetry, a radical critique of the 'violence' exercised by the dominant mainstream thought in relation to society and the individual subject. Addressing nineteenth century as "foolish", he pointed out in *Wild Broom*: "You pursue freedom, yet want thought to be slave of a single age again."[81]

Writing against the currents of Neo-Catholicism and nationalistic liberalism that swept the intellectual elite in Italy, he derided their concern for the 'happiness for all':

> But a new and almost divine counsel has reached the elevated souls of my century,"- he referred in sarcasm to the intellectuals of Naples in his Palinode (1833) - "who not being able to bring any kind of happiness to anyone on this earth and forgetting the individual, are now busy looking for 'collective happiness', and that found easily they are turning the many unhappy and the all miserable into a happy and joyous people, and the news of this discovery, even before being explained by the pamphlets, journals and gazettes, are being lapped up by the civic herd.[82]

Placed against the background of a growing interest in the *masses* or 'the collective' in the ideological and literary projections of nineteenth century thought, Leopardi upholds the voice of the individual, denouncing the mindless conformism of the *civic herd*. He astonishingly foresees the insidious role of the media, which through books (*pamphlets*), journals and newspapers (*gazettes*) would be projecting the new culture, spreading portents of prosperity and happiness, and would encourage consumerism in the society. In a letter of 24 July 1828 to Pietro Giordani, he wrote in a similar vein:

> I ask in all humility how can the people be made happy if the individual remained unhappy?" and to Fanny Targioni Tozzetti in a letter of 5 December 1831: "You know that I hate politics, because I believe, rather I see that individuals are unhappy under every form of government...and I laugh over the happiness of the *masses*, because my small brain cannot conceive of a happy *mass*, composed of unhappy individuals.[83]

In the nineteenth century, in an epoch of historical transition, Leopardi's subject is a dissident but unwavering spirit, in polemics with the idea of absolute values institutionalized in the Grand Narratives of nineteenth century: the discourse of freedom and social progress through liberal humanism, scientific development, and the logic of industrialization in which he sees the system of enrichment of few at the cost of many ("the hunger of many for the well being of the few").[84] He counters the rational Cartesian subject with the pure subjectivity of Being, located at the pre-rational stage of consciousness. His thinking subject is melancholic in the knowledge of the ultimate reality but his speaking subject is not defeated; it addresses men and rejoices in the essential force of poetry, in its elation and illumination, as an ultimate grip on truth that is not contingent. Leopardi's poetry, through different phases of its evolution reinvented its classicist matrix with nuances of contemporary sensibilities, and anticipated, in its affirmation of individual subjectivity and concept of selfhood, as in its expressions of existential pathos, the emerging profile of modern consciousness.

NOTES AND REFERENCES

1. See Note '*A*' at the end.
2. While for the individual compositions of *Canti* I have used Anthony F. Kline's translation as mentioned in the concerned footnotes, the English translation of the passages quoted from this and all other Italian texts are mine.
3. Mario Fubini (ed.) with the collaboration of Enzo Bigi, in Introduction, *Canti*, Turin: Loescher, 1964, pp. 3-20.
4. Cfr. Leopardi translated Idylls of Mosco, a Greek poet of 2nd century BC, and published his comments on the works in *Discourse on Mosco* in 'Spettatore', Milan, 1815.
5. Leopardi, *Zibaldone*. 4234, in Walter Binni (ed.) with the collaboration of Enrico Ghidetti, in *Tutte le opere* [Complete Works], Florence: Sansoni, 1969, p. 1123.
6. Leopardi, *Zibaldone*, 4356-7, *op. cit.*
7. Leopardi, *Zibaldone*, 1228-29, in *Tutte le opere*, *op. cit.*, I.
8. Leopardi, *Zibaldone*, *op. cit.*, I, p. 10.
9. Leopardi, *Zibaldone*, *op. cit.*, II, p. 845.
10. *Ibid.*, p. 812.
11. Leopardi, *Zibaldone*, 56, 57, *op. cit.*, I.
12. Cfr. Gina Martegiani, *Il romanticismo italiano non esiste* [*Italian Romanticism does not exist*], (Florence: Seeber, 1908). An ample debate on this question can be read in the writings of Giuseppe Antonio Borgese, *Storia della critica romantica in Italia*; Antonio De Paz, *Il Romanticismo europeo*, Naples: Liguori, 1987; Michel Orcel, *Il suono dell'infinito*, Naples: Liguori, 1993.
13. See Note '*B*' at the end.
14. Leopardi, *Zibaldone*, 4234, 15 December 1826, in *Tutte le opere*, II, *op. cit.*, p. 1123.
15. Leopardi, 'Discorso di un italiano intorno alla poesia romantica' [Discourse of an Italian over Romantic Poetry, 1818], in *Tutte le opere*, I, *op. cit.*, (trans. mine).
16. Leopardi, *Zibaldone*, 4074, 19 April 1824, *op. cit.*
17. Mme. Germaine De Staël Holstein, 'Sulla maniera e utilita` delle traduzioni' [Over the method and utility of translations] in Anco Marzio Mutterle (ed.), *Discussioni e polemiche sul romanticismo*, Roma-Bari: Laterza, 1975.
18. Leopardi, 'Lettera ai Sigg. Compilatori della "Biblioteca Italiana"' [Letter to the Editors of 'Biblioteca Italiana',1816], in *Tutte le opere*, I, *op. cit.*, p. 882 (trans. and italics mine).
19. Cfr. Cesare Luporini quotes Leopardi in *Leopardi progressivo* in *Filosofi vecchi e nuovi*, Florence: Sansoni, 1947.

20. Leopardi, *Zibaldone*, 30 November 1828, *op. cit.,* II, p. 1196.
21. Eugenio Montale, 'In limine' in *Ossi di Seppia*, *Tutte le opere*, Milan: Mondadori, 1984, p. 8.
22. Leopardi, *Zibaldone*, 4513, 29 May 1829, *Ibid.*, p. 1234 (trans. and italics mine).
23. Leopardi, 'Disegni letterari', XII, 1828, in *Tutte le opere*, I, p. 372 (Eng. trans. mine).
24. Leopardi, *L'infinito*, C. X11 [*The Infinite*], Eng. trans. by Anthony F. Kline, *Canti* of Giacomo Leopardi, www.tonykline.freeonline.co.uk/ Leopardi.htm. December 2003, No. 2, p. 8 (Italics mine).
25. Luigi Pirandello, 'Leopardi cieco' [Blind Leopardi], in *Roma Letteraria*, vol. 8, no. 3, 10 Feb. 1900, pp. 51-54.
26. *Ibid.*
27. Meyer Howard Abrams, in M. Pagnini, (ed.), *I Romantici* [*The Romantics*], (Bologna: Il Mulino, 1986), p. 183.
28. Rainier Maria Rilke, *Elegie Duinesi* [*Dunigio Elegies*], V Elegy, It. trans. (Turin: Einaudi, 1978), vv. 97-98.30.
29. Leopardi, *Zibaldone*, 168-171, 12-13 July 1820, *op. cit.* (trans. and italics mine).
30. Leopardi, *Zibaldone*, 1744, 20 September 1821, *op. cit.*
31. Leopardi, *Zibaldone*, 1928-29, 4293, *op. cit.*
32. Leopardi, *La sera del dì di festa*, C. XIII [*Evening of the Holiday*], trans. by Kline, No. 3, *op. cit.*
33. Leopardi, *Il sabato del villaggio,* C. XXV [*The Village Saturday*], trans. by Kline, No. 5, *op. cit.*
34. *Ibid.*
35. Leopardi, *To the Moon*, [*Alla luna*, C. X1V], trans. by Kline, No. 4, *op. cit.*
36. *Ibid.*
37. Lucio Felici (ed.), in 'Introduction', *Leopardi*: *Canti*, Rome: Newton Compton, 1987, p. 14.
38. Leopardi, *A Silvia*, C. XX1 [*To Silvia*], trans. by Kline, No. 1, *op. cit.,* pp. 6-7 (Italics mine).
39. Mikhail Bachtin, *Estetica e romanzo*, It. trans. Turin: Einaudi, 1976, pp. 372-373, 398.
40. Leopardi, 'Zibaldone', 4388, 21 September 1828, in *Tutte le opere*, (ed. 1976), *op. cit.,* p. 1186.
41. Leopardi, 'Letter to Pietro Giordani, 6 May 1825', in *Tutte le opere*, *op. cit.*
42. Leopardi, *To Himself* (*A se stesso*, C. XXVIII,1833), Kline, No. 6, *op. cit.,* p. 14.
43. Percy Byshe Shelley, 'Ode to the West Wind', quoted by Jerome J. McGann in *The Beauty of the Medusa: A Study in Romantic Literary Iconology*, article on-line, p. 3, reproduced as part of The Romantic Circles Electronic Edition of Shelley's 'Medusa', from Studies in Romanticism

11 (1972) pp. 3-25. www.rc.ud.edu/editions/shelley/medusa/mcgann.html, 12 May 2003.

44. Shelley, *Fragment 'On The Medusa of Leonardo da Vinci in the Florentine Gallery'*, quoted by McGann, *op. cit.*, pp. 2-3.
45. Leopardi, *Sopra un basso rilievo antico sepolcrale*, C. XXX [*Bas-relief on an Ancient Tomb*], Eng. trans. by Kline, No. 17, *op. cit.*, p. 49.
46. Leopardi, *Zibaldone*, 4485-86, 11 April 1829, *op. cit.*
47. Leopardi, in the lines dedicated to his friends in Florence in the Preface of the first edition of the *Canti*, published in Florence in 1831.
48. Walter Binni, *La protesta di Leopardi*, Florence: Sansoni, 1988, pp. 278-285.
49. Cfr. Binni, *La nuova poetica leopardiana,* Florence: Sansoni, 1979.
50. Leopardi, *Wild Broom*, *La ginestra*, C. XXXIV [*Wild Broom*], trans. by Kline, No. 13, *op. cit.*, p. 30.
51. *Ibid.*
52. *Ibid.*
53. *Ibid.*
54. *Ibid.*
55. *Ibid.*
56. *Ibid.*
57. Cfr. Carlo Ferrucci, *Leopardi filosofo e le ragioni della poesia*, Venezia: Marsilio, 1987.
58. Leopardi, *Zibaldone*, 2492, 23 June 1822; 2402-4 and 2549-55; *Pensiero* VI, *Tutte le opere*, *op. cit.*
59. Sebastian Timpanaro, *Classicismo e illuminismo nell'Ottocento italiano*, Pisa: Nistri-Lischi, 1969, p. 40.
60. Leopardi, *Bas-Relief on an Ancient Tomb*, *op. cit.*; *On a lovely lady's image*, *op. cit.*
61. Neuro Bonifazi, 'Genesi della poesia leopardiana' [Genesis of Leopardian Poetry], in *Il genere letterario*, Ravenna: Longo Editore, 1986, p. 106.
62. *Ibid.*
63. Leopardi, *Ad Angelo Mai*,C. III [*To Angelo Mai*], trans. by Kline, No. 37, *op. cit.*
64. Leopardi, *Zibaldone*, 72, *op. cit.*
65. Leopardi, in *Tutte le opere*, *op. cit.*, 1, p. 1382.
66. Leopardi, *Sopra il basso rilievo antico sepolcrale*, C.XXX [*Bas-Relief on an Ancient Tomb*] in Kline, No. 17, *op. cit.*, pp. 48-51 ; *Sopra il ritratto di una bella donna scolpito nel monumento sepolcrale della medesima*, C. XXXI [*On a lovely lady's image*], in Kline, No. 18, *op. cit.*, pp. 52-53.
67. Gennaro Saverese, 'Il figurativo e Leopardi' [The figurative in Leopardi] in *La Rassegna della Letteratura*, Florence: Le Lettere, July-December 2002, no. 2, pp. 414- 418. Contains references to the detailed analysis of this theme in Francesca Fedi's monograph *Mausolei di sabbia. Sulla cultura figurativa di Leopardi* [*Mausoleums of sand. On the figurative culture of Leopardi*]; Cfr. Leopardi, *All'Italia*, C. I [*To Italy*], trans. by Kline, No. 35, *op. cit.*

68. Ricoeur, *op. cit.*, p. 41.
69. Cfr. Mario Ricciardi points to the link indicated between *Canti* and the oral traditions of ancient Greek lyrics, in *Giacomo Leopardi: la logica dei 'Canti'*, Milan: F. Angeli, 1986.
70. Leopardi, 'Zibaldone', 18 September 1827, in *Tutte le opere*, II, *op. cit.*, p. 1149.
71. Leopardi, 'Lettera ai Sigg. Compilatori della "Biblioteca Italiana"' [Letter to the Editors of 'Biblioteca Italiana', 1816], in *Tutte le opere*, I, *op. cit.*, p. 882.
72. Paul Ricoeur, *Interpretation Theory: Discourse and the Surplus of Meaning*, Fort Worth, Texas Christian University Press, 1976, p. 44.
73. *Ibid.*
74. Cfr. Sergio Solmi touches upon a singular aspect in his poetry in the following lines: "The highest poetry of Leopardi came out with the Idylls only...it unfolded with the supreme innocent simplicity of a sigh, and a purity of inflections that Italy had not known since Petrarch. The verse which rhymed more with the measure of the inner voice of the poet than with the play of syllables and accents, created enchanted suspensions and delicious prospects, where, in the evocations of place and time the motions of thought and heart were rendered, purged of every turgidity and affectation, essential as the Greek lyrics." - Sergio Solmi, *Studi leopardiani. Note su autori classici italiani e stranieri*, Milan: Adelphi, 1987, p. 190 (trans. mine).
75. Leopardi, *Zibaldone*, 19 April 1827, *op. cit.*
76. Antonio Prete, *Il pensiero poetante*, Milan: Feltrinelli, 1980.
77. Ricoeur, *op. cit.*, p. 53.
78. *Ibid.* p. 51.
79. Anthony. J. Cascardi, 'Introduction', *The Subject of Modernity*, Cambridge, Cambridge University Press, 1992, p. 2.
80. Leopardi, *Zibaldone*, 19 April 1827, *op. cit.*
81. Leopardi, *Wild Broom*, *op. cit.*, p. 30.
82. Leopardi, *Palinodia al Marchese Gino Capponi*, C. XXXII [*Palinode to Marquis Gino Capponi*] in *Tutte le opere*, *op. cit.* (Eng. trans. and italics mine).
83. Leopardi, 'Letter to Pietro Giordani in 24 July, 1829 and letter to Fanny Targioni Tozzetti' in *Tutte le opere*, *op. cit.*
84. Cfr. Leopardi, *Zibaldone*. 1172, 3: 1182, 3, *op. cit.*, [In these notes and elsewhere, as also in *Palinode*, Leopardi denounces the violence and exploitation hidden behind the façade of progress; mentions the pitiable condition of the labourers working in the mines, in the textile mills of Manchester, and the state of slavery in the cotton plantations of the southern states of America; mentions the spirit of egoism, competition and the abuse of resources promoted by the mercantile ideology and the credo of utilitarianism.]

A. *The Life and Works of Leopardi.*

Not one to seek solace in false prospects of happiness, Leopardi embraced his misfortunes with stoic fortitude and evolved a critical philosophy that gave him the courage of truth, to live life in his own terms, in defiance of destiny. We provide here a brief account of his life and works, considered fundamental for our understanding of the poet. Born in 1798 in a noble family of the Marches in central Italy at Recanati, Giacomo was a child prodigy who translated Homer and Horace and composed poetry in old Greek before he crossed his early teens. Leading a cloistered existence in the paternal mansion and starved of affection in a cold family atmosphere, noted especially in his mother, he spent time mostly in the family library surrounded by books, developed physical deformities and soon fell victim to a crippling illness. While he suffered in solitude and despair, his unhappiness was compounded by experiences of unrequited love that dogged him throughout his life, and its echo can be found in the lyrics addressed to different feminine figures in the *Canti.* Finding the closed, provincial atmosphere of Recanati insufferable Giacomo tried to leave home and live in cities with a broader cultural milieu, in Milan, Florence, Bologna, Rome and Pisa, even facing acute financial hardship. He reached Naples in 1833 where he passed the terminal period of his life, prolific in writing notwithstanding his failing health and physical pain. He died at Naples in 1837 at the age of thirty-nine, comforted solely in the company of his friend Antonio Ranieri and was buried in the church of San Vitale at Fuorigrotta in Naples.

Leopardi collected his entire poetry in a single volume in the *Canti,* which was published for the first time in 1831 in Florence, followed by an expanded edition in 1833 in Naples. In its final form the *Canti* was published posthumously in 1845 at the initiative of his friend Antonio Ranieri who added two later compositions to the previous edition, i.e., *Moonset (ll tramonto della luna,* C. XXXIII) and *Wild Broom (La ginestra,* C. XXXIV), both of 1836, retaining the sequential order intended by the poet. Beginning with his civil or patriotic compositions, for example, *To Italy (All'Italia* C.I, 1818), or *On the Proposed Dante Monument in Florence (Sopra il monumento di Dante,* C.II, 1818), his poetry proceeded to classical themes in the longer *Canzone* form as in *Marcus Junius Brutus (Bruto minore,* C.VI, 1821) and *Sappho's Last Song (L'ultimo canto di Saffo,* C.IX, 1822) and simultaneously to brief, evocative Idylls like the *Infinite (L'infinito,* C.XII, 1819) or *The Evening of the Holiday (La sera del di di festa,* c.xm, 1820), in this phase between 1819 and 1822. After a long gap of years spent in writing philosophical prose, he returned to poetry again in 1828, with longer Idylls marked by a reflective tone, for example, *To Silvia (A Silvia,* C.XXI, 1828), *The Village Saturday (Il Sabato del villaggio,* C.XXY, 1829), *the Solitary Bird (Il passero solitario,* C.XI, 1829), and speculative poems like *The Night song of a Wondering Shepherd in Asia (Il canto notturno di un pastore errante in Asia,* C.XXIII, 1830), in the years between 1828-1830. Gradually, his spirit of non-conformism in relation to the dominant ideologies of his epoch began to assert in his works, in compositions of satire like *Palinode to Marchese Gino Capponi (Palinodia al Marchese Gino Capponi,* C.XXXII, 1835), and the unpublished *The Newly Faithful (I nuovi credenti,* 1835), or *Paralipomeni della Batracomiomachia* (a parodical sequel to Homer's work, 1830-1833), and in the allegorical dialogues in *Operette morali* (1824-1836), culminating in the *Canti* in a tone of fiery protest in *Wild Broom,* and contemplative in *Moonset,* in the last phase of his poetry, in the years 1833-1836. Thus moments have been individuated in his poetry in phases, which are in a way distinguishable yet also overlapping, with the categorical elements coexistent in each. Leopardi's writings in prose in his *Zibaldone* (notebook of thoughts, dating from 1817 to 1832), *Pensieri* (philosophical reflections, organized in volume in 1832), and Epistolary (931 letters) recorded his musings on poetry and philosophy as also society and culture, covering almost his entire life span, throwing valuable insight into his life and thoughts.

B. *Romanticism in Italy.*

Romanticism as a movement, which gained momentum in the late eighteenth and early nineteenth century Europe, reached late in Italy, and was clothed in the image of German hegemony. Two impulses can be identified in the text of Romanticism and its reception in Italy. Caution, diffidence, if not outright contempt constituted the first impulse that resulted in inhibiting the initial phase of its reception, while subsequently, in a second impulse, constituted by a phase of acculturation in the Italian soil, Romanticism was adapted to meet the specifics of the Italian reality and instrumentalized to lend impetus to the national movement of unification, *Il Risorgimento.* Thus there was a late outbreak, albeit short lived, of the movement in Italy, with the initial span lasting roughly between the years 1816 and the 1820's, when it petered out under the brunt of severe Austrian retaliation on the leaders of revolt. Significantly, the first moment of contact was at Milan, where it was received as a crossover trend of German philosophical thought. A defining trait of Italian Romanticism was its regional character, for its initial distribution spread predominantly in the north, in the regions of Lombardy, the Venetian and the adjoining parts of Liguria, with Milan as the epicenter of the movement. Milan, returned to Hapsburg rule in 1815 after a short experience of French dispensation under Napoleon, had long been the Italian capital of Enlightenment culture. It had a thriving intellectual climate sustained by numerous cultural forums in literary salons, café, journals *(Il Conciliatore,* the focal point of Italian Romanticism, was published in Milan, following the tradition of *café* of the Enlightenment era), which provided the rallying point for a growing ideological ferment, and was developing to be the center of the rising nationalist aspirations in Italy. The Italian intellectuals traced the origin of Romantic thought in the Jena school led by Schelling, Herder, Fichte and Novalis; in the

Berlin school, in the philosophy of Schleiermacher; and most significantly in the movement of Sturm and Drang, beginning in the 1770's that found expression in the writings of Goethe and Schiller, and was articulated in the reflections of the Schlegel brothers. With her book *De L'Allemagne,* Mme De Staël Holstein emerged as the most influential exponent of Romantic culture in Europe. The equivocal nature of Italian response to the aesthetics of the transalpine trend was thus in direct correlation to the view of its purported emanation from Germany, its endorsement on the part of the dominant group appearing as a discourse of power aimed at a proliferation of political subjugation into cultural domination. The whole controversy on Romanticism came out in the open with the publication of the letter of Mme De Staël titled 'On the method and utility of translation', on January 1816, in the first issue of the Milanese journal *Biblioteca Italiana* (founded by Ludovico Di Breme and Pietro Borsieri, leading figures of Italian Romanticism), in which she exhorted the Italian writers to translate works of foreign literature and let in the flow of new ideas across the Alps. She observed that it would revitalize Italian literature caught in the cesspool of classical tradition and repetitions of outdated rhetoric and ornate words, bereft of the power and vitality found in expressions of authentic human feelings that animated the new literature of Europe. Smarting already under Austrian domination, the Italian intelligentsia baulked at the criticism of the classicist culture in Italy and was galled at the suggestion of a Nordic model to replace the prevailing Greco-Roman tradition. Pietro Giordani, a Milanese writer, came out with an anonymous rejoinder *'An Italian responds'* in the same journal, in favour of Classicism, rejecting the so-called suggestion of imitation of foreign models, but affirmed all the same the need for change, which as he sustained, had to take shape out of the culture, history and literary traditions of Italy. A very young Gtacomo Leopardi (only eighteen years then), in a systematic exposition, concurred with Giordani and addressed a letter to the same journal in defense of the elements of mythology and the classical ideals celebrated in the Italian tradition, an important document, to which we refer in our text. Narrative fiction emerged as the new genre of the age, ending the traditional preeminence of epic poetry and tragedy in Italian literature. Unbridled expressions of individual will, still less the Romantic license for 'the aberrant' or the Gothic, which militated against the didactic and nationalistic scope of the movement and the collective spirit, did not feature as a desired trait in Italian Romanticism. It was a historical moment of great hopes and greater disappointments in national life. Napoleon had brought into the fractured body politic of the peninsula prospects of recovery and had kindled the hopes of national unification, expectations belied first by the imperialist ambitions of the Napoleonic regime, and subsequently by its fall and the restoration of the old monarchies to their previous positions, crushing the hopes of a nationstate in Italy. The dramatic moment found expression in tragic poetry, for example, in the *Odes* of Ugo Foscolo, and his *Last letters of Jacopo Ortis*, dealing with the themes of war, death and in *Jacopo Ortis*, that of suicide, or in the element of the 'pathetic' in the poetry of Alfieri, in the ideals of patriotism and heroic sacrifice. Their poetry was neo-classical in form but romantic in inspiration, which imbued the leaders of Risorgimento, such as Mazzini and Gioberti, and widened the popular appeal of Romanticism in the country. While Alessandro Manzoni set the norm of prose fiction with his historical novel *I Promessi Sposi* (1827), a proliferation of historical and popular fictions followed in the writings of Ludovico Di Breme, Pietro Borsieri, Giovanni Berchet, Ermes Visconti, Silvio Pellico. Continuing in a Romantic line, Antonio Fogazzaro and Niccolò Tommaseo wrote significant works of popular fiction, while Giuseppe Belli and Carlo Porta brought out novels in regional dialects, recreating local realities and reflecting regional aspirations, widely popularizing the genre of prose fiction. These trends continued in Italian literature long after the decline of the Romantic Movement and merged into the literature of realism or *Verismo* in the later part of nineteenth century.

LALITA SUBBU

Romantic Quest and Forsterian Vision in *Howards End*

It has often been said that modernism had its roots in the crises of the nineteenth century. A specific line of continuity is observable right through the Romantics and the Victorians into the twentieth century with reference to some of the themes like the industrial revolution, increasing urbanization, the socio-economic disparities of England in the nineteenth century and the loneliness of the self in such a world. What is less often undertaken, however, is an examination of how any aspect of Romanticism emerges for the early modernist writer like E.M. Forster as a vision, a mode, an influence, a history that shapes his own modernism. This paper hopes to consider, not the pressures and challenges faced by the English/European romantics in their time (which is a posited *presentness*—viz, something happening *in* their time), but the choices that lie before modernist authors who are Janus-faced, looking back and ahead. In the transmutation of Romanticism into modernism, the sense of a continuity and a separateness are both entertained. The changes and continuities in theme, form, theory and ideology have to be closely examined, because when a modernist writer is said to deal with issues of Romanticism, the question of how to approach such a writer becomes important. Where do we enter his work and his history? Do we address his social and historical background, or the intellectual influences on him, or the motifs and textuality of his work? There is the resulting problem of his ideology, because one is addressing modernism *and* Romanticism simultaneously here. There is also the question of genre transformation, from Romantic philosophy and poetry to British fiction.

In E.M. Forster's case, it may be argued that he understands his own modernism better through his use of Romanticism. Well before *A Passage to India* (1924) appeared and before the start of the complex critical history that first applauded this novel and then took it apart on the grounds of post-colonial readings, E.M. Forster's liberal humanism has been seen as conservative, flawed and problematic. His novels offer a vision of the self, fractured by industrialisation. The loneliness in the city leads to problems of communication. The new artistic world of the early twentieth century resonates with the music of Wagner and Beethoven. Yet the tawdry is never abandoned. Forster is constantly absorbed in representing the fictional self but unlike T.S. Eliot who represents the dismantled subject before the contours of the city, Forster predicates the self in terms of an older debate from Romantic and Victorian England—a debate between the poor and the rich, the peasant and the landowner, the intellectual and the vulgar, the saved and the damned, the idealists and the materialists, the women and the men.

Forster's claim to a Romantic vision may seem to be thin in the face of his being called "Victorian," "Edwardian," "Liberal humanist," and "conservative." His sense of Romanticism derives from his dissatisfaction with three institutions that betray him in his quest for truth-telling and for following his consciousness on its journey. The first of these is the companionable, intellectually rigorous, but ultimately unfulfilling atmosphere of Cambridge, which introduces philosophy as the systemic pursuit of truth—from Plato to Berkeley, Hume, Kant, Hegel and Nietzsche—down to G.E. Moore's *Principia Ethica* (1903). It is an academic system that does not enter into life's lived mysteries. The second institution that betrays him is the self-regarding public school system and the narrow confines of British philanthropy and utilitarian concerns recreated by him in his 1903 novel, *The Longest Journey* (1907) as Sawston. The hero of the novel, Rickie Elliott, a throw-back to the Forster of the Cambridge years, rejects both Cambridge and Sawston and moves towards Wiltshire, the pastoral home and the roots of the peasantry of England.

The third and last institution to weary Forster is the English spirit itself, though he never sets himself in direct opposition to it. This weariness is seen in the fascination with which he throws all his English characters into settings outside his own country—into places like Italy, Greece, India. Even in *Howards End*, Britain is always judged from the standpoint of another country—Germany—and the heroines Margaret and Helen Schlegel, are cosmopolitan in sensibility, with a German father and an English mother.

Mr. Schlegel, the father of Margaret and Helen, belongs to a prominent class of the Germany of the post-1850s—"not the aggressive German, so dear to the English journalist, not the domestic German, so dear to the English wit ... [but] the countryman of Hegel and Kant—a 'dreamy' idealist." Though he has fought against Denmark, Austria and France, he loves peace:

> he had fought without visualizing the results of victory. A hint of the truth broke on him after Sedan, when he saw the dyed moustaches of Napoleon going grey; another when he entered Paris, and saw the smashed windows of the Tuileries. Peace came - it was all very immense, one had turned into an Empire - but he knew that some quality had vanished for which not all Alsace-Lorraine could compensate him. Germany a commercial Power, Germany a naval Power, Germany with colonies here and a Forward Policy there, and legitimate aspirations in the other place, might appeal to others, and be fitly served by them; for his own part, he abstained from the fruits of victory, and naturalized himself in England.[1]

He hopes that the "clouds of materialism" overhanging Germany will part and the "intellectual light will re-emerge".[2] Margaret's childhood is spent in hearing him explain to relatives that the prioritising of money first, then of intellect, then of the imagination, in that order, is not going to be creative: "Pan-Germanism is no more imaginative than ... Imperialism over here".[3] Both these attitudes in the two countries valorize bigness and quantity. Claiming that the poets and philosophers of Germany who held sway for at least two centuries, are now a thing of the past, he exhorts his listeners to revive the imagination: "[Germany has] learned men, who collect more facts than do the learned men of England. They collect facts, and facts, and empires of facts. But which of them will rekindle the light within?".[4]

Forster uses the parentage of Margaret and Helen to reveal the differences in the English and German attitudes to art. Margaret often pays tribute to the German love of beauty. The average German, according to her, is always asking beauty to enter his life and for her there is salvation in such a quest. She is angered by the tasteful contempt of the average islander for things Teutonic and asserts that though there may be liberty of action in England, the liberty of thought and the quest of beauty are to be located in Prussia. Margaret takes much pride in her half-German status and Forster derives some strategic convenience as a novelist from her distinctive personality and the difference between her and other English characters.

This 'difference' and this quest, accompanied by Romantic predilections is observable in the fiction of both Forster and D.H. Lawrence. They are caught in the problematic circuit of Romantic nostalgia for the unspoilt countryside on the one hand, and a radical awareness and style that look forward to a modern consciousness, on the other. Though very different from one another in terms of ideology and style Lawrence's heroines in *Women in Love* (1920), Ursula and Gudrun and Forster's heroines in *Howards End* (Margaret and Helen Schlegel) show the quest of the women for passion, personal relations, non-conformism, irrationality, poetry, spontaneity and subjectivity. The life of the emotions is valorized and its primacy is all-consuming.

However, it is also necessary to remember that Lawrence expresses his dissatisfaction with Forster for glorifying the business class—the Wilcoxes—into whose family Margaret Schlegel enters. It is also significant that Lawrence expresses his dissatisfaction with the group to which Forster belonged—namely, the Bloomsbury group. Lawrence's suspicious view of Bloomsbury indicates his preference for a less intellectualized, less esoteric and more *social* polemic of art. The Bloomsbury canon is examined in detail by a cultural critic of more recent times, Raymond Williams, who articulates his dissatisfaction in a penetrating account of Bloomsbury in the essay "The Bloomsbury Fraction," in his work *Problems in Materialism and Culture.*[5] Raymond Williams speaks of this group as a cultural group that is too small for statistical analysis—viz. too small to effectively intervene in social matters. It is interesting and significant that he compares them unfavourably with Romantic activists like William Godwin and his circle who were dissenters, and small working professionals who operated from a social and economic position that was sharply different from the ruling and upper class of the day. This Bloomsbury group, though avowing an interest in social conscience like the Romantics, still remains a *fraction* of the existing English upper class. They opposed the dominant ideas and values of this class. Williams dramatizes the paradox of the Bloomsbury group. While recording their private contribution to political and organizational involvement (Virginia Woolf's involvement with the Women's Cooperative Guild meetings, Leonard Woolf's involvement with the League of Nations, the Cooperative Movement, the Labour Party on anti-imperialist questions) he points out that their oppositional value was restricted to the English upper class itself with whom they still maintained relations; the women in this class opposed the men, the critique was intellectual. The level of social intervention is within the professional and highly educated section of the English ruling class and is at best aimed at a kind of liberalization. The interaction with the working class was minimal, according to Raymond Williams.

The Bloomsbury group was to be located in the social and intellectual atmosphere of the reformed universities. The male members of this British aristocracy of intellect went automatically to "the best public schools, to Oxford and Cambridge and then into all the most powerful and respectable professions. ... You found them as civil servants, sitting in the seat of permanent under-secretaries of government departments; they became generals, admirals, editors, judges, or they retired with a KCSI or KCMG after distinguished careers in the Indian or Colonial Civil Services. Others again got fellowships at Oxford or Cambridge and ended as head of an Oxford or Cambridge College or headmaster of one of the great public schools".[6]

Though the group's social pretensions are critically examined by Raymond Williams, he simultaneously recognizes its contribution to a new "structure of feeling," a new style, a new intimacy of social intercourse with the Woolfs, the Bells, the Stephens, Keynes, Strachey, Duncan Grant, Roger Fry, Forster and others. Williams quotes Leonard Woolf's confession that Bloomsbury was a label imposed by the external world and never existed in that form—it was the existence of a group of friends whose roots of friendship were in the University of Cambridge.

The vision of Forster as a product of this circle gains significance. The Romantic poets, Wordsworth and Coleridge had emerged in privatized voices after the failure of their own active participation in and support of the French Revolution and its aftermath. Forster is all along aware of the *dangers* of Bloomsbury individualism in the public world. Yet it is Bloomsbury that gives him his sense of art and aesthetics in the true Romantic sense of autonomy.

Forster's Romanticism, which comprehends a sort of philosophical idealism combined with a sense of ethics, emerges as somewhat helpless in the face of his growing awareness as a writer that this idealism and ethics cannot adequately combat the realities of the money-grabbing and rapacious system of capitalism. Yet, the private sensitivity of a Bloomsbury writer is self-referential and aesthetic, almost mystical.

Forster moves towards a commitment to an inner vision where art is important. Forster believes that the artist's vision is an important expression of his unique, individual feeling. The spirit expands with the inner transcendental idea of beauty. Art is to be upheld, not because it is noble or beautiful or enlightened or original or sincere or idealistic or useful or educational. It may embody any of those qualities, but more importantly it is upheld because it is the only material object in the universe which may possess internal harmony. Art is seen as an imaginative construct. The work of art is both detached from social existence and is a part of it. Through the experience of art there is the pleasure of entering such an autonomous world, and there is also the moral influence gained obliquely from this entry. What had been earlier criticized as an ivory-tower mentality is now seen by Forster not as a 'retreat' but as an expression whereby the artist critiques society from his own private site, *Howards End* is itself the site from which the business class is criticized.

In Forster's time, a writer who cared for the countryside and for personal relations would feel indignant at the moneyed class emerging after the industrial and financial progress of the age. Art itself being a despised thing in such circles, the art for arts sake motto is a new challenge put forward by the Bloomsbury aesthetic. Roger Fry, artist-writer, critic for the Athenaeum, director of the Metropolitan Museum of Art, New York, and a prominent member of the Bloomsbury group, expresses the idea of the autonomous, self-contained internal harmony of the work of art, whether it is church architecture, a symphony of Beethoven or even the harmony within a country house like Howards End with its wych-elm. According to Fry, the individual consciousness evolves due to this emotional response to art.

The *Principia Ethica* by G.E. Moore[7] is the philosophical work published in October 1903 and Lytton Strachey speaks enthusiastically of its sense of dialogue with Aristotle, Herbert Spencer, Bradley. It proposes at once an ethical theory, as well as a celebration of the value of art and Love. Moore initially grounds his work in the acceptance of the idealist thesis that the familiar empirical world is a web of appearances grounded in a timeless reality that transcends our perceptions. Later, he switches to a more sceptical attitude towards transcendent reality and instead speaks of values as abstract objects detached from empirical reality, yet also part of them. His interaction with his philosophy teacher, Henry Sidgwick who taught ethics, leads Moore to develop and expand ideas about ethics, ideal utilitarianism which can be non-hedonistic. While both Sidgwick and Moore are in agreement that ethical concepts are irreducible, they have different ideas about how to connect these concepts with human relations. Ethical judgements, according to Moore, should be expressive of emotions or attitudes. So while goodness or the intrinsic value of things is unanalysable, the sense of social utilitarian obligation is also present. However, Moore's defence of conventional morality in *The Principia Ethica* is ignored by the Bloomsbury Group which, instead, takes up his later thesis that the most valuable things are the states of consciousness that give rise to pleasures of intercourse and the love of aesthetic objects. The thesis that art has intrinsic value is not a new one and goes back to English Romanticism (Keats's statement that a thing of beauty is a joy for ever or that what the imagination seizes as beauty must be truth or that he is certain of nothing, but the holiness of the heart's affections). Where the Romantics advocate the creative process itself (because of their confidence in the active agency of creation and prophecy) G.E. Moore seems rather to highlight passive appreciation of objects of enjoyment for their own sake.

Moore seeks the good and the beautiful in terms of relations with others. A predicate good is symbolic and indefinable, an *a priori* consciousness which is a sense of good in the individual mind. The question that arises is that if we have to lead an ethical life in the world outside how do we reconcile our moral obligation to others with our private sense of pleasure?

This enquiry throws up some related questions. The English Romantics had based their idealism on the notional difference between the transcendental and timeless eternity on the one hand and the ephemeral, human, finite prison of the world on the other. Their vision dramatizes this difference as, for example, Kant's transcendentalism, Shelley's dependence on Platonism to lift him from a suffering world into a mansion of ideal forms, or Wordsworth's immortalising of certain moments in the purity of unspoilt Nature. The ideal and the actual coexist and the vision of Romanticism gives expression to both. But the English Romantics speak out of a pastoral world that is rapidly changing. By the time of Forster, it has changed much more and the social stratifications of England and Europe are different. Thus every modernist writer who offers a glimpse of Romantic vision also offers us his own sense of its limits or failures. The individual's quest for personal salvation or social betterment has to contend with the material and public world.

In *Howards End* both the Schlegel sisters make mistakes in their quest. Margaret, the elder sister is pragmatic and unattractive, desires proportion and harmony and conviction in her life, even with as powerful and moneyed a family as the Wilcoxes. This is a family which inaugurates the impulse of Europe with its Imperial and West African Rubber Company. It also ushers in the automobile age with its car that raises dust in the village. Margaret defends her marriage even though she discovers that Mr. Wilcox has had a mistress. Her pragmatism represents the decency and intellectual cosmopolitanism of the safe variety that is to broaden into the complacency of a woman of property. Margaret's open support of empire builders like Mr. Wilcox and her assertion that such men constitute the 'progress' of England bear damning testimony to the fears of early Romantics like Blake or Wordsworth about England's future. Her only saving grace is her affection for Mr. Wilcox's first wife, Ruth (who is represented as a Romantic symbol in the novel) and her love for her sister Helen. Ruth Wilcox's dying wish that Margaret should inherit Howards End shows her recognition of Margaret's depth of character and her sensitivity. The scene of Ruth Wilcox's funeral is turned by Forster into a lament for the passing away of a rural order (a Romantic theme) and only the woodcutter who watches the procession while attending to the trees, provides a choric comment "The old sort were dying out".[8]

Helen's mistakes in her quest are of a different and an extreme kind. She insists on her preference for a totally inner world and hates the panic and emptiness of the outside world. She "entices" and is "enticed." She is the first to fancy herself in love with one of the younger Wilcoxes (Paul, the second son) but is the first to fall out of love with the whole family, except for Mrs. Wilcox. For Helen the Wilcoxes signify brute authority, insensitivity, people who, importantly, fear emotions and fear the inner life.

We can see how in Helen the Romantic sensibility of the women in Emily Bronte or Hardy has become more vulnerable and more aware of the disruptions of the external world. The standards by which Margaret and Helen (Schlegelism) live demand a constant commitment in theory to art, truth, social activism and the poetry of mood. In the light of such commitment, their meeting with Leonard Bast (a lower middle-class clerk whose family ancestors are yeomen) leads to their interest in his social upliftment. What is usually discussed with mock seriousness in the women's club is now a serious matter for Helen. On a tip-off from Mr. Wilcox that the finances of Leonard Bast's office are about to smash the Schlegels force him to leave the company. As he is then left without a job, and as Mr. Wilcox now declares carelessly that the Company was actually quite safe and has tided over its earlier anxieties, Helen is outraged at what she sees as Bast's lapse into poverty. Her Romantic sensibility drives her to fight with Margaret and Mr. Wilcox, to try to help Leonard and his wife financially, ultimately to try and save him from dying due to unemployment, starvation and disappointment. And here is the Forster mystique—that the idea of death saves a man but that death destroys him. Helen, in one last attempt to stave off her sense of guilt, consoles Leonard Bast, offers herself to him and is later bearing his child. The situation is further complicated by the fact that Leonard Bast's wife, Jacky, has been the mistress of Mr. Wilcox, but this fact comes to light only later. When Margaret demands that her pregnant sister should be allowed to rest and sleep at Howards End, the beautiful country house of the Wilcoxes, Mr. Wilcox, though choosing not to live there after marrying Margaret, forbids Helen to enter, claiming that he has his dead wife to think of. Driven out of her pragmatism for once, Margaret points out with emphasis that double standards cannot now operate and that rich and poor be treated alike:

> Do you see the connexion? Stupid, hypocritical, cruel—oh, contemptible!—a man who insults his wife when she's alive and cants with her memory when she's dead. A man who ruins a woman for his pleasure, and casts her off to ruin other men. And gives bad financial advice, and then says he is not responsible. These men are you. You can't recognize them, because you cannot connect.[9]

The novel's later events are bizarre for Leonard Bast is hunted down as he comes to meet Helen, and dies, not from a weapon that was used against him by Charles Wilcox but heart trouble and a bookshelf of books that falls on him.

The tragedy of Leonard Bast is complete. He dies in abject poverty, and has lived as a lower middle-class citizen. He has no claim to his just inheritance—the land which his ancestors may have worked on. All his life he had hoped to rise above his ugly station by acquiring culture, pronouncing foreign names accurately, being well-informed, attending music concerts, perfecting his manners, reading Ruskin to improve his language, talking of Monet and Debussy. The Forsterian critique is double-edged for it does not spare either Helen or Leonard Bast. Helen in her interference has cost him his life. Leonard Bast's attempt to "connect" with the intellectual Schlegels has resulted in disastrous social meetings and in a final desperate moment of physical contact with Helen.

It is suggested that Helen's child will now inherit the estate. The child is a Romantic symbol of a past which no longer exists. Bast's dead father is one connection with the peasantry. The first Mrs. Wilcox is another, for she hails from the original family of Howards who possessed Howards End. It is the end and the beginning of the Howards for the Schlegel sisters now have each other, the child of Helen and Leonard and a broken Henry who does not object any more to Helen's presence. Like Lawrence's heroine Ursula who sees the rainbow at the end of *The Rainbow*, Margaret derives inspiration from the rainbow-bridge that will connect prose and passion, the inner and outer worlds. Yet along with this inspiration is the uneasiness, at the impending advance of urban reality upon Howards End. This moment of vision is more modernist than Romantic.

The precarious Romantic moment of vision coupled with a dread of modern living is perhaps sustained only once in the entire novel. This is in the symbol of Beethoven's 5th Symphony, carefully presented by Forster in the early pages of the novel. The symphony is highlighted in three different ways by Forster. Firstly, it is approached at various levels by its listeners in an introductory passage that is mildly ironic:

> It will be generally admitted that Beethoven's Fifth Symphony is the most sublime noise that has ever penetrated into the ear of man. All sorts and conditions are satisfied by it. Whether you are like Mrs. Munt, and tap surreptitiously when the tunes come—of course, not so as to disturb the others—or like Helen, who can see heroes and shipwrecks in the music's flood; or like Margaret, who can only see the music; or like Tibby, who is profoundly versed in counterpoint, and holds the full score open on his knee; or like their cousin, Fräulein Mosebach, who remembers all the time that Beethoven is 'echt Deutsch'; or like Fräulein Mosebach's young man, who can remember nothing but Fräulein Mosebach: in any case, the passion of your life becomes more vivid and you are bound to admit that such a noise is cheap at two shillings. It is cheap, even if you hear it in the Queen's Hall, dreariest music-room in London, though not as dreary as the Free Trade Hall, Manchester.[10]

Secondly, Forster highlights Helen's response to the Symphony and to its meaning. She sees the constant reappearance of the goblins in the universe as a reminder of the ugly world outside of panic and emptiness. Just when the goblins are accepted by us, they disappear and just when we have relaxed at their disappearance, they appear or can appear. This motif highlights the fragile happiness in life that is threatened by mutability, the inner, private world by the outer public world.

Thirdly, Forster presents Beethoven himself as the Romantic artist who knows the chaos and the order, who controls and creates scenes of magnificence and storm:

> For, as if things were going too far, Beethoven took hold of the goblins and made them do what he wanted. He appeared in person. He gave them a little push, and they began to walk in major key instead of in a minor, and then—he blew with his mouth and they were scattered! Gusts of splendour, gods and demi-gods contending with vast swords, colour and fragrance broadcast on the field of battle, magnificent victory, magnificent death! Oh, it all burst before the girl, and she even stretched out her gloved hands as if it was tangible. Any fate was titanic; any contest desirable; conqueror and conquered would alike be applauded by the angels of the utmost stars.
>
> And the goblins—they had not really been there at all? They were only the phantoms of cowardice and unbelief? One healthy human impulse would dispel them? Men like the Wilcoxes, or President Roosevelt, would say yes. Beethoven knew better. The goblins really

had been there. They might return—and they did. It was as if the splendour of life might boil over and waste to steam and froth. In its dissolution one heard the terrible, ominous note, and a goblin, with increased malignity, walked quietly over the universe from end to end. Panic and emptiness! Panic and emptiness! Even the flaming ramparts of the world might fall.

Beethoven chose to make all right in the end. He built the ramparts up. He blew with his mouth for the second time, and again the goblins were scattered. He brought back the gusts of splendour, the heroism, the youth, the magnificence of life and of death, and, amid vast roarings of a superhuman joy, he led his Fifth Symphony to its conclusion. But the goblins were there. They could return. He had said so bravely, and that is why one can trust Beethoven when he says other things.[11]

If Beethoven orchestrates the chief Romantic leitmotif in the novel, the thematic centre of the novel's Romantic concerns is obviously Helen, and not Margaret. However, we need to underscore the fact that Forster does not foreground Helen, refuses to grant the possibility of her happiness with a living Leonard Bast and instead re-instates Margaret as the centre at the conclusion. Forster here concedes the limits of a Romantic perspective within the social realities of his modernism. In doing this, Forster's position as a writer with Romantic ideology is seriously weakened. Here is no Radical. At the same time, we cannot at any point, dismiss his narrative by concluding that its chief tone is conservative or utilitarian. The narrative is poised precariously between the presence and the absence of the goblins of disquiet in Beethovens symphony.

Forster here re-enacts the Romantic dilemma, for like the poets of that movement, his own poetic sense emerges not out of the vision of individual happiness he might have, but out of the knowledge that this vision is obstructed by the pressures of modernisation.

NOTES AND REFERENCES

1. E.M. Forster, *Howards End*, 1910; rpt. London: Penguins, 1946, p. 28. All subsequent references are to this edition and page numbers are given within parentheses.
2. *Ibid*., p. 29.
3. *Ibid*., p. 29.
4. *Ibid*., p. 29.
5. Raymond Williams, 'The Bloomsbury Fraction' in his book, *Problems in Materialism and Culture* London: Verso, 1982.

6. Leonard Woolf's remarks in *Sowing*, London, 1960, p. 186 is quoted by Raymond Williams in *Problems in Materialism and Culture* London: Verso: Selected Essays, 1980, p. 161.
7. G.E. Moore, *Principia Ethica* 1903; rpt. Cambridge: Cambridge Univ. Press, 1993.
8. E.M. Forster, *op. cit.*, pp. 83-84.
9. *Ibid.*, p. 287.
10. *Ibid.*, p. 31.
11. *Ibid.*, p. 33.

KRISHNAN UNNI. P.

'Can You Locate Us in the Past'? English Romanticism's Response to Modernism

In English Romanticism, there has always been a tendency to resist any systematic and cogent idea of uniformity. The idea of definition, as conceived by the Romantic writers and theoreticians, similarly has been a battleground over the last two centuries. An intricate, at the same time complex and tenuous, relationship with the enlightenment tradition and a confused attitude in the engagement with the social problems of London as well as of other parts of the world typically mark the emergence of Romantic literature. A literature thus formed shares a lot of problems with its predecessors in its construction of language, the verifiability of communication and the question of its addressing. The outcome of this Janus-faced outlook of Romanticism was a partly mythographic and elusive notion of nature, self and subject, which again was an arbitrary construct dependent on a particular social culture and a sense of withdrawal deliberately made by the writer. Any process of theorising English Romanticism, therefore, has to be rooted in a cultural context.

Immanuel Kant in *Critique of Judgement* outlines three fundamental ways by which art can be distinguished from nature. Art, Kant says, should be distinguished from nature, science and all mercenary art. Kant's insistence of distinguishing art from other mercenary art had its impact on Romanticists all over Europe. The ontological nature of the work of art, as Kant conceives it, disrupts any singular way of interpretation. Once the work of art is complete, the artist is invariably separated from it. This separation again as the Kantian epistemology says is related to the 'apriori of senses'. The separation of the artist from the work, in other words, can be understood as a fusion of the artist's intellect with other forms and objects of the world. To treat any form, which has a beauty in nature, implies the idea that the whole panorama of natural beauty can only be introduced through the artistic creation. The Kantian epistemology, thus, by its insistence on the continuous addressing of the work of art questioned the age-old assumption of the evolution of an artistic work. It will be fallacious to assume that Kant was addressing all the Enlightenment debates, particularly the one between reason and unreason. It is equally misleading to conclude that Kant was looking for a space of transcendence or a mode of expression. What Kant was primarily concerned about was a different trope of artistic engagement, an engagement that involves the idea of metaphysics, nature and human constructions of the 'selves' (in their plurality). As opposed to the Renaissance model of constructing supernaturals from myths and texts, Kant seems to suggest the construction of myths depending upon one's perennial conditions of the society. The constant separation and the immediate union of the artist with his/her work, as some of the post-enlightenment critics of Kant would argue, 'forms the ground of looking inward while confounding the public'.

A more vigorous examination of Kant's understanding of the transcendent faculty of reason is made in Thomas Pfau's statement: "for Kant, judgement in its most general sense identifies the moment of conscious recognition of the possibility of representation in general, irrespective of the specific material content of such representation".[1] The evolution of a conscious and exemplary subjectivity, as some of the Romanticist historians have argued, paved the way for a distinctive style. It is in this context that the Romantic opposition between politics and culture has to be examined. As the Romantic historiographers have widely differed themselves, we have, now, before us a whole range of questions, contradictory and contesting in their nature. An early work by Crane Brinton titled *The Political Ideas of the English Romanticists* highlights the disparities prevalent in London by focusing on the class tensions. Carl Woodring in *Politics in English Romantic Poetry* undertakes an effort to study poets like Wordsworth, Coleridge and Keats in the light of 'a politics of marginality and lone recognition'.[2] The often victimized factor of Romanticism, a victimisation of the innocent before the reader brings to the fore the self-contradictoriness of the English romanticists, and for critics like Paul de Man who adopted a synchronic approach in looking at things, the "victimisation of the innocent contradicts the reality of the moment".[3] The recent development of feminist studies on English Romanticism particularly by Margaret Homans and Mary Jacobus makes it clear that a radical victimisation deliberately made by the Romantic poets twisted and thwarted the idea of political action and consequently helped in the formation of a denuded subjectivity. Modelled on the theoretical premises of French Feminist theoreticians like Helene Cixous, these English theoreticians have even gone a step further to critique the dominant conception of language and a predominant masculine identification. Even some metamorphic female figures like Coleridge's Christabel and Keats' Lamia are not free from their criticism. All these observations tend to raise some questions: What is Romantic subjectivity? Is Romantic subjectivity an outgrowth of the enlightenment tradition? How far do the notions of gender, class and binary oppositions remain unsolved, and how far did the writers address these issues from their marked point of similarities?

All attempts by the Romantics to create a private space totally shut off from the objective had resulted in a specific modelling and construction of a space of unipolar perception. Much before Karl Marx's publication of *The Eighteenth Brumaire* and *The German Ideology*, a current of radical bourgeois humanism emerged in the poetry of Wordsworth, Coleridge and Shelley. Wordsworth was moved by the baffling winds and disturbing political scenario set in the matrix of an imaginative mind more doubtful in its nature, while Coleridge in *Biographia Literaria*_emphasized the need of civic education and Shelley aimed for a humanistic platform based on freedom. If, more than any other English Romantic poet, Shelley represented an 'archangel beating his luminous wings in the void', it is because of the bric-a-brac of the politics generated by the social convulsions and the Graeco-Romanic wisdom the poet had inherited. A new language and an ancient wisdom in Shelley are translated into a mythographic human association of pain and salvation. If Wordsworth's subject is a quest for some form of certitude, Shelley's is one of dispute and regression. Unlike the great Romantic trio - Wordsworth, Coleridge and Southey, Shelley never wanted to diffuse and amalgamate disparate strands of imagination. To examine Shelley's central concern about the subject, one must look into the poet's premises of poetry in *The Defence of Poetry*. Shelley writes: "A poet is a nightingale who sits in darkness and sings to cheer its own solitude with sweet sounds; his auditors are as men entranced by the melody of an unseen musician, who feel that they are moved and softened, yet know not whence and why".[4] Shelley's observation about a lone nightingale singing songs to enchant itself in solitude is not derived from any Graeco-Roman idea of art and imagination. On the other hand, the popular Romanticist notion of the nightingale as the one which, by its music satisfies everyone, is a contrast against an omnipotent God who is stern in the medieval times. The medieval god was far away from human perceptions, but the Romantic conception of it, still though far away, can be communicated. Shelley relates the Greek concept of music to poetry. A kind of music is infused in poetry. The poet who is given a space, that is, an area of darkness, is not enclosed by anyone surrounding him/her. But it is the music or poetry, which he produces that makes the communication possible. It must be noted, however, that in Shelley's terminology a poet is not completely a society being, but a being for the society.

Shelley creates a difficult private space in *Alastor*. In his attempt to dramatize the conflict of allegiance between the natural law and the law of love, Shelley incorporates into his poem a structure of deviance: Alastor as a Greek evil genius is undercut by the poet and a more working Alastor, synonymous with the nineteenth century English labourers and factory employees, is presented. The poet's idea of solitude, to take a step further from Blake's *Chimney Sweeper*, can be seen as a pre-condition of an average worker's rest, after his daily work. Shelley does not mystify solitude.

> But on his heart its solitude returned
> And he forebore.[5]

At other levels also, this solitude Shelley creates is different from a daily course of recluse from wantonness. It is a private space of introspection. An introspective mind, more than its powers of perception taken from the Graeco-Roman ideas, is modeled upon the Renaissance. The Renaissance introspective creed propagated by Montaigne is suffused in the poetry of Shelley and a private space as the poet conceives it, secures its own value after getting into this introspective creed. Shelley's subjective nature, by discarding binary oppositions such as nature/art and scepticism/acceptance, to a great extent is well taken up by the moderns. In the words of Andrew Cooper, the poem deconstructs "the dualism initially established between idealist poet and skeptical narrator" and reformulates it "as a dualism within each of them".[6] One should also note the subtle nuances of the poetic questionings of the self. For Shelley, a necessary mediation of the self with a present of intense crisis and a past derived by serious meditations and artistic expressions are the only possibility of a poetic transcendence. Shelley's questioning of the self is inextricably related to the economic, cultural and political spheres which in a New-Historicist point of view decenters all assemblages from the past, and posits a new dimension of economic labour. The metaphoric synonyms of labour and exploitation, which recur in the poems of

Shelley, in their totality, constitute an ideal realm of class-consciousness. Moreover, it is the poet's belief in faith that makes an ideal construction of the self. For instance, in a long poem, *Epipsychidion*, the poet sways between a mystical infatuation and the difficulty to attain it. A hymn to love, which we read at the end of the poem, operates on a series of linguistic paradigms.

> We shall become the same, we shall be one
> Spirit within two frames. Oh! Wherefore two?
> One passion in twin-hearts, which grows and grows.
> Till like two meteors of expanding flame,
> Those spheres instinct with it become the same.
> Touch, mingle, are transfigured....
> One hope within two wills, one will beneath
> Two overshadowing minds, one life, one death.
> One heaven, one Hell, one immortality,
> And one annihilation.[7]

We find in *Epipsychidion* some answers to the problems raised before. The poem is an example of creating a new subjectivity and self from the premises based on the enlightenment tradition. Any movement of the senses from sight to sound is undercut and passion, angér and energy consume all human faculties. The lovers in the poem are struggling more to gain a sense of vision. A constant emphasis on action is repeated: "I pant, I sink, I tremble, I expire!".[8] The repeated pronouncement of "I" is an assertion of individual liberty and artistic freedom. Since it is always this "I" which meditates and intervenes, any sense of human engagement as Shelley perceives, makes his deep-rooted ideology in this power of questioning unlike a Wordsworthian solitary reaper. In the words of Jay Clayton, "Shelley tries to circumvent the entire problem by denying that there is any necessary conflict between visionary experience and ordinary life".[9] Shelley's belief in this inseparable alliance between experience and its aftermath, and his insistence that both these are in our ordinary life, not only destabilises the notion of art as something transcendent outside the human potentialities, but also makes the awareness of this 'inseparability' clear. Moreover, from the same platform laid down by William Blake, Shelley moves a little forward and anticipates Marx's critique of Feurbach's religion: "the reform of consciousness consists entirely in making it form its own consciousness, in arousing it from its dream of itself, in explaining its own actions to it".[10] The much debated Romantic subjectivity, as I have tried to show, is a constant reform of consciousness as Shelley had expostulated and it is this consciousness that makes the imagination possible. The opposition between imagination and reason is not something preordained. It is reason that makes possible the twilight of imagination. On the other hand, Romantic imagination in its various modes of operation is not reason per se. Geoffrey Hartman in his article titled "Romanticism and Anti-self-consciousness" makes rather a sweeping generalisation. According to Hartman "the Romantic poets do not exalt consciousness per se".[11] Hartman's statement seen in the light of the distinction between imagination and reason suffers from some fundamental drawbacks. On the one hand Hartman's reflection of consciousness stems from his study of religion and politics. The nineteenth century political spectrum of London, anticipating a series of class wars as a miracle from other parts of Europe, cannot be simply minimized into separate compartments like religion and politics. Shelley's poetry specifically exemplifies the disquieting process and the strange results of a consciousness freed from the constraints of fixing it to a locus. Raymond Williams takes another stand. For him Shelley's axiom in *The Defence of Poetry*, that "the poets are the unacknowledged legislators of mankind" is nothing but a defensive reaction against their "actual and political isolation".[12] On the mode of operation of imagination Paul de Man states that 'the apostrophe to imagination comes to be written' in the wake of the revolution.[13] All these observations originating from a materialist point of view do not exclude the possibility of an evolving relationship between the subject and imagination.

Romanticism's engagement with language and the subject is further studied by Maurice Blanchot. Blanchot points out several ambiguities of Romanticism of which the most important one is the revolutionary desire to write a great novel or poem of the modern world and the failure to bring the desire to completion. Blanchot's observation on the Jena Romanticism regarding the question of discontinuity and difference is a perverse corollary to English Romanticism. An ardent zeal for revolution initially expressed and later suppressed by poets like Wordsworth makes it clear that a discontinuity operated inside the poets. Blanchot further states that "Romanticism is essentially what begins and what cannot but finish badly: an end that is called suicide, madness, loss, forgetting.[14] It is in this context that the formulated private space in Shelley's poetry has to be examined. As has been shown by the poet several times, the realization of the need for an action, which constitutes the private space in Shelley's poetry, never circumvents the idea of withdrawal. For Wordsworth, the selves merging with the profound harmony of nature themselves formed a background of action. But it is an action interiorised. But in Shelley, a more elusive private self is presented which never can finish badly in loss and forgetting. The self's interaction with nature is a concomitant absence so that not only the self but also the nature which partakes of joys and despair are metamorphosed into action. It is this radical divorce from a popular notion of seclusion that marks the development of selfhood and subjectivity in modern literature.

Modernity in English literature is unquestionably related with several factors of which Romanticism's foremost concerns are with an evolving self-consciousness and a dialectical unfolding of the subject. The philosophical core of modernity has been explained by Hegel in his theory of *Bildung*. Hegel states that "the existence of this world, as also the actuality of self-consciousness, rests on the process in which the latter divests itself of its personality, thereby creating its world. This world it looks on as something alien, a world, therefore, of which it must now take possession... we may say that self-consciousness is merely a 'something', it has actuality only in so far as it alienates itself from itself; by so doing, it gives itself the character of a universal, and this its universality is its authentication and actuality".[15] For Hegel the dual aspect of all culture as will and representation and the dialectic operating between the political ideas and the forms of their representation constitute the meaning of existence. Therefore, the Romantic subject in its development into a modern one undergoes the traumatic and transitional change of capitalism and the notions of the state. However, in modern literature, there is a difficulty to chart this development systematically. But to a great extent, the partial dissolution of the Romantic subject and a symptomatic admixture of it with 'bourgeois individualism' take their cue from the phenomenal conditions laid by Hegel. But it should be noted that Hegel was not a full apostle of modernity all over Europe. Hegel's fundamental concern was with the tension of the society, individual alienation and with the role of language in signifying this tension. The post-Cartesian epistemological and ontological break begins with modernity. A significant importance of Hegel's assumption lies in the fact that any phenomenal compulsion encompassing the market, commodity and the self makes it clear that a true recognition of the subject characterises the time. It is the awareness and recognition of the subject's consciousness that make the tenets of modernity. What was often regarded as the Romantic hero's quest, wanderings, and the involvement with nature assumes a different stage in modernity. Outlining the philosophic question of modernity Heidegger examines Descartes' question of the subject. Heidegger comments that after Descartes, "subjectivity becomes turned in upon itself in such a way that the subject is subject for itself. The essence of consciousness is self-consciousness. Everything that is, is therefore either the object of the subject or the subject of the subject".[16] Heidegger doubted the Cartesian cogito and the subject's dependence in time.

Modernism all over Europe posited the question of the self adhering to the psychoanalytic theories of Freud and the critiquing of institutions and traditions by Friedrich Nietzsche. The constant seeking to prove that the self is in fact unconscious because it underwrites all kinds of conscious action and thought has been one of the characteristic features in Romanticism. But a constant reshuffling of the self and its operation based on the disparate strands of time is a new development in modernity. The question of alienation as promulgated by Hegel and Marx destabilises this positioning of the self and it is in this context that several Romantic motifs including the 'solitariness' and the 'meandering' are questioned. One must also take into consideration the palpable Romantic quest undertaken by the hero in his nostalgic recovery of the past. If modernity cannot produce its own search to uncover the past, no wonder, this attempt by writers is marred by the disillusionment with the machine. (Sergei Eisenstein's *October* and Chaplin's *Modern Times* are typical examples testifying to the concept of alienation in this respect.)

Virginia Woolf's texts raise a whole range of questions, several of them being taken from Romanticism, and some with the problematic nature of modernism. The series of internal repercussions concerned with her protagonist's self, and the marked difference of the "I" from other masculine representations take Woolf's text a step further to unbridge the gap between the subject which seeks to get represented in modernism. The reduction of man to a sequence of bits and fragments and the simultaneous disjuncture from all associations has been criticised by critics like George Lukács. But it must be noted that Woolf's representation of a tangible and tenuous human body structured around the fragmentary notion of time mirrors not only the concept of the text as something deviant in its narration but the impossibility to represent the unrepresentable. This questioning is opposed to the Lukácsian notion of the autonomous self, confronting the outer world. Since language necessarily defers truth indefinitely, one basic problem Woolf confronts is that of the representation of an 'absence'. In the *Voyage Out*, Terence's desire to 'write a novel about silence' testifies to the above statement. Any deep-rooted meaning of 'silence' in Romantic literature cornered within the perimeters of a pacifist private self is not the subject of concern for Woolf. For instance, Shelley's retrospective silence embodied in the

Cenci and *Prometheus Unbound* is not a silence of regression but a periodic synthesis. Terence extends this idea and ponders the impossible to achieve. Terence's periodic forays into the language of thought create a meta-language to construct the absence. A writing about this 'void' requires not only introspection but an entry into the safe corners to primarily assert the ego as we have witnessed in the *Episychidion*. Terence abandons all claims of truth. But where does one wander without truth?

Woolf's notion of the subject is also derived from her direct dismemberment of truth. By doing this, she focuses more on women's lives in her texts and undercuts Romantic male heroizations. Her central characters are elusive in their approach to some fundamental precincts of art. In a novel like *Orlando*, Woolf creates an ambiguous linguistic parody with the English pronouns such as 'my', 'we' and 'one'. Consequently, Woolf creates another atmosphere between the reader's desire to know the subject and the subject's unintentionality to deviate from the meaning. Such a tactical construction of the subject negates some of the synchronic historicisms of modernism including Tony E Jackson's assertion that "modernism marks a significant change in Cartesian consciousness, and, further, that the change to modernism involves an adjustment of the human being to the same situation that led to the appearance of the cogito in the first place".[17] This is not to say that Virginia Woolf's writings appropriated any post-structuralist notion of writing. But what Woolf is impelled to construct is itself a subject which can think over an absence. For example, in *Orlando*, Orlando's strange attire involves the lack of male formality. Her changing clothes from one set to another not only typifies a sharp ridicule of the linear time but registers the difficulty to adjust with a masculine notion of time. One would here recall Shelley's insistence in *Episychidion* of the subject's painting, sinking, trembling and expiring. Shelley's subject forms the pretext of Woolf's action oriented character with one difference. Shelley's subject creates a series of action oriented plans like 'panting' and 'sinking' whereas Woolf's Orlando changing her clothes time after time does not directly fit into a 'time present' contained in a future time. Orlando's only action reverses the order of the present moment. But Shelley's lover, by anticipating the future, groups a series of actions in the present.

Woolf's texts stand at the crossroads of the synchronic and diachronic readings of human consciousness. Her acknowledged reverence for the past as in *Orlando* and *To the Lighthouse* largely accounts for the orientation of the Romantic private space. However, it is difficult to categorise this private space as something distinct of modernity. Woolf tries to solve an inherent puzzle embedded in Romantic underpinnings of the self. For Makiko Minow-Pinkney "Woolf's dissatisfaction with plot, sequence, narrativity is, in short, a protest against the symbolic, which by excluding multi-sensory living experience calls into being the unconscious".[18] In *To the Lighthouse*, the Romantic predicament of the search and artistic perfection are inverted to the narrow time scales of reversion. Lily Briscoe's completion of the painting and the arrival at the lighthouse are two separate but intertwined components of the feminine consciousness. The structure of the text addresses the vociferous desire of another Romantic quest. As the Romantics believed in the perfection of art, it was assumed that a craving for this perfection had to be started by a mutual recognition of love and affection. If Woolf disrupts the clock time by her repeated puncturing of the dialogism between Mr. Ramsay and Mrs. Ramsay, it is in order to prove that any veritable perfection of art is impossible if one acknowledges the totality of time and freedom. The dejected selves of Romanticism in Woolf are more scrutinised and their contentment in a narrow space is questioned. The subversive strategy Woolf employs makes her 'selves' participate in the 'slices of time' rather than a unilateral time given to them.

It is interesting to note the phenomenal change happening to the subject of modernity in the light of industrial expansion and empire building. What needs to be underlined is the fact that the industrial expansion and the colonial mechanism of London at large did not directly affect a knowing or contemplating subject. In Virginia Woolf, the deliberate switching off of the clock time has its internal undertones in the middle class values; some of them, I would say, have been taken from a system of objects: flower vases, lawns, beech trees, pineapples, sherries and paintings. What Woolf does here again is to create some semiological codes to destabilise certain standards of life. The irresistible pull of objects to the modern subject represents Derridean 'differance' that creates history as a product of loss and return and the successive inclusion/exclusion of energy and order. Lily's thought of Mrs. Ramsay in 'the shape of a dome' and a 'purple triangular shape' testifies to this infinite play of signifiers, the paradoxical question of art and especially the task of the expressionist painters who juggled with the idea of expression and representation. Further, in *To The Lighthouse*, in the section 'time passes' we have a series of visual images to express emotions. Every minute detail is interiorised within the mind's landscape. Here again, we encounter L.J. Swingle's basic question about Romanticism that "what greatly complicates the Romantic inclination of thought is its instability. The trap has enticements, even for the mind that would escape it".[19] The Romantic private space of interiority is the one which not only functions as a centre of absorption, but something which radiates a kind of energy as in Wordsworth's *Immortality Ode* and Keats's *Grecian Urn*. But the modern private space functions more as a kind of black hole; in other words, as a trope which absorbs the reader's interpretation. The modern private self functions more as an organism of desire. Language, as a result, becomes a scheme, a ploy or a code that germinates this idea of desire. In Woolf, we have an abundant terrain of this desire. What exactly is the function of this desire? There have been attempts from several theoreticians to redefine the idea of desire. Deleuze and Guattari in their influential work *Anti Oedipus* have outlined this desire to the paranoia of the post-enlightenment thought - 'like a cry suspended between life and death'.[20] Deleuze and Guattari's emphasis on the capitalistic development and the schizophrenic development characteristic of our time have unburdened some fallacies concerned with the rigid notions of modernism. A critique of Woolf's characters does not help us to differentiate this desire associated with the nascent capitalism. Paradoxically, the Woolfian private selves show an impossibility to represent the women characters and the narrow percolations of capitalism inherent in all modern societies. The dignified platform set by the Romantics, such as a Don Juan and an aristocratic class, are seriously transformed here into dining rooms, portraits and books.

An indivisible vocabulary of Romanticism makes its reassertion over and over upon the empirical and ontological aspects of literature. This leads more to a recuperation of wonder than to a strange recollection of the past. The private space in Virginia Woolf as we have seen is a specimen of that. Our assumption of this space mutually interjected and conflicted by a variety of social forces is another standpoint of a strange desire ever produced. Where does this desire lead us? Would it lead us to the chasms of a retrospective past, a past again in its wide tenacity questioned by a Wordsworth, a Coleridge or a Byron? Or would it lead us to the presumptuous notion of a wavering nature subjecting human beings to a chain of endless sufferings and eternal wanderings? Perhaps these questions have yet to be answered, and not from a straitjacketed Woolfian sense of the self.

The traditional postulate of an eternal alliance between the reproductive drive of the individual and the economic prosperity of the nation has to be rewritten with respect to this subjective self-awareness. The question of language at the threshold of its unfolding, as Blanchot repeatedly warns us, is 'paradigmatic in nature'[21] and it unwinds the threads of our mind's unfolding. All linguistic, aesthetic and ethical systems now become endangered by the return of this selfhood. If Woolf had by any chance written a sentence like 'my enchantment never fails', I would say, her whole project of defamiliarising objects and constructing a selfhood would have collapsed. Writing, in its essence, itself is a disjuncture.

This paper, written in the context of a bombardment of simulations virtually blocking the path of identification, does not aim to create divisions in the unburdened ontological terrain of human thought. If the modern subject still keeps on patting our shoulders, it is not because of a nostalgic recuperation, nor any asymmetrical disinvestment, but because of its tenacity, opaqueness and the sheer cynical despair among the masses about what is constructed and what one wishes to be constructed. A looming moonlight, the voice of a skylark in all its 'unpremeditated joy', a wandering and dithering local hermit, a hamlet with a glow and a Blakean ashen sky would perhaps relieve this tension. Locating subjects by all interjections of social forces therefore ought to be liberated from the constraints and disemboweled assumptions of creating narrow margins. Who knows, one day even a primordial darkness can cover all of us?

NOTES AND REFERENCES

1. Thomas Pfau, *Wordsworth's Profession.* California: Stanford University Press, 1997, p. 87.
2. Carl Woodring, *Politics in English Romantic Poetry.* London: Oxford University Press, 1949, p. 174.
3. Paul de Man, *The Rhetoric of Romanticism.* NewYork: Columbia University Press,1984, p. 162.
4. P.B. Shelley, 'The Defence of Poetry' in *English Critical Texts.* Ed. D.J. Enright and Ernst De Chickera. Delhi: Oxford University Press, 1988, p. 932.
5. P.B. Shelley, 'Alastor' in *The Complete Poetical Works of Shelley.* Ed. Thomas Hutchinson. London: Oxford University Press, 1952, pp. 144-45.
6. *Ibid.*, 'Things Not as They Were', p. 118.
7. *Ibid.*, *Epipsychidion,* pp. 573-87.
8. *Ibid.*, p. 591.
9. Jay Clayton, 'Introduction: Transcendence and The Novel' in Jay Clayton, *Romantic Vision and The Novel.* London: Cambridge University Press, 1987, p. 18.

10. Karl Marx, 'Letter to Ruge', September, 1843, in *The Marx-Engels Reader.* Ed. Robert C. Tucker. New York: Norton, 1978.
11. Geoffrey Hartman, 'Romanticism and Anti-Self-Consciousness' in *Romanticism and Consciousness.* Ed. Harold-Bloom. New York: Norton, 1970, p. 47.
12. Raymond Williams, *Culture and Society.* New York: Columbia University Press, 1983, p. 42.
13. Paul de Man, 'Kant and Schiller' in *Aesthetic Ideology*, p. 23.
14. Maurice Blanchot, *The Infinite Conversation.* trans. Susan Hanson. Minneapolis: University of Minnesota Press, 1992, pp. 352-53.
15. G.W.F. Hegel, *The Phenomenology of Spirit.* trans. A.V. Collins. Oxford: Oxford University Press, 1997, p. 350.
16. Martin Heidegger, *The Question Concerning Technology and Other Essays.* trans. Ralph Manheim. New Haven: Yale University Press, 1964, p. 100
17. Tony E. Jackson, *The Subject of Modernism*, p. 15.
18. Makiko Minow-Pinkey, *Virginia Woolf and the Problem of the Subject.* London: Harvester, 1987, p. 163.
19. L.J. Swingle, *The Obstinate Questionings of English Romanticism*, p. 33.
20. Gilles Deleuze, and Felix Guattari, *Anti-Oedipus.* trans. Robert Hurley, Mark Seem and Helen R. Lane, London: The Athlone Press, 1984, p. 18.
21. Maurice Blanchot, *The Writing of the Disaster*. trans. Ann Smock Lincoln: University of Nebraska Press, 1986, p. 111.

MARGIT KÖVES

Inverted Sights

In the early nineteenth century romantic aesthetics made a radical shift from the classical ideal. It did away with the classical notions of reflection, classical notions of beauty and didacticism and introduced the artist, his experiences and states of mind as the center of the work of art. In Eastern Europe Romanticism was the first comprehensive literary movement which created the framework for the establishment of academic institutions, literary establishments and printing houses, the ground for the 'renewal' of the nation.

The Romantic movement initiated the reform of languages, like Polish, Czech, Croatian, Hungarian, Serbian and Russian. So while in Western Europe the artist, the individual became the subject in the philosophical sense, in Eastern Europe romantic literature along with the creation of the romantic personality of the artist also created the collective subject of the nation. Romantic poetry was defined by Friedrich Schlegel as a progressive universal poetry with the aim to unite philosophy and art. The ambivalence of the identity of the poet in Hungarian poetry as part of the collective community of the nation and as its isolated critic fitted in well with Schlegel's definition. The dual and often contradictory task of forging an individual subject and a collective identity of the nation brought about the formulation of the relationship between individual, community and universe.

In this paper I would like to argue that the radical shift which took place in literature and the arts in the 1960s and the 1970s reconstituted the language of the arts and literature in Hungary in a way which transformed aesthetic taste and ways of reception in Hungary. These attempts resulted in the break up of genres and their fusion. The aesthetic change also attempted to reformulate the relationship between individual, community and universe, and this led to a new synthesis of art and philosophy, an aim of Romantic poetry also defined by Schlegel.

This paper will look at a poem by Ákos Szilágyi, some short stories of István Örkény along with some references to Hungarian 'concept art', alternative theatre and the films of Miklós Jancsó in the 1960s to show how literature and art went beyond closed definitions of the subject and object in a manner which is similar to the Romantics in the nineteenth century.

The changes in literature and art were called forth by the economic reforms in the 1960s in Hungary and the renaissance of Marxism in the Lukács School, in Hungary, in Poland, in Yugoslavia and in Czechoslovakia. The cultural revival which took place in Eastern Europe in the 1960s connected praxis to theory, individuals and the role of institutions and dealt with events of East European history of the past fifty years.

Milan Kundera's novels, like *The Book of Laughter and Forgetting* are based on a private interpretation of East European history. In his *Jerusalem Address: The Novel and Europe,* Kundera describes the novel as antithetical to universal history and says that the task of the novel is the struggle against 'kitsch'.[1] 'Kitsch' is defined by Kundera in the context of the Austrian writer Hermann Broch as the translation of received ideas into the language of 'beauty' and 'feeling', the gap between reality and its preconceived notions.

In the 1960s parody, joke and black humor on the periphery of official literature undercut the reader's disposition towards banality and built up a different sense of history. They were introduced into poetry and prose at the time in the 1960s when both public and private poetry lost credit with the audience. Black humour and joke initiated a new voice into literature and the arts and bridged the gap between the audience and work of art. Our contemporary sensibilities, tastes and mode of reception of art and literature are based to a great extent on the artistic voice established in the 1960s and 1970s.

In poetry there were a number of experiments in the 1960s by poets like Dezsõ Tandori (1938-), Ferenc Juhász (1928-), Petri György (1946-2000) and others.[2] Tandori's experimental poetry broke down the boundary between poetry and fiction, Ferenc Juhász's poetry ushered in a new poetic world with images from contemporary biology and sciences and Petri's antipoetic verse introduced political polemics into poetry through the brutal description of private worlds.

In this paper I would like to focus on a poem by Ákos Szilágyi entitled "Parade", ("Díszszemle" in Hungarian) written in 1968.[3] Military parades emptied out of political content were normal events to the average citizen during the Cold War in both camps, in Eastern and

Western Europe. Szilágyi's poem written in 1968, in the year of the Warsaw countries military invention in Czechoslovakia brings out the hollowness, the vacuous pomp of military parades in semiotic rather than military categories. This acoustic poem in its sound effects recalls, imitates and punctures military parades. Parade, one of his first poems points to the direction Szilágyi followed in his poetry in the 1970s.[4] A similar acoustic poem is "Anti-clapping" (1975) which similarly undercuts clapping at political functions. The essay "Comradely Kisses" deals with a special phenomenon of East-European politics after 1956,after the Twentieth Party Congress kisses exchanged by the leaders of the Eastern block at major public functions.[5]

This acoustic poem consist of about eighty to hundred bars.[6] "Parade" is built on the tension between the rhythmic structure of the lines and the content of the words. In Hungarian the stress falls on the first syllable of the word and rhythm is made up of the combination of stress in the language and the length of the syllables. Stresses in "Parade" strengthen or ridicule the meaning of the words. *Dísz*' means 'decorated'. It figures in a range of combinations. The repetition of the first syllable of the word dísz- in other words (*dísz*szemle, *dísz*tribün, *dísz*galamb, *dísz*be öltözik) builds on the ability of Hungarian to create new words by the conjunction of two nouns, and that as an agglutinating language adds suffixes to the roots of words.

Many words in the poem are used because of onomatopoeia. For example, *döccen* – 'bumps' – shares a head-rhyme with *dac* 'stubbornness'. The tension in the poem becomes obvious where the acoustic sphere meets the visual sphere. An example of this is the use of the word *százlábumm* – 'my centipede' – where the third syllable *bumm* imitates the sound of drums. The meaning 'centipede' refers to the visual sight of the parade when the lines of the army look from a higher point, the tribune like a centipede. The reference to the tribune with decorated Generals and Minister with their inflatable bosoms who 'speak, speak, speak' and the flags in the breeze undercut and parody the values attached to the parades, to military power.

The written presentation of the poem is not adequate for the complex aesthetic experience of the meeting of sound, musical phrase, the sequence of semiotic signs of the scene of the parade and logical content which comes through in it's performance. The analysis of the poem is based in the first place on the verbal meaning of the Hungarian text. The English translation is available in the note below the Hungarian text.

In Szilágyi's poem the transformation of the subject is signaled by the absorption of visual and acoustic experiences in a combination where joke verges on cruelty. In the part where 'The glass eye' 'stares', the scene of the parade overlaps the scene of the butcher's shop, the cables of the parade overlap the sight of freshly cut animal intestines.

"Under our feet decorated intestines
Cables spilt out right now
Darling, feel them! They are still warm."

This anti-military poem works on the acoustic, visual and as the above quoted lines show the tactile senses of the audience. The poem is open-ended which also leaves space for the listener for the continuation or revision of the poem. The Russian avant-garde, the futurists Mayakovski, O. Brik, S. Tretyakov composed acoustic poems to break down the hierarchy of institutions and literary genres and expected their listener to respond to poetry more at a sensual than a cognitive level.

In an essay "Lyric and anti-lyric poetry"[7] Szilágyi refers to the acoustic poem in the context of the change of the traditional subject. He considers it an aesthetic experiment that initiates a different participation by the audience and the poet. He connects the emergence of traditional subject with the rise of bourgeois individual who constitutes himself in cognitive opposition to the external world. In the "Parade" there is an attempt to overcome this binary opposition through acoustic, visual and tactile stimulation of the audience.

The duality of the thinking subject and reflected object initiated by Descartes continues with Kant even though Kant defines the limit of the extent of knowledge by the categories of consciousness. In the *Hymnen an die Nacht* [Hymns to the Night] Novalis formulates the romantic Subject as the dialectical unity of the I and Non-I. This Subject evolves in the process, which he describes in the following way. The first step is the inward gaze. This gaze/look separates the I from the external world. The second is the lasting, active look at the external world. Kierkegaard introduces the concept of 'feeling mind' which in his case means understanding itself in existence, a combination of thinking subject with moral and religious emotions and experiences. Ernst Bloch reformulates the concept of existential subject in the *Das Prinzip Hoffnung* [Principle of Hope] as a combination of a wide sphere of drives and urges such as hunger, will and hope, contradictory feelings that are sometimes pleasurably united.

Now, I would like to give a brief account of the experiments in the area of art in the 1960s in Hungary. In the 1960s 'concept art', the art dealing with the linguistic and philosophical connotations of existence, became known in Hungary through the work of artists like Henry Flynt, Josef Kosut and the late work of Duchamp. Though official cultural policy was gradually becoming more open in the 1960s, official art and concept art confronted each other. Concept art was transformed in Hungary by absorbing a wide range of philosophical influences from early Greek philosophy, the Bible, Wittgenstein, and a Hungarian contemporary Béla Hamvas who mediated the Upanishads, the Bhagavadgita, Buddhism, Omar Khayyam to many artists in a book entitled *Antologia Humana*.

The transformation of the subject in the Hungarian concept art is reflected in the work of individual artists. Imre Bak (1939) divides the sensual spheres of the face into four different parts in his 1972 picture "Portrait". Some of the artists like Péter Legéndy used fake sociological questionnaires. The exhibition of Miklós Erdély (1928-1986) an architect shows the philosophical content of Hungarian concept art. In a description of Erdély's exhibition László Lakner writes:

> Erdély writes the paradox "the snow is black" on photographic paper with fixing salt. By the time he reaches the word black the inscription becomes black. Then Erdély reads out his 'theses about the language of the film' - the last one is 'existence is made into language and spoken by us, language is made into existence and lived by us.[8]

In the 1960s and 70s the creation of an alternative theatre was another attempt in Hungary to formulate a different subject. After the 1956 Hungarian Popular Uprising, there was no professional theatre based on real group work. Work in the professional theatre was carried on as a one-way process starting with the written piece, leading through the work of the director, finally to the individual actor and ending with the performance. The Halász Group, the leading alternative theatre group described their theatre with the movement from 'life' leading to 'idea' leading to 'theatre' leading back to 'life'.

Meetings of alternative theatre groups took place in University theatres, flats, cultural houses.[9] These groups emphasized space, movement and interaction. After the initial phase in the 1960s of working in the Kassák House of Culture in Budapest, in the early 1970s the Halász Group performed in flats, studios, abandoned churches, on the pier of Lake Balaton in summer. In their performances metacommunicative, ritual, surreal, stylised elements played a more important role than verbal elements. Their productions emphasized links between the different movements, scraps of everyday relationships, surreal configurations, which were not directly rational. These undercut the expectations of an audience used to the time and the rhythm of normal performance. A Hungarian critic, Géza Fodor wrote in 1990

> this different norm of time in their performances was the best method of leading us out of the sphere of rationality into the sphere of experience.[10]

The film director, Miklós Jancsó regularly attended their performances in Hungary in the 1970s. In an interview in 1990 he defined the group as opposition outside the political system in Hungary. He considered himself different from the official cultural policy but placed himself within the given coordinates of the system.[11] In 1976 the Halász group left Hungary.

In the 1960s, after more than ten years of his work as a film director, Jancsó created a number of films which moved beyond the possibilities of traditional film. The first films of Jancsó which took up historical themes and showed his originality in the use of camera work, sound effects and silence were *The Round Up* (1965) – about nineteenth century outlaws and Austrian suppression –, *Confrontation* (1968) – about the 1947 movement of student revolutionaries –, and *Agnus Dei* (1970) – about the 1919 Republic of Councils. In these films Hungarian history was reflected as the history of political power, complicity with power, will, the struggle of various social groups, the process of physical and moral alliances, resistance, reconciliation and breaking up. The protagonists of Jancsó's films are historical subjects engaging in praxis at various levels of historical consciousness.

The reason for this digression was to give a brief summary about how art, theatre and film attempted to transcend established notions of subject, object, time, experience and reception. These on the one hand were fed on the artistic attempts of the international avant-garde, on the other hand they were part of the strategy of resistance to the bleakness of everyday life, monotony, poverty of official ideology and political repression. Poetry, art and film expressed and addressed a different subject with different aesthetics. This meant the re-evaluation of the relationship of experience and art, merging in a new narrative order.

Now, I would like to take up the work of István Örkény (1912-1979) to demonstrate how in his one-minute stories Örkény developed the grotesque as a suitable form to reflect on a different subject. In his case the grotesque was not a style but a narrative form with different norms of composition.[12]

The grotesque of Örkény evolved as a narrative strategy with a change of perspective on history. Örkény's prose in the late forties about his experiences in the Second World War, the time of the Holocaust were transformed into one-minute stories and into the theatre of absurd in the sixties. This was the result of a critical distance to the historical experience of the Holocaust. The narrative strategy Örkény developed in the one-minute stories and theatre went beyond moralizing and countered the overwhelming emotional effect on the reader.[13]

The one-minute story is one of the short literary forms similar to the riddle, the proverb, the epigram, the parable in the Bible. The one-minute story can be read "till the egg boils, the phone answers, sitting or standing in the bus".[14]

Örkény explained the emergence of the grotesque as the relevant view of the world in our age, a philosophical view that emerged out of the experience of the Holocaust and the Second World War.

> The grotesque is the answer of the twentieth century to the nineteenth. At that time the first trains started, the first infectious diseases were defeated and it was generally believed that humanity at last can explain everything and would live according to a morality which would slowly liberate it from sin, stupidity and war. The self-confidence which grew out of this optimism was contradicted by two world wars, millions of civil deaths, concentration camps, unspeakable horrors.[15]

The structure of the one-minute story, the grotesque is built on a dialogue and it is sustained by a paradox. Örkény compared his one-minute story to a mathematical equation to be solved with maximum input by the reader and with minimum information provided by the narrator.[16] This was also possible because by the 1960s a more receptive audience grew up with a greater openness to irony.

Romanticism had a great interest in grotesque and irony and established the theory and the models of these phenomena. While romantic irony is an attitude, a mode of relating to the world, and the simultaneous acceptance and rejection of reality, or a value, the grotesque is based on the contradiction between reality and the world of art and there is a fantastic resolution to this contradiction in the form of a metaphor. The Romantic theorists Jean Paul and Schlegel emphasized the destructive, terrifying aspect of the grotesque; it was appreciated by them as a transfer to the spiritual sphere. Mikhail Bakhtin in his book on Rabelais compares satire with the grotesque.[17] In his definition, satire is a negative exposure where moral criticism is important. The grotesque temporarily suspends norms of behaviour, reflects the hierarchy of everyday life in "gay relativity" and it has a regenerating principle. E.T.A. Hoffman's stories, *Der Nusskracker* [The Nutcracker] and *Der goldene Topf* [The Golden Pot], represent the romantic transformation of the grotesque. In these stories the fantastic challenges the stability of the world and turns it into something alien.

Örkény defines the grotesque as the realization of the unreal which is based on a fantastic presumption which obeys the laws of the real world. It creates a sovereign world where for example the law of gravitation would be valid, but with an inverse sign.[18] Örkény suggests that the grotesque view is similar to the inverted sight of the world as it appears when one stands with legs apart and looks up from between one's legs.

Örkény's one-minute story derives material from the anecdote, the joke and the tale, but it has a philosophical content. The story in most cases functions at two levels, the common place situation presented in the story which is complemented by the fantastic element. Two one-minute stories "Song"[19] and "Two Cupolas in a Snow-covered landscape"[20] deal with the historical experiences on the Russian Front. In both stories information is reduced to the minimum. "Song" is built on the dualism of physical destruction and the unceasing creativity. In the end of the story the death of the song writer Janász underlines the potential creativity in every human being. The narrator's comment "Each of us can do something no one else can do the same way" provides the catharsis in this story. In Örkény's one-minute stories about contemporary themes this kind of catharsis is provided by the element of the fantastic.

In "Two Cupolas in a Snow-covered landscape" information about the identity of the participants and the location of the events is reduced to the bare minimum and the details have to be established by the reader. The photograph with the two snow-covered cupolas and the face of a little girl is a record of the execution of a Russian woman by Hungarian and German soldiers. The focus is on the surrounding objects and the lack of adjectives also adds a special force to the story. The one-minute story "In Memoriam Dr. GHK"[21] is a dialogue exposing an existential paradox. This was the story which Örkény considered "his best piece".[22] Dr. GHK's discussion about German poets in his habitual intellectual style is in direct contrast with his situation as a prisoner of the camp. This contrast is resolved by his execution. The reduction in the text shows the author's disinclination to pass moral judgement in the stories.

The grotesque provides an escape from a negative reality, its aim is not the elimination of the evil, bad, negative. It moves between negative and positive values and breaks out of a negative reality through the fantastic. This fantastic element liberates the reader from the oppression of everyday life, it opens up reality. This is the basis of Örkény's one-minute stories about contemporary themes.

In the story "Ballad about the power of Poetry"[23] the telephone booth comes to life, falls in love, walks all over the favorite park of lovers in Budapest, after the poet rings up his editor and reads out his at the roadside booth his newly written poem. In two other one-minute stories "Thoughts in the cellar"[24] and "As soon as a problem is clarified the next one emerges"[25] the fantastic, the surreal also plays an important role. The presence of the fantastic, the personification of the sweet mignonette flower in "As soon as a problem is clarified the next one emerges" and the daydreaming rat in the "Thoughts in the cellar" show the development of Örkény's grotesque. While in the one-minute stories dealing with the war creativity, 'life saving' activity provide the catharsis, in the one-minute stories on contemporary themes the fantastic, the surreal creates the same effect. In the stories "Thoughts in the cellar", "As soon as a problem is clarified" and "Ballad about the power of Poetry" the presence of the fantastic adds a liberating dimension to the plane of reality, determination.

The grotesque functioned on the basis of different aesthetic expectations, addressed a different audience, developed a new language and literary sensibilities. The one-minute story demands a complex response, a different aesthetic involvement from the reader. Modern Hungarian literature in the 1990s owes much of its language, readership, and possibilities to Örkény's inventions.

The social and existential situation of the nineteen sixties and seventies motivated artists in all spheres to open up the limits of the subject. This reconstitution was not only a "theoretical objective". It was a wish to break out from a complex historical experience, full of anxiety and fear, the experience of the Second World War and twenty years of socialism. Influences of international movements like concept art, new poetry and the new language of film reached Hungary but these forms had different potentials in Hungary and were filled with specific historical context. Concept art and alternative theatre were considered enemies of the official cultural policy. They had to be resourceful to find ways to organize performances and exhibitions, but they could survive for some time in the atmosphere of 'soft dictatorship'.

Art, film, theatre, poetry and short story in the 1960s and early 70s broke down earlier norms of reflection, reception of the subject and interpreted the possibilities of the subject in the world differently.

Though aimed at the reinvention of the subject, like the Romantics, their subject had a different approach to community and to the universe and defined their possibilities in that framework. The traditional subject was the thinking subject, a determined entity existing in a world of abstract morality, and a sphere of inwardness. The artists and writers attempt in the sixties and early seventies was to replace that with a different subject, with an engagement in an open sensual world of reality, identifying with other people at different levels of consciousness. These were the specific ways the acoustic verse, 'concept art' and the grotesque with its existentialist approach were accepted and absorbed in Hungarian art and literature. This was possible because of the aesthetic changes through which they could go beyond the limitations of the immediate community of the nation and could address ideas to a larger audience in the context of our age.

NOTES AND REFERENCES

1. M. Kundera, 'Jerusalem Address: The Novel and Europe' in *The Art of the Novel,* London, 1988, pp. 162-164.
2. Some of them are known in India through Raghuvir Sahay's translations, in Raghuvir Sahay, *Adhunik Hungari Kavita*, Sahitya Akademi, New Delhi, 1989.
3. Acoustic poem in a tape recording is read out by the poet, in *Szilágyi Ákos, Légzõgyakorlat kezdõ haldoklók számára* [Breathing exercise for beginners at the point of death], Budapest, 1994.
4. Szilágyi (1950-) poet, literary historian and Slavic scholar. Beside books of poetry, and author of collections of essays, a reader on Russian nationalism, he is co-author of *Les mondes d'Andrei Tarkovsky,L'Age d'Homme*, 1986.
5. *The New Hungarian Quarterly* No. 127, Vol. XXXIII, Autumn 1992, pp. 13-17.
6. The text was written down on the basis of the voice recording of the poem. See note 3. Shorter pauses in the acoustic space are signified by slashes, longer ones by gaps. The English translation is given below the Hungarian text.

Díszszemle

Szurony, száj, szurony / Szurony, szíj, arc/ Szurony, szárny, arc/ Szurony, szúr, arc/ Szíj, arc, szurony/
Szíj, szurony, száj/ Szíj, száj, szurony/ Arc, szurony, szárny/

Ez a dísszemle/ Ez a dísszemle/ Ez a dísz-szem-le/ Szemle,/ Vigyázz!/ Szemle,/ Pihenj!/

De a díszlépés,/ De a díszlépés,/ De a díszlé-/ De a díszlépés,/
Tíz tisztlépés/ Száz tisztlépés/ Egy döccenés/ Száz döccenés/ A döcce-döcce-döccenés/

Fel láb-fél-láb/ Láb-le/ Derekad roppan/
Harminc centi a földtõl/ Negyven centi a földtõl/ Százhúsz centi a földtõl/ Szakadjunk el a földtõl/

Sorakozzon már/ Sorakozzon már/ Hisz a dísz/ Díszben lépünk/ Döccen a dacunk/ Döccen a dacunk/
Dac, dac, dac./ Díszben lép a díszmenet/ A díszmenet/ A díszletek/ De szép, de szép/ De szép/

Leszé-, leszé-, leszé-,/ Leszédül föntrõl már a/ Tisztelt tábornok/ S hadügyminiszter/ Beszél, beszél, beszél/

Díszbe döccent itt az utca,/ Dísztribün és díszgalambdúc/ Díszbe tisztulsz/ Díszbe pusztulsz/
Díszcelofánba bifszteket/ Díszzubbonyba tiszteket/ Tiszte- tiszte- tiszteleg/

Lábunk alatt díszbelek/
Épp kiontott kábelek/ Érzed kedves? még meleg./ Nagy mesterünk, házmesterünk/ Is díszbe öl-/ Is díszbe öl-/ Is díszbe öltözött./

Újságokban hirdetés/ Ki dísztelen/ Az esztelen/ Hisz tele az üzletem/ Felfújható díszkebel/
Jól mutat a tiszteken/ Díszgyomorba díszebéd/ Díszegekbe díszfenék/
Lent bámulás/ Fent bámulás/
Kint bámulás/ Üvegszemekben tisztelet/ Döccen, döccen, döccen/A díszmenet/ Lobogónyelv lóg/
Lobogó/ Fujja szellõ, fújja szél/ De szép/ De szép/ De szép/

Megfújom hát orbitális trombitám is./

Kicsi százlábumm/ Kicsi százlábumm/ Kicsi százlá-/
Kicsi százlábumm/ Kicsi százlábumm/ Kicsi százlá-/ Kicsi százlábumm/
Szurony, száj, szurony/ Szurony, szíj, arc/ Szurony, szárny, szurony/ Szurony, szúrj, arc/
Szíj, arc, szurony,/ Szíj, szurony, száj/ Szíj, száj, szurony/ Arc, szurony, szárny...

Parade

Bayonet, mouth, bayonet/ Bayonet, belt, face/ Bayonet, wing, face/ Bayonet, stab, face/
Belt,face, bayonet/ Belt, bayonet, mouth/ Belt, mouth, bayonet/ Face, bayonet, wing/

This is parade/ This is parade / This is pa-ra-de/ Parade,/Attention!/ Parade/At ease!/

But parademarch,/ But parademarch/ But march/ But parademarch,/ One officerstep/
Ten officerssteps/ Hundred officersteps/ One bump/ Hundred bumps/ The bump-a-bump-a-bump/

Up leg-half-leg/ Leg-down/ Leg up/ Your waist goes crack/
Thirty centimeters from the ground/ Forty centimeters from the ground/
Hundred and twenty centimeters from the ground/ Breakaway from the ground/

Fall in fast/ Fall in fast/ This is the parademarch/ We march in the parade/ Our stubbornness bumps/
Our stubbornness bumps/ Stubbornness, stubbornness, stubbornness./
In full dress marches the parade/ March at attention/ Set decoration/
Beautiful, beautiful/ Beautiful/

The respected General from high up/ Tumbles, tumbles, tumbles/
Tumbles down/ And the Defence Minister/ Speaks, speaks, speaks/

The street bumps in decoration/ Decorated tribune and decorated dove house/ You are purified in decoration/ Decorated you go to the dogs/
Beefsteak in decorated cellophane packing/ Officers in decorated tunics/
Salute, salute, salute/

Under our feet decorated intestines/ Cables spilt out right now/ Darling, feel them! They are still warm./ Our great master, our janitor/ Also put on his gala, gala dress./

Advertisement in the newspapers/ To be Undecorated/ Is sheer madness/
When my shop is full/ Inflatable ceremonial bosom/ Decorates beautifully officers/ Gala dinner into stomachs dressed in gala,/
Decorated buttocks enrobed in gala suits/ Downstairs stares,/ Upstairs stares/ Stares outside/ Respect in glass eyes/ Bumps, bumps, bumps/
The parade/ The flag is flapping/ Flag/ Fluttered by breeze, fluttered by wind/ How beautiful/ How beautiful/ How beautiful/

I blow my military bugle./

My small centipede/ My small centipede/ Small centi-,/
My small centipede/ My small centipede/ Small centi-/My small centipede/Bayonet, mouth, bayonet/ Bayonet, belt, face/ Bayonet, wing, bayonet/ Bayonet, stabs, face/ Belt, face, bayonet/ Belt, bayonet, mouth/
Belt, mouth, bayonet/ Face, bayonet, wing...

7. 'Líra és antilíra' in *Nem vagyok kritikus!* [I am not a Critic], Budapest, 1984, pp. 21-46.
8. Éva Körner, 'Az abszurd mint koncepció, jelenetek a magyar koncept art történetéből' [The Absurd as concept, scenes from the history of Hungarian concept art], in *Balkon* 1993/1, pp. 22-25; 1993/2, pp. 10-15.
9. Zsuzsa Forgács, 'Én rögtön posztfeministának születtem' [I was immediately born a post-feminist] http://www.extra.hu/kolorlokal/csejdy/forgacsint.htm
10. Fodor Géza, 'A Halász' in *Szinház* [Theatre], Vol. XXIV October-November, 1991, pp. 14-19.
11. Miklós Jancsó, 'Avantgárd gének' [Avant guarde genes] *ibid.* p. 57.

12. Margit Köves, 'Telling Stories of Partition and War, Saadat Hasan Manto and Istvan Örkény' in *Economic and Political Weekly*, Vol. XXXII, Nos 33 and 34, August 16-23, 1997, pp. 2147-2152.
13. Örkény's work spans four decades from 1930s to the end of the 1970s. As a person of Jewish origin he was called up for military service during the Second World War. He wrote plays (*Voronezh*) and novels (*People of the Camps*) about his experiences on the Front in Russia and in prisoners camp, in the Soviet Union in 1940s. His writings in the 1940s presented characters in their attachment to the myth of Hungarian identity. In the 1960s after six years silence following the 1956 Uprising Örkény developed a new narrative form, the one-minute story. Örkény's plays *The Catsplay*, *Bloodrelations* and *The Toth Family* written in the 1960s and 1970s represent the East-European absurd. *The Toth Family* was translated into Hindi by Raghuvir Sahay and performed by the NSD in the 1980s.
14. István Örkény, 'Használati utasítás' [Instruction for Use], in *Válogatott Egyperces novellák* [One-minute stories], Budapest, 1998, blurb.
15. István Örkény, 'Nem találtam meg a zanzacsinálás titkát' in *Párbeszéd a groteszkről* [Dialogue about the Grotesque], Budapest, 2000, pp. 381-382.
16. István Örkény, 'Fehér asztalnál Örkény Istvánnal' [At white table with István Örkény], in *Párbeszéd a groteszkről* [Dialogue about the Grotesque], Budapest, 2000, p. 385.
17. Mikhail Bakhtin, *Rabelais and His World*, 1984, Indiana University Press, pp. 303-367.
18. István Örkény, 'A groteszk válasz iszonyú önbizalmunkra' [Grotesque is the answer to our unshakable self-confidence], *op. cit.* p. 363.
19. István Örkény, 'Dal' [Song] in *Válogatott egyperces novellák* [Selected one-minute stories], Budapest, 1998, pp. 45-46. English translations of Örkény's one-minute stories in *One minute Stories*, selected and translated by LT András and Carl R Erickson, Budapest, 1992; *One minute Stories,* selected and translated by Judith Sollosy, Budapest, 1994.

    The songwriter's name was Jenö Janász. We were thrown together by the Russian offensive that smashed his unit and separated me from mine near Niklayevka.* We stayed together for nearly two hundred miles, occasionally catching a ride. But most of the time we marched on foot, through snow and ice, under constant enemy fire, until he was felled by a short burst from an automatic on the outskirts of Byelgorod.

    Till then I had no idea how songs were written. Who would have guessed that it was so easy? They came pouring out of Janász, they sprang up, gushing forth like springs from the earth. Anything he saw or heard he turned into a song in the blink of an eye complete with lyrics, rhymes and melody. Only the title had to be added.

    A folk song appeared out of a tin can of fruit preserves we scraped out of the smoldering ruins of a bombed-out ware-house. There was also a bridge blown up right under our noses by the partisans. As we floundered across the ice piled under the wrecked remains, Jenö Janász was already singing:

The old wood bridge over the river it came
tumbling down, tumbling down
There is no going back to my beloved town
beloved town
Oh my Good Lord why have you driven me
so far away
Why have you taken me from the arms
of my sweet Annie-May?

I badgered him to tell me how he did it. He said he didn't know. I asked him how many songs he'd written. He didn't know that either. Maybe three thousand, maybe four.

Byelgorod was within view when the snow began to fall. I pulled down my earflaps, but even so I could hear Janász humming away:

Flakes of snow float down slowly
Russian sleigh bells jingle merrily
Flutter, flutter, little flake of snow...

Five rapid cracks sounded. Janász was dead, his song left unfinished. At times I remember and try to go on with it. I rack my brain searching for a rhyme to that flake of snow. But to no avail. Each of us can do something no one else can do quite the same way. That's how it is.

20. István Örkény, 'Havas tájban két hagymakupola' [Two Cupolas in a Snow-covered landscape] in *Válogatott egyperces novellák*... pp. 49-50.

The whole town of Davidovka should have been there. I mean, not just our battalion, but the local inhabitants, too. Somehow, it didn't work out that way. The Hungarians in our battalion were represented by only a few scared eager-beavers, plus those who had something to lose if they didn't obey - chiefly the sick, the clerks, and the supplymen - forty to fifty men. There were even fewer Russians. Those whom the sergeant major had managed to scare out of their homes drifted around the square for a while, then fled back at the first opportunity. Most conspicuous of all was the absence of our battalion commander, Major Holló, who had been present at all the earlier executions, and who had always been so careful to observe the formalities. In the one-minute when he had appeared in front of headquarters, Holló had surveyed the church square, remarked that the weather was cold, not to show up again. Aside from the battalion surgeon and the sergeant major, the only men present with any authority were a German truck driver and a German NCO who had a Leica hanging around his neck. They had brought the offender to Davidovka, where the sentence of the military court was to be carried out. And, of course, there was also Ecetes, a wagon driver who had volunteered to hang the woman in exchange for three liters of rum. The first liter was already gone, and Ecetes stood quite unsteadily on his feet. The woman stood waiting under a tree. She stood there motionless, as though her feet were frozen on the ground. Her eyes were not even moist. From experience, we knew that it was the elderly who died with the least amount of fuss. They were alarmed, of course, as though unable to grasp what was happening to them, but they didn't beg, whimper or scream. This however, was an attractive, well-dressed young woman and didn't utter a word of complaint. She simply stood and watched with burning eyes a little girl who had crawled under the truck and who was now peeping out from beneath it. She was four or five years old. She was thin and dirty, but her clothes, like the woman's, were well-made - a fur vest, quilted pants, thick woolen stockings, and galoshes. When the noose was tightened around the young woman's neck, the girl under the truck gave a bright little laugh, as though she'd been tickled.

Three minutes later, the battalion surgeon pronounced the woman dead. A cold wind rose, and the body began to sway. The girl crept out from beneath the truck. For a while she watched the corpse swing gently back and forth. Then, as though the whole affair were merely a game that had gone on too long, she cried up toward the tree:

"Mama!"

The Russians had gone. The only Hungarians remaining were Ecetes; Sergeant Major Elek Bíró; Tibor Friedrich, the battalion surgeon; and Corporal István Koszta, formerly a bartender at the Golden Bull Hotel in Debrecen, who had repeatedly requested a transfer to a hospital somewhere behind the front lines to be treated for carbuncles. At the moment, Koszta was standing in such a way as to draw surgeon's attention to the dark read swellings on his neck. The surgeon had turned away, however, and was looking in the direction of the Leica. The German NCO motioned to the little girl to get out of the picture. She remained where she was, however, her eyes wide and sparkling as she stared into the Leica. Perhaps she had never seen a camera before.

21. István Örkény, 'In memoriam dr.K.H.G., in *Válogatott egyperces novellák*... p. 30.

"Hölderlin ist Ihnen unbekannt?" Dr. G.H.K. asked as he dug the pit for the horse's carcass.

"Who is that?" the German guard asked.

"The author of Hyperion,"said Dr. G.H.K., who had a passion for explanations. "The greatest figure of German Romanticism. How about Heine?" he tried again.

"Who are they?" the guard asked.

"Poets," Dr. G.H.K. said. "Haven't you heard of Schiller either?"

"Him I know. "the German guard said.

"And Rilke?"

"Him, too," the German guard said and, turning red shot Dr. G.H.K. dead.

22. István Örkény, 'Fehér asztalnál' ... p.385.
23. István Örkény, 'Ballada a költészet hatalmáról' in *Válogatott egyperces novellák*...pp.105-107.

24. István Örkény, 'Gondolatok a pincében' in *Válogatott egyperces novellák*...p.176.

Through a broken window a ball fell into a corridor in the basement. One of the children, the fourteen year old daughter of the caretaker hobbled down for it. One of her legs had been cut off by the tram and she was happy when she was allowed to collect the ball for the others. There was semi-darkness in the basement, but she saw that something moved in the corner.

-Pussycat- said the girl with a wooden leg. -How did you get here, my little pussy?

She picked up the ball and went off as fast as she could.

The old, ugly and smelly rat - it was taken for a pussycat - was surprised. Nobody had spoken to it so far this way.

Till now it had been hated, pelted by coal, or some people ran away from it scared.

For the first time it thought how differently things would have turned out if it happened to be born a pussycat.

Or - since one is so insatiable! - it started building castles in the air. What if it was born a caretaker's daughter with a wooden leg?

But this was far too beautiful. It was not able to imagine that any more.

25. István Örkény, 'Hiába sikerül egy vitás kérdést tisztázni' in *Válogatott egyperces novellák*...p.177.

A sweet mignonette flower went to the washroom and sat down on the toilet-seat. Then something set it thinking. But then it is a plant, it has no rectum, it has no stool. Then what is it's business here?

At least this has been cleared. The sweet mignonette flower got up and without doing it's job went back to the guests. When the mistress of the house (a lady of royal English blood whose namesday was being celebrated) gave her a questioning look the sweet mignonette smiled back and only said explaining:

- There was a small misunderstanding.

And it went to the bar because it felt like having a champágne. It will be really funny - it thought, - when it saw the champagne glasses -, if I can not drink either.

DOMINIQUE DE GASQUET

Romantic Response to Modernity: New Consciousness of Time through the Ball Scene

This paper will explore the new consciousness of time in Romanticism and Modernity through "the ball scene". Starting from *Spirite* by Théophile Gautier via Baudelaire's *La Fanfarlo* (1857), it will end with *Le Ravissement de Lol V. Stein* by Marguerite Duras (1964) (*Le Vice Consul, India Song*) and Mishima's *Le Nô: Sotoba Komachi*.

We will consider the scene of the ball as a chronotope as defined by Mikhail Bakhtin[1], as time-space that signifies a correlation between spatial and temporal relationships. This is a metaphor taken from Mathematics and Einstein's Physics that signifies the fusion of spatial and temporal signs in a concrete and understandable whole.

In the novel, the chronotope of the ball introduces a major change in the conception of time, a change of perspective similar to the "mise en abime". This process is incorporated, for example, in the "movie inside the movie" by Truffaut in his film *American Night*. The party and the ball bring together at the same instant suspension, retrospection, retrogression, without temporality, flashback into other times and other spaces, elements which bring a redefinition of the subject and its metamorphosis.

The ball builds and destroys, it announces the recomposed story and predicts the future.

Social interactions are characterised by representations of time and space and social representations of time and space belong to poetics, i.e., an artistic creation giving structure and sense to the text. "Writing dance" implied describing a space and its architecture and exposing the time of the party and relating the social event where an individual story is happening.

The ball is thus the description of social life and its risks. As a privileged social space, the ball, as it was the case of conversation during the Ancien Régime, is a dynamic place of social interaction with its movements and its displacements on the social scale. The ball symbolises power, the social power of a world showing itself.

Modern Response of Romanticism

The social power comes with an erotic power which is brought by clothes ("and when Mlle de Fontaine noticed how elegant the clothes and shoes are."[2]). These two powers, social and erotic, constitute a very rich frame made of events and meanings.

One of the essential marks of the ball in the nineteenth century is the illusion of equivalence between wealth and love which denounces the pale morning corresponding to the end of the ball and the end of the love story.

The first ball has an initiating value, it means the introduction to the world, the birth of society and the love story. In *Spirite* by Théophile Gautier, the novel is organised around two scenes, the first one of Lavinia at the scene of the ball and of the ice-skating, one as seen by the heroin and the other one by the hero.

Gautier wrote that a first ball is an important matter for a young girl. Erotic and social positions are in an asymmetrical and conflicting relation, typical of that historical period. To quote Théophile Gautier,

> *Les Bals sont nos batailles, perdues ou gagnées – c'est là que la jeune fille, sortie des ombres du gynécée, brille de tout son éclat [....]; mais bien souvent le petit carnet où elle inscrit les invitations qu'on lui a faites parmi une longue liste, ne contient pas la seule qu'elle eût désirée.*[3]

This special space of freedom, the first ball is for the young girl, the passage from interiority to exteriority, the transition from private space to public space, from darkness to light. The ball of Lavinia is like a military fight and it is not different from the social strategy of Mme d'Ymbecourt. The costume of the ball is a poem "It's not without irony" because of the identification between poetry and strategy, dream and calculation, idealism and materialism. In this pursuit of man – the ball of Lavinia takes place in an architectural and mythological space, we have gone back in time, we are somewhere else.

The very big hotel of "Faubourg St. Germain" has got a prestige, it allows luxury and a crowd. The Louis XIV style evokes Versailles. Evocation and elocution of painting are those of Poussin Dughet. This world does not belong to the present time and big mirrors are a special sign of this description allowing a narcissist showing off and an aesthetic duplication making the room look bigger and infinite.

The game of mirrors also represents the temporal devices. The scene of the ball with its metamorphosis is also a way to find the past again, to go back in time and ward off death. At that specific moment, we break the normal rhythm of life and find eternity. The scene of the ball d'Onuphrius by Théophile Gautier evoked by Balzac in *Une Fille d'Eve* is evocative of the Walpurgis night. It is not only a show, a fantasy and a scene of a voyeuristic vision but a piece of dream, a fragment of poetic prose, where the description changes from the ephemeral into a very beautiful painting, *Songe d'une nuit d'été*.

> *Un beau tableau sur ma foi! Les girandoles de cristal étincelaient comme des étoiles; des gerbes de lumière, des iris prismatiques s'échappaient des pierreries: les épaules des femmes, lustrées, satinées, trempées d'une molle sueur, semblaient des agates ou des onyx dans l'eau; les yeux papillotaient, les gorges battaient la campagne, les mains s'étreignaient, les têtes penchaient, les écharpes allaient au vent, c'était le beau moment; la musique étouffée par les voix, les voix par le frôlement des petits pieds sur le parquet et le frou frou des robes, tout cela formait une harmonie de fête, un bruissement joyeux à enivrer le plus mélancolique, à rendre fou tout autre qu'un fou.*[4]

This adjournment of time goes with the possibility of meeting someone. Lavinia is Cinderella, in a state of anxiety while she waits to see her partner who is absent and whom she has never met.

> The evening was one of the most brilliant and looking at the scene, one was spell-bound. One was struck by the decor, by the women, by their clothes, by the movements of their feet and by the music. This atmosphere created the festive harmony which could intoxicate the most melancholic and could render everyone mad but for the insane.

Théophile Gautier was inspired by Hoffmann's Tales, *Le Conseiller Crespel* for example, which is a remarkable *mise en scène* between inside and outside worlds through architecture, through violin and voice, and it demonstrates that the desire cannot be realised because it is prohibited. This is the same as in the modern *Nô* of Yukio Mishima, *Sotoba Komachi*, where we are in a ball scene, a waltz more precisely, and during this waltz, the metamorphosis of Sotoba Komachi happens. She had warned the poet that if he says she is beautiful, he would die. Ignoring the magical power of this ugly and rather old woman of ninety-nine years, who rejuvenates into a very beautiful young lady of nineteen, the poet will dance with her and will tell her his desires and he will then be found dead. He will discover through the words, "you are beautiful", that beauty can kill. We can also see the influence of Oscar Wilde upon Mishima with Dorian Gray whose fatal beauty has the same power. Those who fall in love with him are fated to kill the object of their love:

> Yet all men kill the thing they love.
> By all let it be heard.
> The coward does it with a kiss,
> The brave man with a sword.[5]

Coming back to Hoffman, we see the relationship of conflict with society becoming the impossibility to sing in certain conditions of death penalty. If here singing provokes death, for Théophile Gautier dance takes the place of songs.

This finds its counterpart in the waltz of Mishima's *Nô*, in the scenic indication in Marguerite Yourcenar's translation[6] which specifies the music of the waltz and a ballroom of the nineteenth century. Moreover, the three young couples from the generation of the 1880s dance a waltz and come very close to the couple of the young poet and the old woman. The waltz abolishes distance and creates proximity of bodies and souls. In his book *La Valse*, Rémi Hess shows very well the scandalous nature of this dance, that is not only the fast movements of the partners but also the proximity of their bodies. There is also the way in which the woman gives herself to a "close hold" and to physical intimacy during the dance. This is a socio-political dimension of the waltz, which becomes the expression of a struggle against authority and the reassertion of an individual's liberty.

The rhythm, the lightness, the absence of effort deliver the couple from the grave situation, isolating them from the rest of the world, wrapped up in a circle of subjective infatuation, in a privacy that mocks time and experiencing the sense of eternity within the instant. In Sotoba Komachi's *Nô*, the waltz in its transgression has an evil aspect that separates the living from the dead, individuals from the society.

Death, taking place during the dance or just after, corresponds to a sort of punishment after a violation of social rules. We can mention in this context Victor Hugo with his physiology of the Polka in the *Feuilles d'Automne*. Hugo calls *la valse impure, au vol lascif et circulaire*. This topos of death during the ball or at the end has been used by Hugo *Elle aimait trop le bal, c'est ce qui l'a tuée*, i.e., "She liked dancing very much, that was what killed her." It means collapsing after having dreamt and becoming sober after drunkenness. It echoes to Théophile Gautier again:

O temps! Que nouse voulons tuer et qui nous tues.[7]

Another form of chronotope appears with Gautier on the opposition between the body and society with the confrontation between Occidental and Oriental dance. Classical dance is criticised because it denies the body and the differences between the sexes. The classical dancers have *l'apparence d'arraignées qu'on inquiète dans leurs toiles et qui se démènent éperdument.*[8]

Gautier discovered the first Spanish dances in which the "southern" blood is reflected: *C'est un poème écrit avec des ondulations de hance* (*Fusains et eaux fortes*).

We find this oriental dance later, at the end of the century, in Oscar Wilde's *Salomé*. It concludes with the tragic death of the dancer: *La danse des sept voiles*. This oriental dance was referred to by Gautier in *Voyage en Algérie.*

> the dance is formed by the perpetual body movements. Arms, legs and all other parts of the body move with an agility insurmountable by any master of opera. The figure evoked a gust of wind filled with love and eroticism which is the symbol of the mysterious drama of voluptuousness.

As we said, Salomé's dance belongs to that association of exoticism and dance mixed with death and this death is the final step. Salomé agrees to dance for Herod, her father-in-law, in spite of her mother's protests. The dance will leave Herod in ecstasy, ready to grant the reward he has promised. She demands the head of Iokanaan, the prophet. Horrified, the Tetrarch tries to dissuade her, offering all his treasures in exchange. Salomé stands her ground, reminding him of his pledge. Herod capitulates. Having received the reward for her dance, Salomé takes it and kisses the mouth that scorned her, reiterating in a monologue her desire to be loved. Herod orders the soldiers to kill Salomé.

Et le mystère de l'amour est plus grand que le mystère de la mort: the mystery of love is greater than the mystery of death. These words pronounced by Salomé at the end of the opera of Richard Strauss, which used the text of the poem by Wilde, demonstrates that this composer, one of the most important figures of the *Avant Garde de l'époque*, had a sense for subversion and provocation.

We have to add also that the Salomé-dance is a solo which is the beginning of modern dance and which we will find in the fifties in what is called in the USA *la danse non littérale* with Merce Cunningham and Lucinda Childs. Salomé expresses the desire, of the self and of the other, by making people aware that the world, since it was christianized, had repressed sexuality. Here it is not ballet but body language. Salomé is an apparition as Gustave Moreau has painted her and she is going to disappear. Salomé starts to become the incarnation of dance at the beginning of the nineteenth century. She reappears in modernity with Maurice Béjart who has performed Salomé in 1969, 1970, 1983 and 1985. She appears in 1961 in Bolero. The woman in a circle surrounded by men, even if she is not called Salomé, evokes her. "How Princess Salomé is beautiful tonight" in 1970 with Josiane Consoli evokes *l'entreé en danse, l'éssence de la danse*.

We can say that dance and literature have been mixed together since the nineteenth century, they represent a social act ensuing from the ideology of history. In fact, dance during the nineteenth century was very important not only in novels but also in art, theatre, through romanticism, realism, naturalism, representing the society of that time.

Examples that can be cited are "livrets de ballet" of Théophile Gautier, Francois Coppée, Ludovic Halévy, La Sylphide, 1832, Giselle 1841. After the role played by dance in the Encyclopedia, Théophile Gautier, St. Mallarmé, Paul Valéry will express the metaphor of the ideal through dance. Dance and poetry establish correspondences and analogy. Dance evokes a model for poetry. From 1800, with Germaine de Stael poetry begins to imitate dance.[9] The magic power of dance stimulates the imagination of those who are watching it.

> While dancing, Corrine passed on to the spectators the musical and colourful language which passionately charged her sensible imagination. Her dance transports the audience to an ideal existence out of this world.

In fact, in 1847, Baudelaire in *La Fanfarlo* spoke about dance being more important and suggestive than poetry or music.

> *La danse c'est de la poésie avec des bras et des jambes.*

Baudelaire establishes the connection between elements from the North and South of England and Italy to capture this *matiére en mouvement qu'est la danse*. Dance can express what words cannot. From Diderot, de Staël, to Théodore de Banville, Théophile Gautier, Mallarmé, Gerard de Nerval, Pierre Louys, Alphonse Daudet, one can see how its silence provokes poets and artists to make it talk, that is to say how dance had an artistic and social importance in the culture of that century. The romantic ballet belongs to the 'intrigue' (plot). Baudelaire, in *La Fanfarlo* changes little his language tools while speaking of the dance:

Every culture, antique, Indian or Arabian, has cultivated dance as equal to poetry. Dance has also the same stature as that of music. Those, whom the music gives ideas of paintings, can understand me better. Dance can reveal whatever music leaves mysterious and at the same time can be human and concrete. Dance: it's poetry with arms and legs, it's gracious, terrible while animated by the movement.[10]

The illusion of the scene of the ball corresponds also to the perception of the rules and codes of society. Here is a choreography of textuality *le rhythm ternaire de Salomé* of Wilde for example. One could read *Le Bal de Sceaux* by Honoré de Balzac as the following three scenes:

a) public ball - 'intrigue' (plot)
b) private ball birth of feelings of lovers
c) ball given by the Napolitan ambassador - dénouement

There is a combination between "contredanse" and syntax. Without going into any detail one could also recall the scene in Madame Bovary's ball when Emma is invited by a Vicomte to dance a waltz during a *contillon*. We have the description of a private ball in *La Monarchie de Juillet*. We have the position of the narrator and that of the character.[11]

The Vice Consul, in a quick movement, disappeared pulling her along till the end of the hall, where she almost fainted, [...] then [...], gently he led her to her place. The furniture, the lamps, the tapestry and the floor, all seeming to roll around them, like a disc in the gramophone.

Without description, *La scéne du bal de Sceaux* is made of the syntax of "contredanse". And *Le Bal de Sceaux* and *Madame Bovary* themselves become dance showing at the same time, with realism, the socio-cultural context of the historical period. In fact, texts that insert dance in the story tell more about dance than the critical essays about dance. There is a sort of reflection inside fiction, texts imitate in their style the movements and rhythm of dance; inserting a ball room scene creates the "dancing text": *l'écrit dancent*. This is testified by the word choreography which means dance and writing.

From Romanticism to Modernity or a Romantic and Modern Questioning of Consciousness of Time and Space.

In the twentieth century, the scene of the ball is very present in the novels of Marguerite Duras (*le grand Meaulnes d'Alain Fournier et Marcel Proust*). The ball takes place in a close room. Casino de S.T. beach

"Ambassade de France à Calcutta". The octagonal room that we can see or discover in *Le Ravissement de Lol V. Stein*, *Le Vice Consul* (*India Song*, text and film) shows us how in modernity dance has something to do with a new consciousness of time and oneself.

During the ball, when she is nineteen, Lol will see her own fiancé going away at the end of the night with another woman: Annie Marie Stretter. Lol will look at them while they are going away, then she will collapse. Since that day, even if she gets married to another man, even if everything seems to have been regained again, Lol will be haunted by the ball. She will come back to the casino on the same beach where the event happened and she will find peace but the event has turned into a fixed image. It is quite the same story as that of the little girl aged fifteen and a half, crossing the river and meeting for the first time the Chinese book which will be called the lover and represent *l'image absolue*, the first title of the book.

Annie Marie Stretter, the Vice-consul, and "voices off-stage" will increase the impression of disturbance. We are not in front of events happening in present time but we are in front of dreams come alive again. The ball is the experience of emptiness, it is a real poetic moment, an access to ecstasy.

During the ball, conversation is difficult. That is why Lol will collapse and the Vice consul after having exchanged some words with Annie Marie Stretter will shout and scream desperately "keep me, keep me with you", knowing perfectly that it is impossible. [But he has been so happy to dance, that means to be so close to this wonderful Anne Marie Stretter he loved so much]. Both in Duras and in Mishima's *Nô*, during the ball we don't see real characters but ghosts who are already dead and possessed again by their past life, they live again in their passion. Dreams start again as if they were a part of reality. But the mirrors' reflection shows us that what we are looking at belongs to the kingdom of Death, to the past, to illusion.

We can see from the sixties to the seventies, Duras evoking dance and creating the space of dance in her novels, theatre, plays and films. The words delegate their power to bodies. It is always during the summer, close to the seaside, during the night, and the ball reveals the deep nature of feelings. It is a magic moment, the proximity of death as in Romantic literature does not continue because even if people meet each other it is an illusion, the morning will chase them, they will have to leave, what they have seen, is fascinating and corresponds to a metaphysical moment.

Visual impulses mixed with sounds and the physical meeting of bodies during the waltz allow transgression. The vice-consul, a 'pariah', an outsider, because he comes from Lahore, where he had a very strange and violent behaviour, will be accepted during the ball and recognised by Anne Marie Stretter. During the ball scene, the dance with the music also introduces a revolution in the style of writing. Dance turns the text into a field where cinematographic work is in progress. Dance takes the place of conversation.

> They were dancing and dancing without speaking to each other.[12]

In the several meanings of the ball, the end is the most important — this event of her separation from the couple between Anne Marie Stretter and Michael Richardson.

How dance and writing are mixed together, is demonstrated in Robert Wilson's adaptation of *The Illness of Death* (*La Maladie de la Mort*) in 1997 at the Bobigny Theatre. Micheal Piccoli was the actor and Lucinda Childs the dancer, as a result of which the audience did not know which was more important - the words of Marguerite Duras or the dance.

During the dance we do not know who is the leader, who is following. As Paul Valéry says *dans la danse dans le bal, je ne sais plus si je suis objct ou sujct, si jc possédc ou suis possédé.* Time changes into space, vision into fascination. Lol will be in touch all the time with the ball. It turns into a picture and an obsession. The ball is the symbol of meeting, separation, loneliness, it will produce an apparition which will succeed in disappearing. The paradox is that, when it is over we can read it, when we are inside, it is blinding. It is a picture of the eternal return of time. It allows differences of position and perceptions. The ball proposes a prodigious perspectival system that plays continuously with opposing concepts: permanent / becoming, inescapable / fugitive, memory / imagination.

In Marguerite Duras, the ball has escaped real time. It has entered into the imagination as in a fairy tale or legend and this is part of a modern revolution, of a new consciousness of time.

NOTES AND REFERENCES

1. Mikhail Bakhtine, *Esthétique et théorie du roman*, Gallimard, 1978.
2. Honoré de Balzac, *Le Bal de Sceaux*, Pléiade I, p. 135.
3. Balls are similar to battles. The young girls have got a relative freedom but very often even if they accept to dance, they will never dance with the one they would have liked to dance with.
4. 'Onuphrius' in Théophile Gautier, *L'Oeuvre fantastique*, Classiques Garnier-Bordas, 1992, t. 1, pp. 45-46.
5. Oscar Wilde, 'Ballad of Reading Gaol'.

6. Mishima Yukio, 'Sotoba Komachi' in *Cinq Nô Modernes de Yukio Mishima*, trans. and adaptation by Marquerite Yourcenar, Gallimard, 1984, p. 35.
7. Théophile Gautier, *Poésies Complètes*, 1970, p. 98.
8. *Feuilleton de la charte de 1830*.
9. Germaine de Staël, *Corrine Ou l'Italie*, D. Appletown & Cie. 1876, p. 119.
10. Charles Baudelaire, *La Fanfarlo, op. cit.*, pp. 47-48.
11. Gustave Flaubert, *Madame Bovary*, Moeurs de Province, Garnier, 1947, p. 54.
12. Marguerite Duras, *Le Ravissement de Lol V. Stein*, Gallimard Folio, p. 15, p. 46.

KAVITA BHATIA

Rahel Varnhagen's Berlin Salons: The Question of Emancipation

> What a history! - A fugitive from Egypt and Palestine, here I am and find help, love, fostering in you people. With real rapture I think of these origins of mine and this whole nexus of destiny, through which the oldest memories of the human race stand by side with the latest developments. The greatest distances in time and space are bridged. The thing which all my life seemed to one the greatest shame, which was the misery and misfortune of my life - having been born a Jewess - this I should on no account now wish to have missed.
>
> (Rahel Varnhagen, on her death bed, March 7, 1833)

The cosmopolitanism resulting from the Kantian Enlightenment at the turn of the eighteenth century had brought with it the hope that it would resolve the question of Jewish identity as with its help it would become part and parcel of a German and therefore European society. Similarly, it was in the premises of an Enlightenment modernity that the emancipation of women was also sought to be premised. However, experience as well as struggles have brought to the fore problems associated with this belief system built around the notions of modernity and its emancipatory potential.

The turn of the century also saw the emergence of ideas developed by the Romantics in their response to modernity, ideas which were on the one hand politically and socially chauvinistic in that they took the form of the glorification of the past, particularly of the Middle Ages, support to reactionary feudal rulers and to characteristic brands of nationalism, and a literary cosmopolitanism on the other, together with an understanding of art, society and politics, reflecting the various processes of political and social change in Europe. The Romantic worldview, conscious of the contradictions of the modern era, evolved a modern aesthetic that privileged creativity and imagination, the autonomy and open-endedness of the work of art, its anti-representational conception of language, its emphasis on the fragment and on irony, its problematisation of the subject, a new consciousness of time, and conflicting processes of development.

For women, the Romantic emphasis on the right of subjectivity and individualism also led to increasing emancipation and to their greater participation in the literary movement in various ways. Well-known amongst the women were Dorothea Schlegel, Caroline Schlegel, Sophie and Bettina Brentano.[1]

For the two Jewish women, Henriette Herz and Rahel Varnhagen, both the emancipatory potential of modernity and the contradictions inherent in Romanticism are symbolized in their Berlin Salons of the late eighteenth and early nineteenth century. These salons reflect the specific form of the struggle between emancipation and assimilation, a struggle characterizing the position of the Jewish community as a Diaspora in various countries of Europe for decades. Individuals within the community with their varying social and historical backgrounds responded to the question of Jewish identity by developing diverse strategies of survival located in their immediate life-situations.[2] This paper attempts to trace the form this struggle took in the life and salons of Rahel Varnhagen (1771-1833), moving between the two poles of assimilation and emancipation, between an enlightened modernity and the contradictions of Romanticism at the turn of the century.

For Rahel the contradictory liberal demand for assimilation and the impossibility of integration found expression in her world-view, which was shaped both by German Romanticism and Classicism (the two major influences on her intellectual development were Goethe and Fichte, both of whom she admired.).[3] Historically German Romanticism and Rahel's life coincide with the major political upheavals of the French Revolution and the Napoleonic Wars resulting in the defeat of Germany, its occupation and reorganisation. With the attempt at the restoration of the old absolutist order at the Congress of Vienna (1815), hopes of fulfilment of the slogans of 'Liberty, Equality, Fraternity' were belied, with apparent consequences also for the struggle for Jewish identity and emancipation in the nineteenth century.

I

This section takes a closer look at the trajectory of Rahel Varnhagen's life and attempts to deal with some aspects of the complex problems of assimilation and emancipation, viz., the concrete manner in which assimilation to the intellectual and social life of the environment took place in the history of an individual's life, thus shaping a personal destiny.[4] Her two famous salons as the site of the struggle for emancipation exemplify both the opportunities for as well as setbacks to emancipation as Jew and woman at the turn of the century in Germany.

The Enlightenment of the eighteenth century led to the constitution of an "enlightened society", comprising the bourgeois - not as economic class, but a rising middle-class of educated people -, civil servants, lawyers, clerics, entrepreneurs, as well as officers and landowners. Predominantly, these sections were not from among the highly privileged. They did not subscribe to, or had discarded, the outlook on the world and on life of the older class societies. A basic consensus of moral, social and political attitudes emerged. Partially transcending class barriers and crossing denominational and religious dividing lines which no longer had any justification in the intended "bourgeois constitution" and in the face of an enlightened rational religion, the consensus did not just remain that of intellectual assent but found practical forms of realization. These, on the one hand, resulted in an extensive system of publications, journals and reviews, and on the other, in new "bourgeois" forms of associations - the salons, clubs, reading groups, patriotic societies, Freemasons' Lodges etc.[5]

The salons especially, became symbols of the change in the form of social interaction, for the coming together of the feudal and bourgeois spheres. Already at the end of the reign of Frederick the Great, before salons actually emerged, it was access to artistic talent more than money or a title which made entry into feudal circles and those of the educated bourgeoisie easier. The actual models for the salons were to be found however not in Germany, but in Milan, Vienna and especially Paris. In pre-revolutionary Paris there were fashionable circles in which writers and philosophers of the French Enlightenment came together with politicians and the nobility, besides numerous cafes where a lively intellectual exchange took place between writers, philosophers, actors and musicians.[6] In the Berlin salons of Henriette Herz and Rahel Varnhagen French still represented the culture of the *ancien régime*, with German being the language of philosophy and literature.

Though both women belonged to the urban Jewish community of Berlin, the difference in their social and historical backgrounds helped shape vastly different trajectories of their lives. Henriette Herz, with her marriage to the respected doctor Marcus Herz at the age of 15, in 1779, belonged to the small circle of privileged Jewish families in Berlin. The privileges did not mean emancipation for those that enjoyed them but allowed them to be active in trade, banking, etc., with a majority becoming businessman.

The philosophical writings of Moses Mendelssohn, in whose house these families regularly met, provided the bridge to an enlightened Judaism. Known for his friendship with Lessing and Nicolai, there lay at the centre of Mendelssohn's thought the idea of the invisible church which would unite people of different confessions: Jews, Christians and Muslims in mutual respect. Developing the idea of a religiosity based on rationality and tolerance - which deviated decisively from the old Jewish tradition and rituals -, Mendelssohn's writings exemplify the spiritual bridge to the Enlightenment philosophy of Immanuel Kant, in which the belief in the existence of God and in the immortality of the soul, and the possibility of a moral freedom of choice were understood not as analysable certainties but "postulates of practical reason". It was Kant's teachings which were widespread and accepted in all of the Berlin salons at the turn of the century.

With the general interest in philosophical problems being so large in this generation that the well-off Jewish homes soon became reputed for their knowledge of the dominant philosophy, which resulted in a far more rapid and radical turning away from the older traditional way of life than had been believed possible.[7]

For Henriette Herz, the proximity to Moses Mendelssohn through her friendship with his daughter Dorothea Schlegel was decisive. Equally significant was her interaction with her husband's pupils (Marcus Herz was himself a Kant disciple), who taught her Latin, Greek, some Sanskrit, Mathematics and Physics. Jewish tradition, as an obstacle to assimilation was thus overcome early on in her youth, as is evident in her "Jugenderrinnerungen" (Memories of youth).[8] The many languages she learnt in the course of her life helped her enlarge her social circle. They also helped her financially after the death of her husband.[9]

The trajectory of Rahel Varnhagen's life was quite different. Unlike Henriette who had found full support for her education from her husband, Rahel's father, though he made a fortune as a dealer in precious stones, remained without any understanding for her intellectual activities. Only after his death could she continue unhindered with her efforts at improving her literary and philosophical knowledge, French and playing the piano. Deprived of an education and dependent upon her mother's allowance and the generosity of her brothers, she believed herself without weapons in her struggle as a Jew for a secure social existence.[10]

This struggle against the facts of her life, especially that of her Jewish identity, tragically turned for her into a struggle against herself.

Choosing to be a typically "romantic" personality, comparing herself to the "greatest artists", Rahel believed that "life itself was the assignment", so that one had to live life as if it were a work of art, that by "cultivation" one could make a work of art of one's own life. In her desire to expose herself to life, so that it could strike her "like a storm without an umbrella", she believed she could neither choose nor act, because choice and action in themselves would anticipate life and falsify the purity of life's happen stance". All she needed to do was become a "mouthpiece for experience, to verbalize whatever happened, which could be accomplished by introspection, constant alertness and the capacity for pain being what were required within oneself.[11] Despite close friendships in the early years (1771-1795) she is supposed to have noted carefully with a "cruel joy" every confirmation of her being a *schlemiel*: not rich, not beautiful and Jewish.[12]

In her biography of Rahel Varnhagen[13] written in 1933, Hannah Arendt, political and cultural critic of the twentieth century, for whom the question of Jewish identity and history remain central, sketches out Rahel's struggle for emancipation as determined by the facts of her life. Thus, between 1795 and 1799, believing that in the circumstances the only course open to her was social assimilation through marriage, Rahel attempted to marry Count Karl von Finckenstein, who belonged to one of the oldest noble families of Prussia, but failed.

The idea that it was the "courage for happiness" which she lacked, shadowed many of her relationships, but strengthened her resolve to develop other talents, to take over the role of a "human magnet", a sibyl in her salons. Already after her father's death she had made it a practice to receive guests, so that the attic room in the house in Jägerstrasse became the site of her first salon, receiving guests who like the Jews had been denied entry into bourgeois homes. In the years 1797 –1802, her own interest in the aesthetic and literary ideas of the Schlegel brothers made her salon into the favoured meeting place of Berlin Romanticism, though visitors from all the social circles of contemporary Berlin also met: Prince Louis Ferdinand, ministers and diplomats, the Humboldt brothers, Clemens von Brentano, Friedrich de la Motte-Fouqué, Ludwig Tieck, Adalbert von Chamisso, Friedrich von Gentz, Friedrich Schleiermacher, Jean Paul. It was the Jewish Salon which became, at a time of social transition when a rejection of rigid social norms and connections was taking place, the kind of neutral zone where the coming together of the bourgeois and the feudal, the Christian and the Jewish circles was possible.[14]

Already, however, at the beginning of the century, a wave of anti-Semitism propagated and represented by Grettenaner's Pamphlet "Against the Jews" spread through the Prussian provinces in the midst of the process of assimilation. This proved especially harmful to the Berlin Jews. With 1806, the age of Friedrich II in which Jews were allowed to live in peace was over. Towards the end of the French occupation of Germany, Rahel's salon had also practically broken up, with friends either dead in the war or forced into a wandering existence. After this it was no longer possible for her to be the actual centre of a representative circle revolving around her own personality.

By 1813-14 anti-Semitism was clearly evident, manifesting itself more openly after 1815. Once again, marriage seemed to her the only way out. After being baptised as a Christian, Rahel married Karl August Varnhagen von Ense, whom she had met in 1808. Having rid herself finally of Rahel Levin, the baptism and the social status acquired through marriage however brought the realisation that she did not want to be Mrs. Karl August Varnhagen von Ense either.[15]

On returning to Berlin in 1819, attempts to revive the old salon proved difficult. Salons were now formed around persons of name and rank, officialdom was to the fore together with the hereditary landed nobility and high-ranking officers of the army. In deliberate contrast to the Jewish Salons, the new groupings had all the hallmarks of patriotic secret societies. They were highly exclusive and sought a form that would keep the circle more closely-knit. An attempt in this direction was the "Zeltersche Liedertafel" out of which emerged the "Christliche Deutsche Tischgesellschaft" (the Christian German Table Society) started by Achim von Arnim. Of the forty nine founding members, two thirds belonged to the Prussian nobility, though the Romantics set the tone: Brentano, Eichendorff, Fichte, Fouqué, Iffland, Kleist, Adam Müller, Schleiermacher. The society had written by-laws that banned admittance of women, Frenchmen, philistines and Jews. Each of the meetings had a fixed programme, a serious story read aloud followed by a second reading in which the same story was told in a grotesque and farcical variation, obviously representing the Romantic element.[16]

With the defeat of Prussia and the dissolution of the Holy Roman Empire in 1806, the cosmopolitanism of the early Romantics, which was apparent in the reception and translations of literary works from England, Italy, Spain, Persia, India and the Far East (translations of Shakespeare by August Wilhelm, Ludwig Tieck and Dorothea Schlegel, Dante's "Divina Commedia" and Calderon's religious dramas, Cervantes' *Don Quixote* and Friedrich Schlegele's *Über die Sprache and Weisheit der*

Inder[17]), was replaced by a militant period of German Romanticism with its valorisation of the German national past through its aestheticisation of certain basic ideas bound to the Middle Ages, as for example in the various collections of German folk songs and fairly tales by Achim von Arnim, Clemens Brentano and the Grimm brothers. The contributions to German philosophy by the Grimm brothers in their *Deutsche Grammatik* (German Grammar) *Geschichte der deutschen Sprache* (History of the German language) *Die deutschen Heldensagen* (The German Heroic Sagas) as well as Ludwig Tieck's modernisation of medieval love poems in his *Minnelieder* (1803), his edition of sixteenth and seventeenth century dramas (1817) were all equally reflective of the concern with the German past, as were Ludwig Uhland's collection of Old High or Low German Folk songs and Adalbert von Chamisso's ballads dealing with medieval history.

For German Romanticism, this preoccupation with the Middle Ages was also a reflection of its confrontation with the complexities of modernity, resulting from its desire to return to that lost sense of unity, where human beings were still part of an all-encompassing organism as was presumed to have existed in the political, social or religious order of the Middle Ages, the Catholic church and Catholicism being amongst the pillars one could cling to in the face of this confrontation. Essentially a Catholic movement, strong Catholic leanings were evident for example in Brentano's *Romanzen vom Rosenkranz* (Romances of the Rosary).[18]

This cult of the Middle Ages was something which remained alien to Rahel Varnhagen. Even though her second salon became a meeting place of intellectual Berlin, Rahel herself was forced to become conscious of the contradictions and tensions of the changed times. The fact that a "pariah" remained nothing but a "parvenu" and that despite baptism she could not escape anti-Semitism in the form of personal insults brought the realisation in the years 1820-1833 that no assimilation could be achieved merely by surrendering one's identity and past. In the face of anti-Semitism, in a society hostile to Jews, it was possible to assimilate only by assimilating to anti-Semitism as well. With the wave of pogroms sweeping Prussia in 1819, the earlier unhappy existence seemed more real than the new.[19]

Rahel staved off an actual politicisation for long in her salon. However, confronted with hardened political fronts in the form of a Heinrich Heine, the historians Ranke and Raumar, and the Hegel student Eduard Gans, this no longer remained possible. No longer wanting to deny her Jewishness, Rahel at the close of her life affirmed with Heinrich Heine that not assimilation but the emancipation of Jews as Jews was needed.[20]

II

Emancipation in the German context had meant assimilation, despite the hope generated by the European Enlightenment. German Romanticism's conservative return to the Middle Ages and Christianity, with its strengthening of a patriotic exclusionist nationalism, had determined the process in which the nation was defined, with difference either sought to be denied or allowed in an order of hierarchy.[21]

For middle Europe these debates ranging around the question of Jewish emancipation extended over a century. Clearly, even the various edicts in the nineteenth century - starting already with the earlier Emancipation edicts of 1782 and Hardenberg's Jew edict of 1812 - had contained within them the expectation that the Jews in the process of emancipation would make a break with their inherited traditions, give up their own group structures and identity, and adapt to their environment as Austrians and Germans. Even the 1781 Dohm programme "Über die bürgerliche Verbesserung der Juden" (On the civil improvement of Jews) under the direct supervision of Mendelssohn had included "denationalisation" as tacit agreement of the price to be paid. Whenever in the course of the nineteenth century similar impulses with a cosmopolitan intent were heard, the postulate of equality contained equally its offset, making it clear that emancipation and the erasure of Jewish identity were linked.

That even up to the Seventies, the social adaptation of European Jews had not smoothly taken place, was due neither to a denied legal equality nor to the strong consciousness of Jewish identity, but to the ideological-political process of formation of the European nation-state. The idea of the nation-state as laid out in its form in the French Revolution already contained too many historical aspects which became apparent in the course of the nineteenth century, to allow the 'denationalisation' of the Jewish population to succeed completely. Thus after 1870 there is the peculiar picture of a majority of Jews being, in a certain sense, "over assimilated" but precisely because of this standing out again from the rest. A look at the social profile brings out the double fact of the Jewish population being more bourgeoisified and more intellectualised in comparison to the non-Jewish. This is evident in demographic data, the spectrum of professions, choice of political parties, and the situation in school and in the sphere of education in general.

Clearly, emancipation and integration did not lead to the disappearance of Jews as Jews. They remained a clearly recognisable social group, defined or held together not only by the external anti-Semitism, but also due to the primary and secondary characteristics of being a special group. Religion, tradition and the consciousness of "distinction" made the Jews stand out from their environment. Acquired secondary characteristics manifested themselves in demographic behaviour, in professional and social class as also in family tradition.[22]

Economic and social efforts at integration, which preceded the legal emancipation of 1871, did not bring total assimilation. Assimilation in the cosmopolitan liberal sense, which in effect would have meant the relinquishing of Jewish nationality, counteracted the nineteenth century concept of nation that sought legitimacy in a historical as well as religious basis.

The limitations to assimilation in the national sense became apparent in connection with the wars of liberation. Anti-Jewish factors in the Wartburg Fest had already sent out signals. This was clearly spelt out however in the legislative and administrative practices of the German state organs, which under the aegis of the holy (i.e. Christian) alliance opened up public careers only for the price of conversion.[23]

What however became possible after the opening up of the ghettos, the social integration and the economic success was a far-reaching acculturation in a double sense: the German as also West European Jewry accepted a considerable reduction of autonomy in the spheres of religion, schools and education but simultaneously also involved itself actively in the cultural development of the respective majorities. Having rejected offers to buy themselves a place in a "Jew-free" society through the entry tickets of total assimilation, the majority of the Middle European Jews however took over decisive "cultural patterns" of the environment and attempted to protect Jewish cultural specificity within this framework.[24]

In the sphere of religion, for instance, rabbinic jurisdiction was given up almost without a fight, reflecting the separation of "Jewish religiosity" from "Jewish nationality" in general. The "Jewish" could be defined only in "confessional" terms and, with the general decline in the importance of religion for purposes of identity and self-consciousness, the path for a change in the construction of identity was marked out.[25] As mentioned earlier, the historical and intellectual basis for this change had already been laid down in the second half of the eighteenth century in the reevaluation of Jewish monotheism during the Enlightenment. Moses Mendelssohn's interpretation, that the religion of rationality and that of Judaism had more in common than both had with Christianity, as well as his differentiation between the rational religious substance and the revealed law made that the historical moment for a new orientation in Jewish self-consciousness and Jewish identity. Of comparable importance was, secondly, the ethicization of the religious by Kant, in which a certain analogy to the liberal (Christian) theology of the nineteenth century is apparent.

The results of this changed conception of religion were visible primarily in the reform of synagogal worship, which assimilated to the Christian forms of worship including the sermon and the musical setting. Occupying Jewish communities for decades, this resulted in the overall picture appearing as varied and contradictory as that for the Christian: Reform Jews, conservatives and the neo-orthodoxy, with the majority of the middle-European Jewry however belonging to liberal, reformed streams. An indifference to religion and tradition in general appears more in the Jewish than in the non-Jewish bourgeoisie.[26]

The traditional aspects of Jewish education and teaching also receded sharply in this period as a fall-out of Mendelssohn's language reform and the opening up to modern, that is, to an enlightened education. With the Talmudic tradition being gradually separated from education and education consciousness of the German Jewry and with its replacement by an affiliation to German or rather European culture and literature, nowhere was the acculturation carried out so much as in the school and education system at all levels. By 1850 the identification with German culture had been in the main completed with secular content dominating even in Jewish schools.

Simultaneous to the decline of 'Jewish' schools, the integration of a majority of Jewish children into the state education system took place, indicating a bourgeoisification. The fact that a higher percentage of Jewish children visited schools and colleges as compared to the non-Jewish population, reflected further in the participation of the Jews in the cultural, scientific and literary spheres. The literary salons of Henriette Herz, Dorothea Schlegel and Rahel Varnhagen are widely understood, as already discussed, to represent the symptom of this socio-cultural historical situation as they stepped into the "gaps of the missing big bourgeoisie." The increasing participation of Jewish-German citizens in the development of science and culture in the course of the nineteenth century is also well known. It was actually the period between the Enlightenment and Weimar Classicism with its intellectual and literary history, which had provided the grounds for a consciousness towards cultural integration and given rise to the expectation, based on their cosmopolitan orientation of social and cultural life and precisely in the sphere of German language and culture, of finding the acceptance to which they were entitled.[27]

An earlier, similarly fruitful encounter of two cultural streams in Jewish history had happened when Jewish and Arabic culture had met in the heyday of Spanish Jewry. At this moment in the nineteenth century, German Judaism became a phenomenon with its own particularity through the encounter of Jewish tradition with a branch of German culture, namely with German Classicism, towards which the Jews felt a special affinity. The tragic mistake, however, as was proved later, lay in identifying this branch with the whole.

It is to the Herderian component of Classicism, which links in the philosophy of history a cosmopolitan concept of humanity with the idea of a national cultural tradition, that a new historical self-awareness was credited, which gave meaning to the acculturation tendency.

The establishment in 1819 of the "Verein für Kultur and Wissenschaft der Juden" (Association for Culture and Science of the Jews) to which Leopold Zunz, Eduard Gans and for some time Heinrich Heine as also Moses Moser belonged, was a first reaction to the events after the Napoleonic Era and at the beginning of the Restoration. Conceived within the framework of a scientific and historical understanding of the new, the "historical" century, it was established on a belief in the social effectiveness of scientific insight and in the teleology of the self-realisation of humanity. Whereas Mendelssohn's attempt had been to "place Judaism, for which the world was visible only in the form of a warped ghetto being, within its great historical significance", and thus to also lend it moral dignity, the academicians of the Association followed this up with the attempt to bring into general consciousness the cultural achievements of oriental and occidental Judaism for the benefit of the whole of human culture. This aim "for the outside" corresponded "within" to the attempt, as Eduard Gans formulated it, to make the Jewish world "known to itself", i.e. to develop a Jewish self-consciousness through academic preoccupation with itself.

The Cultural Association saw its programme in bringing knowledge of Jewish history and culture once again to large sections of Jews and in teaching them to understand Jewishness as a part of the general culture, and not as opposition.

In so far as Jewish understanding of history broke off from the old talmudic traditional concept and was mediated through the different premise of a European consciousness of history, there was the possibility of basing Jewish equality in the acculturation process and thus creating historical Jewish self-consciousness.

Though the academic research on Judaism produced by the Association did not find academic space in German universities for long, it did bring large areas of Jewish history into general consciousness. Zunz' research on the Jewish Middle Ages or Heinrich Graetz' multivolume *Geschichte der Juden* (History of the Jews), which did not epitomise Jewish martyrs and Jewish intellectuals as the image of Jews and thus countered occidental ignorance as well as the trivialising understanding of Jewish history, played a meaningful role in the historicization of Jewish consciousness after the support provided by religion had lost meaning. In the century of a Ranke, a Droysen and a Mommsen, academic research on Judaism was anyway needed to keep pace and thus to strengthen the acculturation.[28]

In Rahel Varnhagen's second salon, the presence of Heinrich Heine, Ranke, Raumer Eduard Gans and the corresponding debates around the questions of Jewish history and consciousness together with the developments in German history, reflected the changes from the predominance of the German nobility and Romanticism in her earlier salon.

For Rahel Varnhagen, her attempt at assimilation resulted in self-hatred, since it was complemented by internalizing the discourse of anti-Semitism.[29] Lacking access to education, she attempted to make a virtue of "being an ignoramus".[30] Being deprived of an education, she was also deprived of a consciousness of her own history as a Jew, as well as of German history, and consequently lacked the tools for a scientific and systematic understanding of either. At the end of her life, as recorded in Arendt's biography, the disappointment of the expectations through assimilation remained; the hope that with conversion and marriage, barriers for social advancement could be overcome, did not fulfil itself, since the stigma of opportunism often remained with the converted.[31] Historically at the turn of the century, German nationalism had created the framework in which the Jewish question was being negotiated. Confronted with this, the emphasis had to be shifted from the earlier idea of assimilation to the strengthening of Jewish consciousness and preservation of Jewish autonomy, to the affirmation of her own Jewish identity instead of denying it as Rahel Varnhagen finally did with Heine.

NOTES AND REFERENCES

All translations are mine.

1. Werner P. Friederich, *History of German Literature*, New York, 1962, p. 114.
2. Margit Koves, 'Myths and Realities: Jewish Identity in Hungary at the turn of the Century' in *germinal*, Journal of the Department of Germanic & Romance Studies, University of Delhi, Vol. 1, 1994, p. 85.
3. *Sie sassen und tranken am Teetisch. Anfänge und Blütezeit der Berliner Salons 1789-1871.* Ed. by Rolf Strube. Munich 1991, p. 19

4. Hannah Arendt, *Rahel Varnhagen: The Life of a Jewess*, London: Leo Baeck Institute, 1957, p. xiii.
5. Rudolf Vierhaus, 'The Historical Interpretation of the Enlightenment: Problems and Viewpoints' in *Enlightenment in Germany*, Paul Raabe, Wilhelm Schmidt - Biggemann (eds.), Bown, 1979, p. 30.
6. Strube (ed.), *op. cit.*, pp. 10-11.
7. *Ibid.*, pp. 12-13.
8. Hannah Arendt, *op. cit.*, p. 23.
9. Strube (ed.), *op. cit.*, p. 13.
10. Hannah Arendt, *op. cit.*, p. 3.
11. *Ibid.*, p. xi.
12. *Ibid.*, p. 19.
13. *Ibid.*
14. *Ibid.*, p. 46.
15. *Ibid.*, p. 172.
16. *Ibid.*, p. 99.
17. On the language and wisdom of the Indians
18. Werner Friedrich, *op. cit.*, pp. 116-135.
19. Hannah Arendt, *op. cit.*, p. 183.
20. *Ibid.*, p. 185.
21. Margit Koves, *op. cit.*, p. 93.
22. Günter E. Grimm, Hans-Peter Bayerdorfer (eds.), in *Zeichen Hiobs*, Konigstein/Ts., 1985, pp. 9-10.
23. *Ibid.*, p. 13.
24. *Ibid.*
25. *Ibid.*, p. 14.
26. *Ibid.*, pp. 14-15.
27. *Ibid.*, p. 16.
28. *Ibid.*, pp. 16-17.
29. Margit Köves, *op. cit.*, p. 94.
30. Hannah Arendt, *op. cit.*, p. 26.
31. Gunter E. Grimm, Hans- Peter Bayerdorfer (eds.), *op. cit.*, p. 24.

VIRGINIA NIETO-SANDOVAL MILLÁN

Nature and Fear: Two Conditions in European Romantic Painting

It is difficult to define Romanticism as an artistic movement satisfactorily because each country in Europe offers a different artistic response to the new political and social situation of the nineteenth century. It can be considered a new departure from the union of possible connections between the different European modes of artistic behaviour.

The first symptoms of Romanticism are found in Europe from the eighteenth century onwards and it becomes established with Napoleon coming to power and his expansionist wars generating strong nationalistic feelings in the defeated countries. After his fall, a great change came as revolutionary ideas against the more conservative, and still later it took the form of a strong opposition to the *ancien régime*. All these events get translated into a contrast to the classical tradition which had dominated during the Neoclassicist period and had perpetuated the artistic values of Rome and the Mediterranean.

Although the concepts "Classical" and "Romantic" have a very wide significance, they are applicable to the art of each epoch, including the works of each artist at distinct moments of his life. In the middle of the eighteenth century there appears a division between the Classical and the Romantic. This can be observed in two different works appearing at almost the same time - Winkelmann's Thoughts on the Imitation of Greek Art, published in 1755, a basic text for Classicism, and Burke's Research on the Origin of the Sublime, which analyses the themes of Romanticism, in particular the emotion of fear, which is the source of the sublime.

In painting, the prelude to Romanticism can be seen in the works of the Italian Giovanni Battista Piranesi,[1] who was born in Venice in 1720. In his series of drawings known as *Imaginary Prisons* the Roman ruins do not appear as the Happy Arcade any more, neither does one see the old classicism described by Winkelmann. What appears are the agonizing prisons, which restrict artistic creativity and symbolize the despotism of the neo-classical tradition.

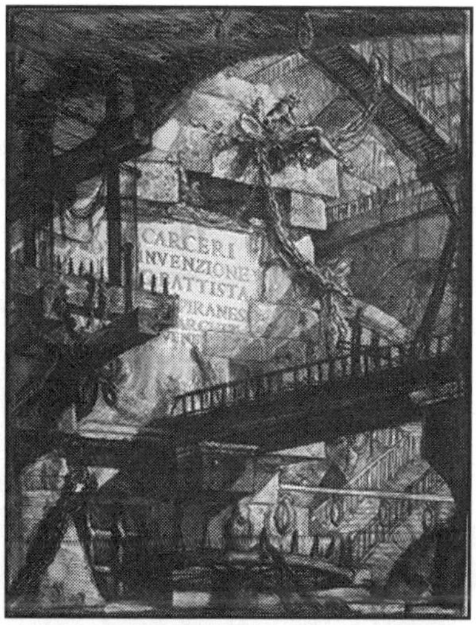

Fig. 1. Giovanni Battista Piranesi, *Imaginary Prisons.*

These *Imaginary Prisons* as great theatrical stage designs contain the crisscrossed gigantic architectures of pessimistic corridors; the staircases which do not lead anywhere, the bars which close the exits, generate in the spectator a deep sense of frustration and anguish, which Burke has called an "aesthetics of fear".[2]

Hereafter the classical ruins would be substituted by Romantic and gothic architecture located in the middle of a landscape. And the Middle Ages, till now considered a dark period by historians, would convert itself into a model of inspiration for the Romantics. The genre of the landscape appears in the thematic of Romantic painting as an answer by the artists to the unstoppable process of industrialisation taking place in Europe and a desire of the emerging bourgeoisie to repossess what they are losing. The representation of nature would collide with different viewpoints and it would develop into the expounding of the aesthetic intentions of Romanticism.

During the course of history, the painting of landscapes had been considered by the essayists as a minor genre, but from the eighteenth century onwards, and especially with the Holland school, it stars to reach its peak and convert itself into a major genre, acquiring special importance in Romanticism, in which the aesthetic education and the ethics of the individual are considered important.

Rousseau, in the *New Eloise* had emphasized the ethical effect of the landscape on the wanderer, creating a sensation of happiness and serenity in the person absorbed in its contemplation. Nature would be considered a medium of elevation of man and also a place of the manifestation of divinity. This idea comes from the Protestant religion, opposed to the image of the church as a house of God, or to the association of the divine with sacred images. They wished to place the divine in an abstract space such as nature. The German painter and essayist Carl Gustav Carus in 'Letters and notes on the painting of

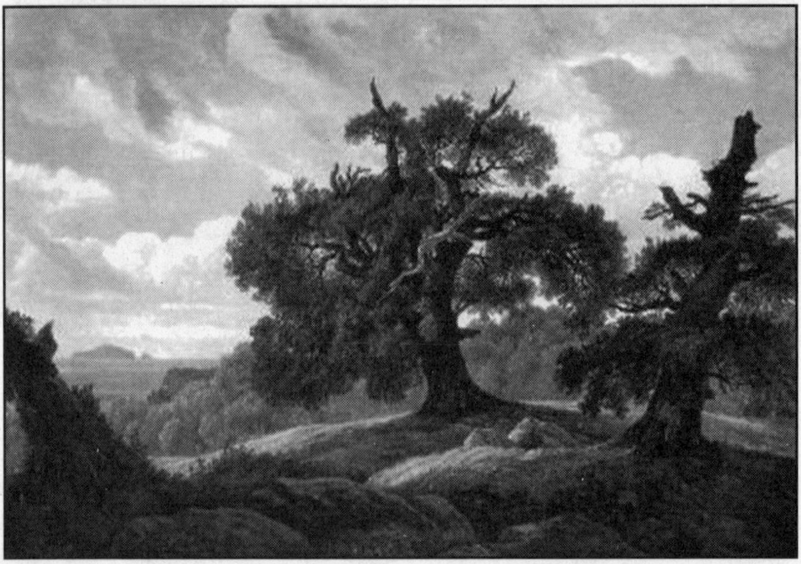

Fig. 2. Carl Gustav Carus, *Oaks at the Sea Shore*.

landscape' insists on this idea. "In a quiet gathering you loose yourself in the unlimited spaces, all your being gets purified gently and your "I" vanishes, you are nothing, God is everything".[3]

In the Romantic landscape, there emerged certain aesthetic categories including terms like the "picturesque" and the "sublime". The term "sublime" was coined by Burke in his "Research on the Origins of Sublime". Burke talks about the studies on the emotions and physiological reactions produced in a human being when standing before the extraordinary motifs of the landscape and defines the "sublime" as a contrary pleasure related to the fear of danger, which provokes an internal tension in the mind. In this manner, the Romantic painters would tend to represent the phenomena of nature such as troughs, tidal waves and threatening skies through emphatic perspectives and at times in fantastic imagery, with confusing points of view. One important object of representation would be the mountain, savage nature, not inhabited nor contaminated by man. The landscapes selected by the Romantic landscape painters would always be local and not Mediterranean as was common amongst the artists of earlier centuries.

One great exponent of the sublime in nature would be the German painter Caspar David Friedrich[4] (1774-1840), who reasserts the Nordic landscape, recreating a magnificent landscape in front of which man stands belittled. Usually in his works one finds close-ups with human figures seen from behind, contemplating nature. The viewer is drawn to immediately identify with the figure, while the background acquires a soft character, creating a great visual tension.

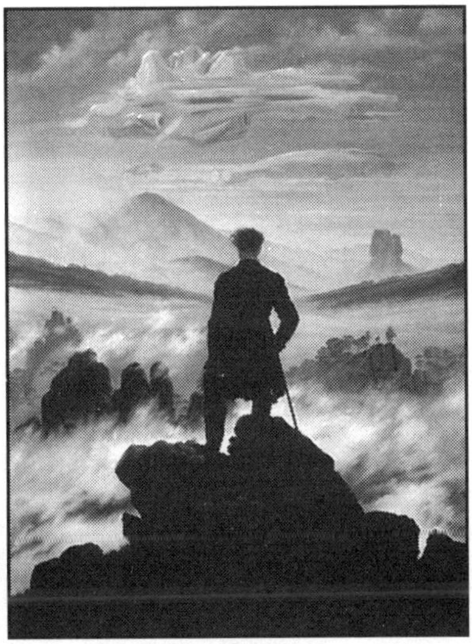

Fig. 3. Caspar David Friedrich, *Wanderer above the Sea of Fog.*

Friedrich consistently creates this visual tension. Technically, he works with the hyper-realistic, meticulously paying attention to each and every detail. In the work of Friedrich, a sequence is developed which takes one to the divinization of nature. In his earlier works landscapes appear as religious symbols, for instance in the form of a cross dominating a mountainous landscape. In his later works, this symbol is substituted by an element of nature, such as a tree or a rick, which maintain the same intention till finally the same nature converts itself into an object of contemplation for the human figures facing it.

In the painting *Wanderer above the Sea of Fog*, Friedrich creates an epic sentiment of form in favour of the sublime. Nature turns into a metaphor for the divinity.

His conception of the sublime differs from the vision of the work of British painter Joseph Turner[5] (1775-1851) who was attracted by such natural phenomena, in which nature condenses all its energy, for example, torrents, tidal waves and mountains. Turner was a great observer of reality and had an extraordinary visual memory. His art was based on instincts, feelings and his first impulse for creation was light and colour rather than an idea.

For this he found watercolour to be the must suitable medium of expression, since it permitted him to show the vitality of the atmosphere with well defined colour schemes. In the artistic creation of Turner there exists a process of independence of colour over the form and the content of the picture, which gives rise to almost abstract compositions.

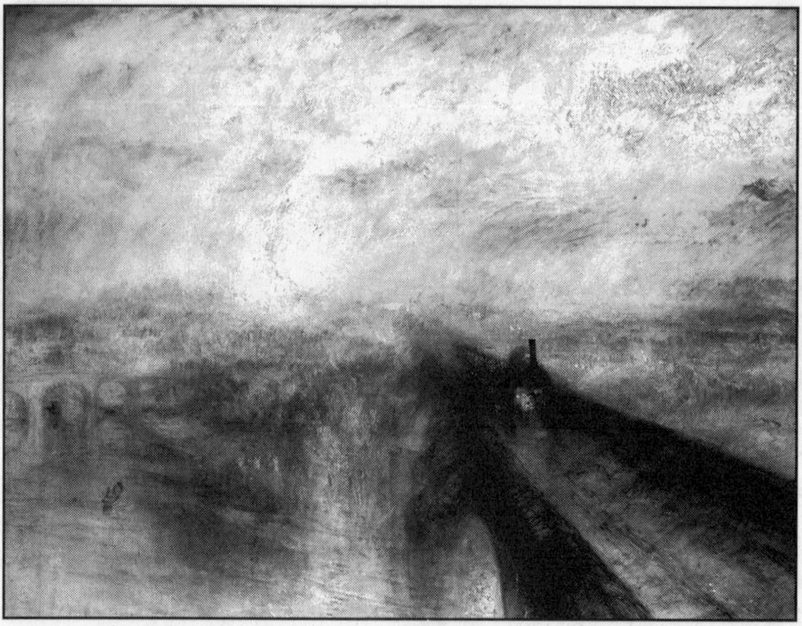

Fig. 4. Joseph Turner, *Rain, Steam and Speed - The Great Western Railway.*

In the landscape painting *Rain, Steam and Speed - The Great Western Railway*, Turner presents the theme of industrial society uniting nature with the effect of movement which is produced by a railway engine, without producing an opposition between nature and the machine.

Both artists, with their distinct pictorial languages, try to paint an image of the universality and abundance of nature.

Contrary to the sublime interpretation of the landscape, the picturesque conception refers to a more lovable nature, of which man can feel a part. Technically, it translates into a throwaway brush stroke. It is free and expressive, and expresses itself thematically through popular and regional images.

In the context of the picturesque, the work of John Constable[6] comes as a milestone in the tradition of European painting. Always accompanied by a small notebook, Constable noted down the finer points of nature and recreated landscapes near to him, in his own ambience. He found his subjects in the land that belonged to his father where he lived most of his life. *The Hay-Wain* is a typical example.

Fundamentally, Constable liked to create the effects of light and shadow in movement transmitting the sensations produced by nature, for example the humidity or the heat of the day, and for such effects he

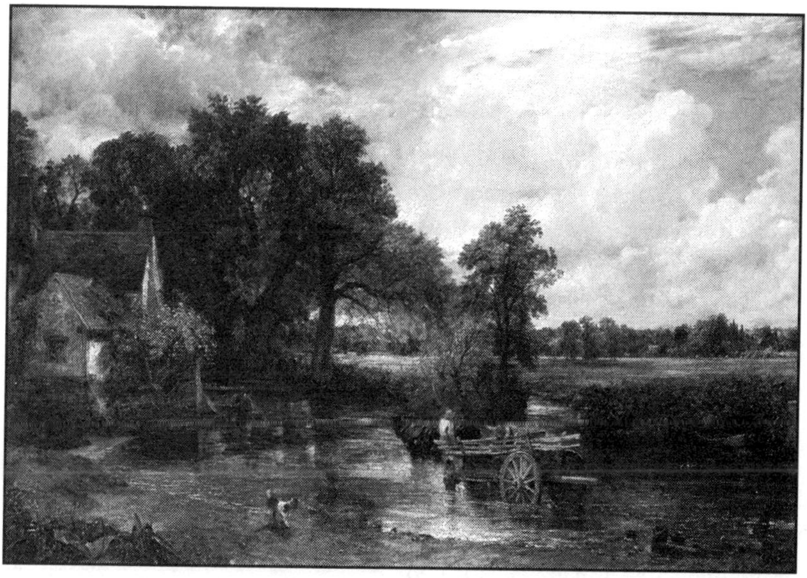

Fig. 5. John Constable, *The Hay-Wain*.

used small and nervous brush strokes of oleo. His fundamental wish was "to paint without affectation and simply what I see and how I see".

Both in the sublime conception of landscape and in the picturesque, the Romantic artist appears as a creator capable of creating works which appear to be alive, as though they were of nature, capable of elevating our spirit and converting it into an intermediary between Man and God. But the reality is that the artist can create only artificial images of fiction, that is, when he wants to act like God, he is only capable of producing a monster, it is here that the myth of Frankenstein, created by Mary Shelley is born. In this manner the monstrous and the fantastic, which are exponents of fear, which are beyond reason, would become part of Romantic painting.

This work of the Spanish painter Francisco de Goya[7] is outstanding, a great creator of images whose personal universe coincides with Romantic themes in some aspects, and again renews this idea. The interpretation of the painting *The Sleep of Reason Produces Monsters* (1799) has been very controversial. But, perhaps it expresses the irrational consequences produced by the bad use of the reason. It can also be seen as a revue, as a critique of the illustration. It belongs to a series of eighty four paintings titled *Los Caprichos* (whims), which, as Goya himself explains in a letter, are "made according to my taste, where the whims and imagination do not have any limits".

The themes he creates are the decline in moral standards, superstition (in particular witchcraft), ideas critical of the church and ignorance. The titles of these paintings, most of the time ambiguous, are as important as the paintings themselves. *Los Caprichos* show a corrupt world that can be made better.

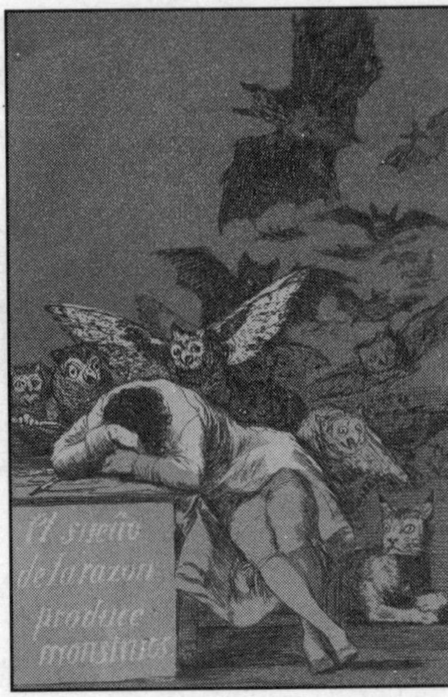

Fig. 6. Francisco de Goya, *The Sleep of Reason Produces Monsters.*

The evolution of the painter coincides with the development of Spanish society, gripped by a radical crisis that not only affects the mode of painting, but also the structure of society. The old forms of life and drawing decline and are substituted by new forms.

In 1790, Goya suffers from an illness, which leaves him bedridden for one and a half years, and this period coincides with the age of terror in France after the Revolution. As a result of this crisis he becomes deaf which further alienates him from the outside world. From this moment onwards, his works follow a line which carries forward the conception of the great works of the War of Independence in Spain, the revolution which resulted in overthrowing the French and brought in at the same time a change in the traditional structures.

The picture *The Executions of the Third of May* (1814) shows a firing squad, a group of soldiers from behind, without faces, who shoot at a group of patriots illuminated by a lamp, the people who face us in the painting and who represent the pain of the country. The man who occupies the central position lifts his arms as though he is being crucified.

The Uprising of the Second of May of 1808 (1814) shows a group of patriots revolting against the Turkish army. In this work, Goya is more interested in the image of the multitude, the common "mass" agitated by the violence and the cruelty inflicted by the war on both sides.

In the same period he creates the series *The Disasters of War*, full of subtle moments of the brutality and irrationality of the war.

From 1816 onwards Goya starts on a series known as *Los Disparates* (blunders), whose principal theme could be the absurd. In this series,

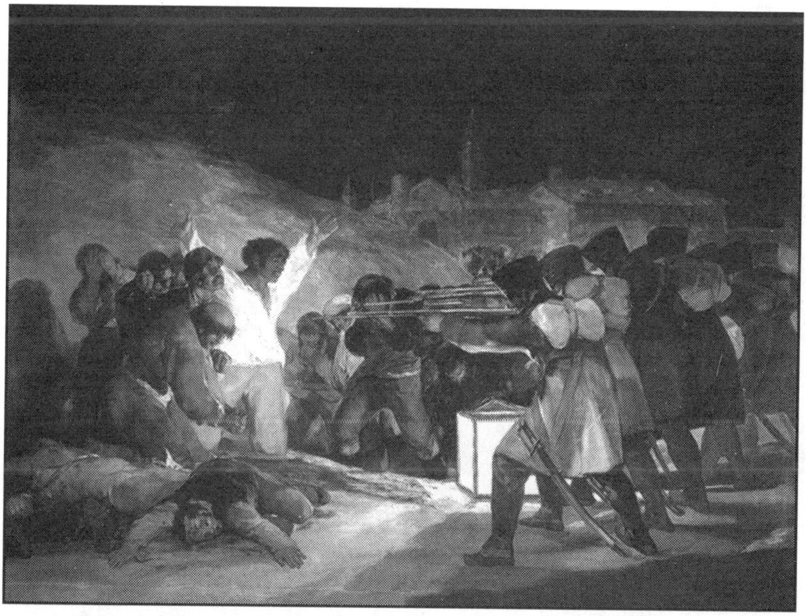

Fig. 7. Francisco de Goya, *The Executions of the Third of May 1808.*

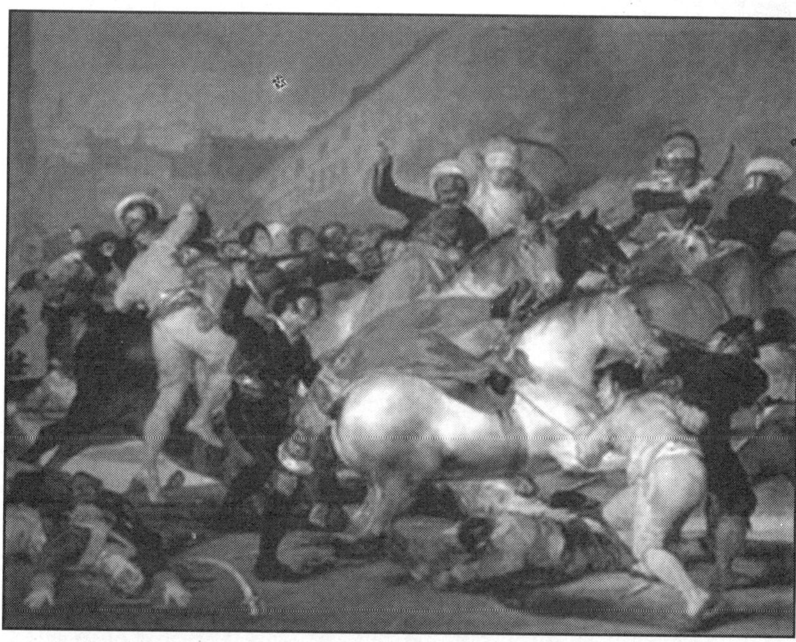

Fig. 8. Francisco de Goya, *The Uprising of the Second of May 1808.*

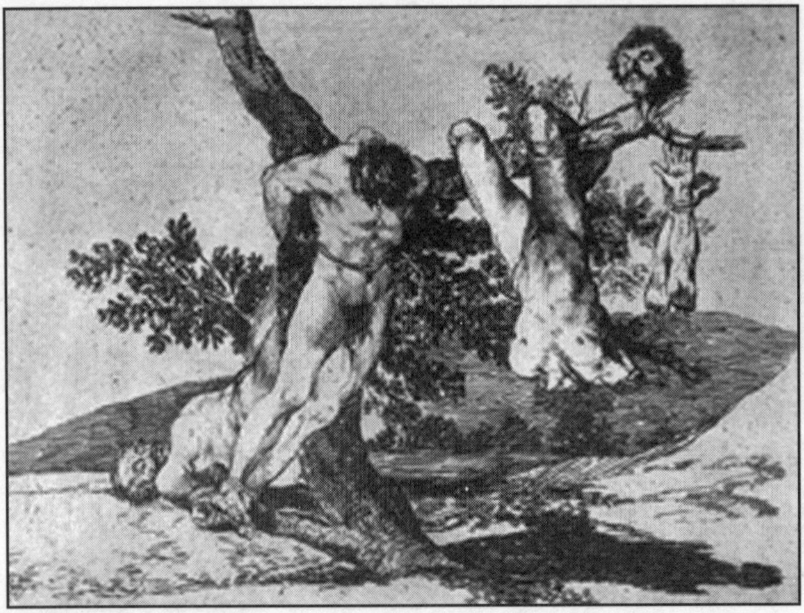

Fig. 9. Francisco de Goya, *The Disasters of War*.

images appear as a world that is "upside down", men fly and walk with their hands. The absurd presents the true face of reality. One must not forget that at this moment the Government of Fernando VII "El Deseado" (The Desired) comes to power. It abolished the Constitution, banned the newspapers, closed the universities and reestablished the Inquisition, creating an atmosphere of conspiracy and cheating, of insecurity and fear.

It is in this atmosphere that he paints *The Black Paintings*, during 1820-22. These are fresco paintings which he did on the walls of his house "La Quinta del Sordo" (the villa of the deaf). He uses a technique which consists in accumulating multitudes in a small space while the rest of the space remains absolutely vacant. Besides, he uses gigantic figures which produce a sensation of terror in front of the smallness of man.

During the "Decada Ominosa" (ominous decade) Goya decides to run away from Spain, under the pretext of taking baths necessary for his illness. He sets himself up in Burdeos with many Spanish intellectuals and from there on his painting become more tranquil.

At the age of eighty two he wrote, "I cannot see nor hear, I lack everything but I have surplus willpower". As a great creator of images, he was able to express this in his last work, a self-portrait in which he

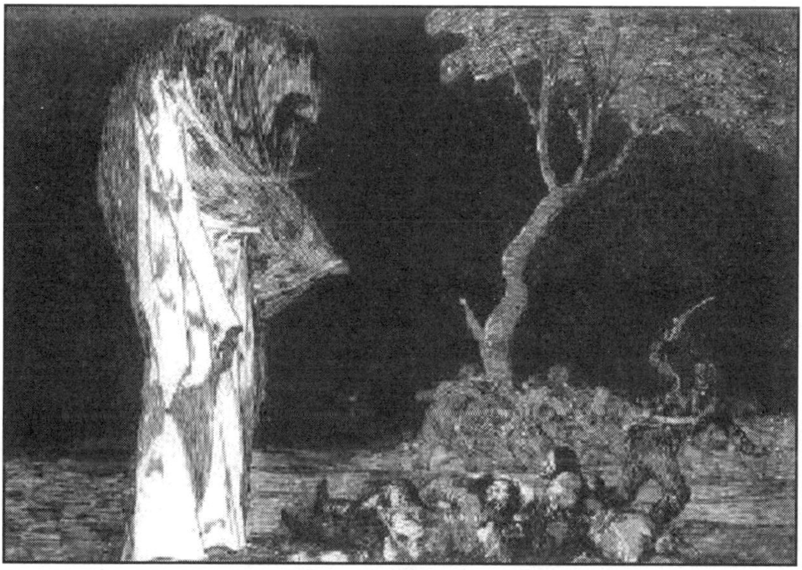

Fig. 10. Francisco de Goya, *Los Disparates*.

utilises a new technique which he had learned in France, lithography, in which an old man appears walking with the help of crutches. The title of the portrait is *I still learn*.

This thematic of fear would also be developed by other European artists. The Swiss painter Henry Fuseli[8] would be the creator of an iconography of the irrational, where nightmares, ghosts, witches and

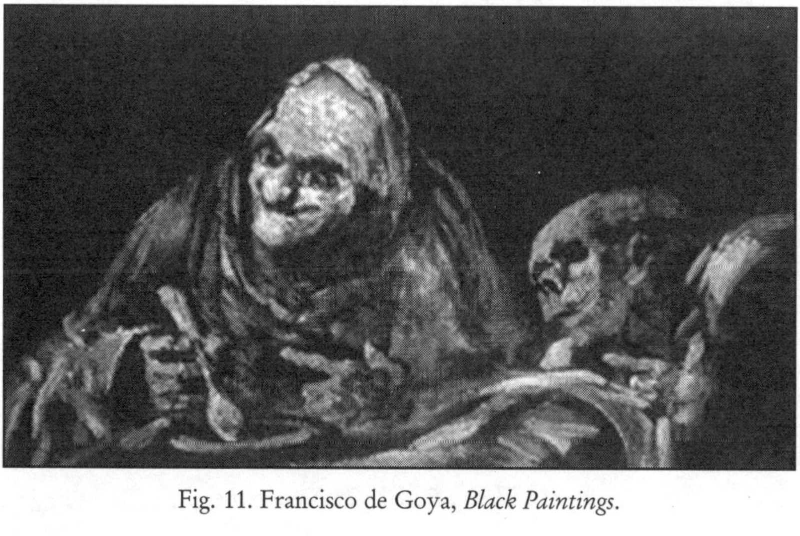

Fig. 11. Francisco de Goya, *Black Paintings*.

giants acquire a new dimension. Ordained into priesthood in his youth, he would soon feel closer to the groups of Romantic young bohemians and would be compelled to go to the British Islands.

Influenced by the works of Shakespeare, he would start working with dramatic themes related to fear, utilising a picturesque and mannerist language, almost on the lines of Michelangelo.

His work, which is very close to illustration, has a great formal liberty with hints of the expressionists. Ghosts, witches, and giants are part of his personal iconography and the horses turn into symbols of passion and sex. He is one of the most important representatives of the engagement with the non-rational in Romanticism.

The painting *The Nightmare* (1781) represents an oneiric universe where the horses, symbolizing the dream, make the women tremble while they are sleeping in bed.

In the works of the Englishman William Blake[9] there exists a prophetic force and he has been considered by critics as a visionary artist. The nature of his visions, images placed in his mind before he knows their meaning, give rise to the symbol which would be repeated time and again. These visions are stronger than the real world and are a great source of inspiration.

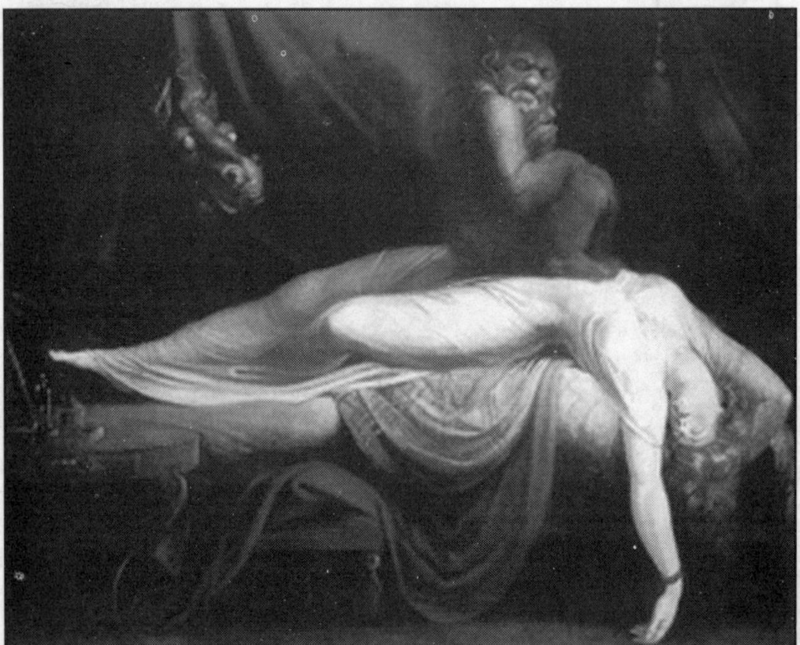

Fig. 12. Henry Fuseli, *The Nightmare*.

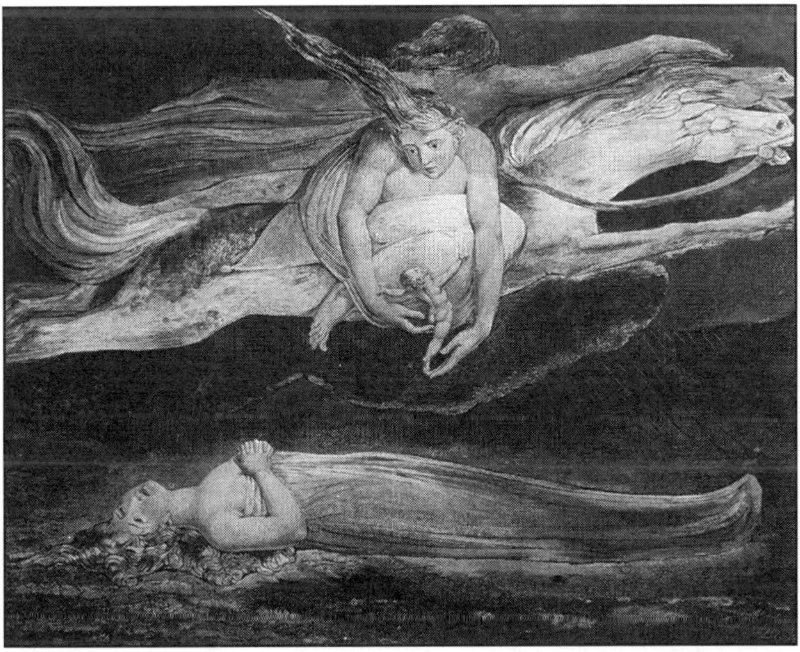

Fig. 13. William Blake, *Pity*.

One should not forget that since his childhood he loved to see prints compulsively and they would remain in his memory forever. Blake never considers nature as a model. "I should create my own system if I don't want to be a slave of anyone."

His medium of expression would be the illustration of books, his source of inspiration the middle ages and the themes he treated generally religious. Blake can be considered as a painter who was capable of giving a new interpretation to religion, as any good Romantic artist would do.

NOTES AND REFERENCES

1. Giovanni Battista Piranesi (1720 - 1778), also called Giambattista Piranesi, Italian draftsman, printmaker, architect, and art theorist.
2. K. Clark. *La rebelion Romantica*. Alianza Forma. Madrid, 1996.
3. Carl Gustav Carus (1789-1869), *Carus. Cartas y anotaciones sobre pintura de paisaje*. Alianza Forma. Madrid.
4. Caspar David Friedrich (1774 - 1840), pioneer of early nineteenth-century German Romantic painting.
5. J.M.W. Turner (1775 - 1851), in full Joseph Mallord William Turner English Romantic landscape painter.

6. John Constable (1776 - 1837), painter who, with J.M.W. Turner, dominated English landscape painting in the nineteenth century.
7. Francisco (José) de Goya (y Lucientes) (1746 - 1828), Spanish artist whose multifarious paintings, drawings, and engravings reflected contemporary historical upheavals and influenced important nineteenth- and twentieth-century painters.
8. Henry Fuseli, (1741 - 1825), original name Johann Heinrich Füssli. Swiss-born painter who settled in London in 1764.
9. William Blake (1757 - 1827), English poet, painter, engraver, and visionary mystic whose hand-illustrated series of lyrical and epic poems, beginning with *Songs of Innocence* (1789) and *Songs of Experience* (1794), form one of the most strikingly original and independent bodies of work in the Western cultural tradition.

REKHA BASU

Kant and the Limits of Rationality: A Reading of the *Groundwork of the Metaphysic of Morals*

Kant considered himself not only part of but also a guardian of the Enlightenment. In his pamphlet *What is Enlightenment* (1784), he answered the question in the title in terms of the process of "man's emergence from his self-imposed immaturity" to have the courage to live his life on the basis of his own thinking. The only condition necessary for beginning the process of enlightenment, for actually beginning to use our reason, Kant wrote, is freedom externally, the absence of institutional restraints on independent thought and public debate, and internally the courage to think for ourselves rather than let others do it for us.

'Reason' was not a monolith during the Enlightenment. It was partly Cartesian, and partly Lockean and Newtonian. Voltaire praised Descartes' methodical doubt which, he hoped, might be extended now beyond metaphysical ideas to social mores and institutions. Reason was Lockean in its distrust of all intellectual "systems", including those erected by the Cartesians on the basis of intuitive certainties. Reason as scientific was epitomised in the person of Isaac Newton who employed all weapons in the scientific arsenal - mathematics, experiment, observation - with equal ease. And finally, of course, it was Kantian or Critical, when it was suspicious of authority, tradition and revelation.

Rationality for Kant had a dual signification, it was a splintered reason - 'pure' reason and 'practical' reason. There was a programmatic similarity between the two sets of analysis: the projected goals for both pure reason and practical reason were to establish objectivity, universality and a priori foundations for their specified spheres of study. By undertaking a reading of *Groundwork of the Metaphysic of Morals*[1] (hitherto abbreviated to read *GM*) I wish to show a Janus-faced scholarship most of the time firmly entrenched in the Enlightenment and acquiescent in its agenda, but sometimes wavering and interrogating its contextual moorings. I believe it is this second Kant, backtracking and drawing boundaries to reason, that lent itself to Romantic appropriations.

Kant's moral theory draws its material from the ordinary person, the peasant, or the labourer. Kant's father had been a harness-maker. Kant believed that a life of privilege produced only a morality of selfish egoism, at whatever cost, to the lower classes. A morality of the people, on the other hand, would have to be objective and impartial. Within Kantian moral theory, this entailed a repudiation of moral relativism. Kant believed that philosophers had misapprehended morality by attempting to base it on experience. In *GM* he talks about 'cultivated reason' which, according to him, concerns itself with the aim of enjoying life and happiness, taking man away from 'true contentment'.

This is why there arises in many a misology, a hatred of reason. Part of Kant's endeavour in *GM* is to rehabilitate the status of moral claims vis-à-vis those of the physical sciences by grounding the former on reason. In Kant's moral theory the dignity of persons and their right to respect is grounded in their freedom - their ability to subordinate their particular desires and inclinations to the universal law of morality. What we subjectively want to do is called into question by a rational ideal of what we ought to do. Kant's parents had been devout Pietists, and his early education had been undertaken in an intensely pietistic school. Pietism emphasised practical faith and searched for the moral world in the ordinary everyday details of human living, and not within rigidly structured, otherworldly, monastic practices. From pietism Kant got his conviction that the morally good character of a person depends on that person's moral disposition of dutifulness or conscientiousness. Kant introduces the concept of a good will which is already present in a sound natural understanding and requires not so much to be taught as merely to be clarified.[2] According to Kant,

> A good will is not good because of what it effects or accomplishes... it is good through its willing alone - that is, good in itself.... Even if, by some special disfavour of destiny... this will is entirely lacking in power to carry out its intentions; if by its utmost effort it still accomplishes nothing, even then it would still shine like a jewel for its own sake as something which has its full value in itself.[3]

Kant lumps all motives other than the purely moral motive of acting solely from duty into the generic class of inclinations or desires.

Hence benevolence, philanthropy and parental love on the one hand, and selfish greed, the desire for sensual pleasure, and fear on the other, all without exception constitute the emotive and the conative which Kant wishes so ardently to exclude from a moral theory that receives its direction from reason alone.

This was the archetypal Enlightenment philosophy, impatient with the kaleidoscopic, the mutable and the inconstant even in the sphere of morality, debunking it in favour of the universal which could only be rationally derived. In the spirit of Newton Kant sought to construct laws for the moral life. The spectacular career of the natural sciences had greatly impressed Kant. Great advances in science - physics, astronomy, mechanics, and mathematics - had altered the conventional views about the nature of the universe. Reason began to be perceived as efficacious enough not only to explain all physical reality with relatively few fundamental and purely mathematico-mechanical laws of enormous scope and power, but also to create a new science of human nature.

Kant endeavoured to do this in *GM.* The Kantian moral agent was autonomous. But the autonomy was not a state of segregation; it incorporated within it a social obligation. In the formulation of one of the principles of moral life, Kant writes, 'I ought never to act except in such a way that I can also will that my maxim should become a universal law'.[4] The moral agent is not simply self-legislative, but must superintend universally. Self-empowerment is linked inextricably to the empowerment of humanity as a whole.

The thesis is corroborated by the second Imperative.[5] For rational beings all stand under the law that each of them should treat himself and all others, never merely as a means, but always at the same time as an end in himself.[6] Kant envisions a society as comprising of dynamic subjectivities, coordinating their moral efforts in the direction of producing a Kingdom of Ends.

Implicit in the Kingdom of Ends is a yearning for an organically connected society, a "...union of different rational being under common laws".[7] This is the vision that would have captured the Romantic imagination. Otherwise, the imperatives are couched in vocabulary (viz., universal law, self-consistency, etc.) that seems suspiciously Newtonian in its inspiration. Besides, Kant's faculty view of the mind, his insistent exclusion of the emotive and the conative from the formulations of moral laws, would have been inimical to the Romantic notion of the 'whole man' as an amalgamation of intellect and emotion, analytical reason and sympathetic, intuitive understanding. Kant, because he located the thing-in-itself *outside* the structures of knowledge provided by the understanding, cannot really attain to the view of the universe as a dynamic organism, which is so central to the Romantic *Weltanschauung*.

Despite these convictions in Kantian epistemology and moral theory, views completely at variance with the Romantic philosophy, the spirit of Kantian thought, synthesis, becomes a leitmotif for the Romantic thought. The Romantic ideal is to try and overcome externality, isolation and division; it knocks down boundaries between knowledge, religion and art. For instance, the creative artist, according to Herder, is also a pedagogue who must not just indulge in solitary exploitation of his talents, but dedicate them to the edification of his fellow men. Fichte, whose derivation from Kant was unmistakable, utilised Kantian 'synthesis of transcendental apperception', combined it with the freedom of the human will (a postulate of Kant's moral theory) and formed his principle of 'Ich', the ultimate principle of knowledge. The 'Ich' did not have connotations of an individual subject, but signified the totality of subjective reality, which is the unifying principle of all individual egos and has the stature of a suprapersonal objective *Ich-prinzip*.

It should be remembered that Kant's own notion of the transcendental self did not possess a principle of individuation. It was a logical construct, and to that extent, presumably belonged to each person. Kant did not even address himself to trying to resolve this tangle; he did not perceive it as a problem, viz., the reality and plurality of the subjects in his epistemology. I believe this is what assimilates the Pure reason to Practical reason. The Kingdom of Ends, though a great respecter of persons and a precursor of socialism in Europe in a sense, is complemented by the requirement of the universalizability. Both in knowledge, and in moral conduct, Kant strove for objectivity.

Kant writes in the *GM*,

> ... a rational being must regard himself qua intelligence...as belonging to the intelligible world, not to the sensible one. He has therefore two points of view from which he can regard himself and from which he can know laws governing the employment of his powers and consequently governing all his actions. He can consider himself first - so far as he belongs to the sensible world - to be under laws of nature (heteronomy) and secondly, so far as he belongs to the intelligible world to be under laws which, being independent of nature, are not empirical but have their ground in reason alone.[8]

This discussion would have been very accessible to the Romantic imagination. Further, writing about freedom in a section called 'The antinomy of freedom and necessity' Kant says,

> Freedom... is a mere idea: its objective validity can in no way be exhibited by reference to laws of nature and consequently cannot be exhibited in any possible reference. Thus the Idea of freedom can never admit of full comprehension, or indeed of insight, since it can never by any analogy have an example falling under it.[9]

This fundamental invulnerability of freedom to the categorising intellect really marks the limits of the Enlightenment rationality. The Enlightenment ideology had definitely intruded into Kant's moral project in terms of his search for the a priori, universal and unvarying imperatives of moral life. But his 'modus operandi' lands him in inconsistencies. Delineating upon the programme of the *GM* Kant writes,

> ... such a completely isolated metaphysics of morals, mixed with no anthropology, no theology, no physics, no hyperphysics, still less with occult qualities... is not only an indispensable substratum of all theoretical and precisely defined knowledge of duties, but is at the same time a desideratum of the utmost importance for the actual execution of moral precepts.[10]

Now, there are clear contradictions in this position because, having resolved not to use experience for a metaphysics of morals, Kant effortlessly resorts to explicitly empirical premises in order to prove, for instance, the unviability of a possible law of lying.

> Keeping promises is a moral law not because of any intrinsic worth that might belong to promise-keeping, but because of considerations, which are purely prudential.[11]

This regress to experience, though incongruent with Kant's self-confessed goals, is fertile with possibilities. There will be many traditions, post Kant, which will retain the experiential and resist its denigration. Within ethics itself you witness a wide breath of theories of conduct that reject a deontologized norm of conduct, and that address themselves to the antecedent conditions of moral choice, which presuppose a moral agent, which is not truncated but feeling, emoting, and ratiocinating as well. To Kant goes the credit for having energized debates in both knowledge and ethics.

NOTES

1. Immanuel Kant, 'Groundwork of the Metaphysic of Morals' in *The Moral Law*, trans. H.J. Paton, London: Hutchinson University Library, 1966.
2. *Ibid.*, 3/397.
3. *Ibid.*, 3/394.

4. *Ibid.*, 17/402.
5. The conception of an objective principle so far as this principle is necessitating for a will is called a command (of reason), and the formula of this command is called an imperative.
6. *Ibid.*, 75/434.
7. *Ibid.*, 74/433.
8. *Ibid.*, 109/453.
9. *Ibid.*, 115/456.
10. *Ibid.*, 33/411.
11. *Ibid.*, 19/403.

REFERENCES

L. Aberscrombie, *Romanticism*, London, 1926.

E. Bernbaum, *Guide through the Romantic Movement*, New York, 1949.

L.R. Furst, *Romanticism Reconsidered*, Columbia, 1963.

E. D. Keyser, *The Romantic West*, 1789-1850. Geneva, 1965.

J.L. Talmon, *Romanticism and Revolt*, London, 1967.

S.S. Prawer ed., *The Romantic Period in Germany*, London: Institute of Germanic Studies, 1970.

R. Taylor, *The Romantic Tradition in Germany*, London: Methuen & Co. Ltd., 1970.

KATHLEEN KERR

What is Modernity? Habermas and/or de Man

In claiming that citations not only legitimate scholarship, but 'remind us of a former way of posing a question, to prove that an answer that has become classic is no longer satisfactory, that it has itself become historical and demands of us a renewal of the process of question and answer,[1] Hans Robert Jauss pronounces on a key issue in the debates over the concept of modernity: does the turn to language in the arenas of deconstruction and critical theory make history redundant or significant in the formation of theory? In the case of the question of modernity, is an understanding of history necessary for the formulation of a theory of modernity or should 'the formation of theory reflect on the history of its formation'.[2] In Jauss's view, citations initiate the repetition of the process of question and answer in the light of an historically redundant answer. Thus, when Locke cites the classic Cartesian description of the 'I' as *res cogitans*, he reissues and historicises the question of subjectivity by indicating the problem of the perpetuity of personal identity when the substance of the thinking thing changes, and posits a new theory in which a natural association of ideas is secured through experience, each idea marked for reference by a word. In re-historicising subjectivity, Kant cites both Leibniz's 'noogony' and Locke's 'sensualised...concepts of the understanding' in proposing a bifurcated 'empirical' and 'transcendental' 'I', and Hegel cites Kant in raising the problem of grounding such a diremptive 'I' when he makes it a self-reflexive concrete universal. For Jürgen Habermas, on the other hand, this renewal of the question of the philosophical 'I' is more than a response to the redundancy of an earlier description: the repetition is the grounding principle of modernity, and the main theme running through the philosophical discourse of modernity.

In fact, the concept of modernity has been configured in various ways, which accord with methods of research and ideological interests. In the nineteenth century, for example, Marx viewed modernity as the constant renewal of the impulse toward change (changing modes of production) and thus as an (alienating) effect of the dynamics of capital accumulation.[3] By contrast in the twentieth century, someone like Matei Calinescu, whose concerns are more aesthetic than social scientific, sees modernity as both unrepeatable sequential historical time which is enlightened and secular and yet unavoidably linked with Christian eschatology as developing industrialisation, and contradictorily, as a self-questioning connected with the death of God which fractures the 'human' with political, linguistic and cultural constructions of subjectivity that compromise any easy faith in progressive teleology.[4] For Peter Osbourne, modernity is primarily a temporal concept which has nevertheless been made possible because of certain spatial preconditions: these are the unification of the globe through colonial navigation which allows for the thought of history as a whole, and the hierarchical distinction of European from non-European cultures, in which an historical differentiation could be introduced within the present.[5] For Christopher Norris, modernity is to be understood as a turn to subjectivity which starts with Descartes' quest for knowledge self evident to reason and secure from all the demons of sceptical doubt: it is invoked to signify the currents of thought that emerged from Kant's critical revolution in the spheres of epistemology, ethics and aesthetic judgement.[6] In all of these descriptions, modernity as a concept is doubled: on the one hand, it is monologically rational (or rationalising), evolutionary and attached to some notion of progress; on the other hand, it is in conflict with history, bound to 'recapitulate the break brought about by the past as a *continuous renewal*'.[7] In this paper I want to take up this theme of doubling by comparing Jürgen Habermas's view of modernity as an 'unfinished project' with Paul de Man's view of it as a concept at odds with history.

Putting Habermas next to de Man – that is the claims of critical theory next to those of deconstruction – would be anathema for most. Habermas is a social theorist and a philosopher and is concerned with theorising the intersubjective conditions that would facilitate a public sphere capable of continuing the Enlightenment project; de Man is a literary critic concerned primarily with pitting signification against the inescapable forces of institutionalisation upon which the concept of modernity rests. Habermas's concern is to theorise a unifying context for communicative action; de Man's main concern is to contextualise resistances to the unity and universality of theory. Habermas explicitly eschews the kind of postmetaphysical thinking that dismisses a lifeworld background which would make possible a public sphere of communicative action; de Man scrupulously analyses - especially in his later work – how literariness, 'the use of language that foregrounds the rhetorical over the grammatical and logical function', persistently disrupts the inner balance of the *trivium* (grammar, rhetoric, logic) and its articulation with the *quadrivium* (arithmetic, geometry, astronomy, music).[8]

This dissimilarity between Habermasian critical theory and de Manian critico-linguistics can, in fact, be reduced to a single difference: that of defining what philosophy is and should aspire towards. This difference prevents any productive synthesis of the two. But my claim here is that the debate over the value of one perspective over another, and the investment that thinkers have put in maintaining the mutual exclusivity of the two approaches, has thus far precluded a potentially useful critical engagement between them on the question of modernity. For Habermas the project of modernity - that is the pursuit of progressive intersubjective action that leads to a maturity of thought in the linking of the One with the Many - is still unfinished, and the linguistic turn in philosophy, pace Derrida's reading of Saussure and others, has not rendered the project redundant, but provided the opportunity for rethinking communicative action. By contrast, for de Man, the term 'modernity' papers over the inescapable *aporia* that exists between two orders - the phenomenal and the material - that are so different in kind as to prohibit any synthesising dialectic. Whereas Habermas reformulates the marxist notion of *praxis* – understood as political, economic or ethical action instigated through the union of subjective and objective realms - by distinguishing between what Marx understood as 'work' or 'purposive rational action' and what he himself understands as 'interaction' or communicative action, de Man couples *theoria* with *aesthesia* in order to reveal the source of the problem of *praxis*. And whereas Habermas restricts his speculations to the discourse of philosophy, de Man works with writers/thinkers that straddle the two domains of philosophy and literature. Finally, whereas for Habermas aesthetic discourse, which reaches its apex with romanticism, represents a strong counter-discourse within the philosophical discourse of modernity, for de Man, the institutional framework in which the work of the so-called 'romantic' writing is housed, precludes its functioning as the radical counter-discourse that it strives to be.

Habermas reads a clear distinction between aesthetic discourse and the philosophical discourse of modernity: in aesthetic discourse, before the rise of philosophical aesthetics, the problem of the 'modern' emerges with the problem of conceptualising the 'new', rather than configuring subjectivity. By way of example, in the seventeenth century, Jonathan Swift's *Battle of the Books*[9] memorialised in a fictional context what would emerge in the eighteenth century as the *querelle des anciens et des modernes* which represented the struggle between two different world views brought on by the advance of modern natural science. In this context what becomes an issue is the new *ethos*, rather than the logical grounding so important to the epistemologists. Swift's *Battle* threw into focus the character of the *Moderns*, their Enlightenment emphasis on individuation, progress and reason in contrast to the *Ancient's* orientation toward scholarship: the *Ancients* - described as bee-like in their productivity and endowed with studiousness, range, and judgement - declare war on the *Moderns* - who are spider-like in their laziness, contemplative and proud, entirely self-nurturing and scorning any obligation to outside influences. The war constitutes a theoretical, aesthetic and linguistic impasse: action is anything but dialogic. The dramatic outcome (the *Ancients* arise supreme in eradicating the *Moderns*) radicalises the importance of the *Ancients* found in the work of men such as John of Salisbury and Michel Montaigne, for whom the *Moderns* were like dwarfs, standing on the shoulders of the earlier *Ancient* giants, products of earlier accomplishments rather than examples of personal and independent achievement.

In focusing on the temporal element in art history and philosophical history, eighteenth century French *philosophie de l'histoire* circumnavigated the problem of the mutual exclusivity of the standards of perfection represented by the *Anciens* and *Modernes*.[10] Thus the French Enlightenment represents an 'epochal turning point' where singular history wins out and emerges as a new beginning, a new grounding, a new 'self understanding' as the meaning of classical imitation is critiqued and a new aesthetic is posed, conjoining, following the model of modern natural science, the notion of perfection with that of progress. Later eighteenth century German philosophical aesthetics carries this theme forward in overturning the pre-eminence of reason over the imagination.

The philosophical discourse of modernity, on the other hand, can be thought to begin with Descartes' *cogito* and the formulation of the ground for the rise of the modern sovereign rational subject. Jacques Derrida describes this event as an internal modification in the history of Western metaphysics in line with the determination of being as presence and the final reduction of the trace which continues through Rousseau, Kant and the Enlightenment philosophers arising again with Ferdinand de Saussure's *Course in General Linguistics* and structuralism.[11] The philosophical discourse of modernity turns on this rise of the sovereign subject, rational and moral and, after Kant, governed by *a priori* categories. The concept is preserved in the eighteenth century with the removal of rhetoric from the classical trivium: aesthetics then achieves autonomy with 'disinterestedness' as it is distanced from the immediate concerns of *logos* and *ethos*. This allows for the individuation of the dual domains of mind/body, reason/unreason, philosophy/literature imbedded in a value hierarchy where the philosophical, the rational, and the spiritual are prioritised over the literary, irrational and material. In this the important cognitive function of the literary is suborned to the theorising interests of philosophy.

But the rise of aesthetics in the eighteenth century also provides the opportunity for a counter-enlightenment discourse to develop: from Schiller and the romantics to Nietzsche, Marx, the left Hegelians, Heidegger, Adorno and Horkheimer, Derrida and those poststructuralists that follow a new counter-discourse directed toward the 'desublimation and de-centering' of the sovereign rational subject. This new discourse affirms the values of contingency, conventionality, plurality of worlds, heterogeneity, semiotic systems lacking foundations, the economy of desire, and the historical and cultural character of categories of thought and structures of action. Modernity thus comes to designate both the discourse of reason and a radicalising counter discourse. From this perspective, romanticism, modernism and postmodernism can be viewed as aesthetic categories that participate in, but cannot be reduced to, the philosophical discourse of modernity. All of this is distinguished from the process of modernisation which is rationalisation through technology and the development of bureaucratic state apparatuses operating in conjunction with capitalism.

Now Habermas and de Man enter the counter-discourse of modernity, or what Habermas calls 'postmetaphysical thinking', from very different angles: de Man's interest in the late part of his career is with the technical aspects of 'critico-linguistics', while Habermas's late linguistic turn takes the form of wresting a lifeworld and a domain of communicative action from the process of rationalisation. This difference is of course crucial, because de Man's linguistic turn exacerbates his earlier phenomenological insights in not merely fracturing understanding, but exploding it; Habermas's turn, on the other hand, opens up new vistas for understanding. After *Knowledge and Human Interests*, in fact,

Habermas's linguistic turn necessarily includes the embracing of certain truths about language that are already assumed by de Man in his early writings of the '50's and 60's. Habermas clearly admires de Man's early work, though this respect is not matched by a closeness to it, for he gets it wrong when he groups de Man in with critics who he describes as 'levelling of the genre distinction between literary criticism and literature.'[12] In actual fact the incisiveness of de Man's thinking depends upon a clear, albeit temporary, circumscription of generic, categorial and cognitive domains.

Nevertheless, de Man and Habermas can be thought to enter the debate with significant points of connection in their thinking, that is in the area of methodology, in the importance attributed to romanticism, in the centrality of their respective critiques of Hegel and Nietzsche. After Habermas wrote *Knowledge and Human Interests* he realised immediately that the Kantian notion of self-reflection was ambivalent - that the distinction between self-reflection as the grasp of 'universal and necessary conditions for the very possibility of theoretical knowledge, practical reason and teleological and aesthetic judgement' and the freedom-oriented, emancipatory sense of self reflection was not made clear. In *Theory of Communicative Action* he redresses this oversight by preserving the Kantian programme of transcendental philosophy, but without a foundation in *a priori* concepts. In other words, in making his own inquiry scientific he proceeded on the basis of empirical testing of hypotheses.

So, to his earlier category of empirical/analytical sciences (such as the natural whose interests were technical and were served by instrumental reason) he added the reconstructive sciences, whose aims are to provide explicit theoretical knowledge of implicit 'pre-theoretical' knowledge; in other words, rather than being a form of transcendental philosophy, reconstructive sciences seek to make explicit 'universal species competences' in the context of empirical research verified by canons of truth and falsehood. But reconstructive sciences differ from empirical sciences in that, rather than seeking to 'replace' 'pre-theoretical' knowledge with a more adequate scientific explanation of the world, they explain and clarify the basic grammar of our 'pre-theoretical knowledge'. Now the theory of communicative action and rationality (also called Universal Pragmatics because it seeks to isolate, identify and clarify conditions required for human communication and because, for Habermas, all human symbolic competence presupposes the universal species competence of communication) is a 'reconstructive science' but it differs from the others in that it has a more 'universalist thrust' than the others ('linguistics and theories of psychological and moral development'). It is precisely that reconstructive science which enables us to specify the contributions and limitations of reconstructive sciences that have more restricted domains.

De Man's critical methodology also eschews Kantian *a priori* imperatives: his work consistently seeks to provide explicit theoretical knowledge (knowing that) from implicit pre-theoretical knowledge (knowing how). Unlike the social sciences, however, what is at stake for de Man is precisely the 'transcendental' status of theoretical knowledge on literature. Theory in the area of literary studies is 'a controlled reflection on the formation of method' which uncovers a tension, or a resistance, between truth and method, or scholarship and theory. Literary language cannot be contained by the 'Cratylism of the name' since the phenomenality of the signifier (where sound links the thing named and the name) is reduced to the materiality of convention in the relationship between the signifier and the signified. He calls this 'non-phenomenal linguistics' and views it as a way of freeing the discourse on literature from uncritical aesthetic and mimetic (and its counterpart, pure verbalist) conceptions of art. Although he recognises that this view of language is epistemologically unreliable; nevertheless,

> ...in a genuine semiology as well as in other linguistically oriented theories, the referential function of language is not being denied – far from it; what is in question is its authority as a model for natural or phenomenal cognition. Literature is fiction not because it somehow refuses to acknowledge 'reality', but because it is not a priori certain that language functions according to principles which are those, or which are like those, of the phenomenal world. It is therefore not a priori certain that literature is a reliable source of information about anything but its own language.[13]

He drives this point home when he says that

> No one in his right mind would try to grow grapes by the luminosity of the word 'day' but it is very difficult not to conceive the pattern of one's past and future existence in accordance with temporal and spatial schemes that belong to fictional narratives and not to the world.

The 'linguistics of literariness' is a double-edged sword: on the one hand, in blindly ignoring the difference between linguistics and natural reality, or the difference between the referential function of language and phenomenalism, it participates in both the production of, and unmasking of, 'ideological aberrations.' Built into the very question of literary theory, then, is the notion of 'resistance', defined as the 'resistance to the use of language about language'.[14]

Hegel and Nietzsche function importantly for both thinkers: Habermas sees Hegel as having inaugurated the discourse of modernity, and the first philosopher to view modernity as an epochal concept. Hegel viewed the problem of modernity as couched in the constellation of modernity, time-consciousness, and rationality: elevating Spirit to the Absolute obviated the conditions under which it achieved itself and this made modernity conscious to itself. In this Kant's third antimony of causality becomes a dialectic of freedom and determination. *Phenomenology of Mind* tackles the problem of appearances by claiming that we can only know Reality when we have completely mastered appearances. Appearances (material and mental phenomena) both hide and reveal Reality (noumena, *Geist*, spirit, mind) - the history of human consciousness consists of appearances, images and illusions as consciousness itself moves through various stages and levels of development on its way toward Absolute Truth. Hegel, as Habermas points out, was the first to think 'modernity' as a resistance to both the religion of reason and religious Orthodoxy: both forms were guilty of what he called *Positivität*[15], or the authoritarian linking of the two worlds of finite and infinite by faith rather than reason. As Habermas says

> 'Positive' applies to prescriptions according to which the faithful are supposed to earn God's benevolence through works instead of moral action; to the hope for compensation in the beyond; to the divorce of a doctrine in the hands of a few from the life and possession of all; to the detachment of priestly knowledge from the fetishised belief of the masses, as well as to the detour that supposedly leads to morality only by way of the authority and miraculous deeds of one person; to all the assurances and threats aimed at the sheer legality of action; finally and above all, to the separation of private religion from public life.

The Enlightenment had mistakenly raised understanding (*Verstand*) which is finite, to the level of the Absolute. This idolatry of Reason - achieved only by sublating the understanding to the status of Reason itself which inevitably leads to a relapse when the activity of Reason is fixed in opposition - pretentiously and groundlessly assumes rationality. Both the religions of reason and Orthodoxy used Biblical exegesis as a means of critically founding their independent directions. The religion of reason, the felicity of which depends on the condition of subjective freedom, only reinforces modernity's diremptive condition rather than, as Hegel would have it, 'shaping religion into the ethical totality of an entire nation and of inspiring a life of political freedom'.[16]

But Hegel's thinking, as Habermas indicates, is recuperated precisely by the thinking it critiques: Hegel makes the finite understanding posit the infinite as absolute even before it is *demonstrated* that 'a kind of reason which is more than an absolutised understanding can convincingly reunify the antithesis that reason has to unfold discursively.'[17]

With Nietzsche, subject-centred reason is submitted to an immanent critique and he gives up the dialectic of the Enlightenment. By following 'the road not taken' by Nietzsche and subsequent poststructuralists, Habermas seeks to transpose the dialectic of consciousness into that of intersubjectivity. This entails both a recognition that operates reciprocally and non-coercively, and is directed toward mutual understanding. The totality of ethical life becomes paramount here: unification and reconciliation are based on rational agreement conducted in the everyday lifeworld through communicative action. The de-centred subject participates, through the medium of language, where the relation between meaning and validity claims is both conditioned and continually revised, but ultimately directed beyond local contexts. Validity serves as the foundation of an existing consensus. Hence the foundation of 'discourse ethics' is in the universalisation of moral norms and the development of ethical personal identities. But all of this is dependent upon a clear distinction between the structural intentions of philosophical and literary discourses.

In *The Philosophical Discourse of Modernity*, Habermas describes two versions of the *posthistoire* that he claims arise after the discursive shift that occurs when social-scientific functionalism supersedes Weberian classical sociology. Whereas the earlier tradition focuses on modernity as both cultural secularisation and the institutionalisation of the dual systems of purposive rationality taking shape around capitalist enterprise and the bureaucratic state apparatus emerging in the wake of Christianity, the latter concentrates on the cumulative and mutually reinforcing processes of modernisation such as the formation and development of capital, centralisation of political power and the rise of national identities, formal schooling, voting rights, etc. The effect of this discursive shift is to abstract modernity from its situated historicity - that is as a phenomenon peculiar to the European Occident - thus making modernisation the theory of evolutionary development with universal application. What gets lost in this is 'the historical objectification of rational structures', the internal linkage 'between modernity and the historical context of Western rationalism, in other words, 'the conceptual horizon of Western rationalism'. On this abandonment of the historically situated condition of modernity, two post-Enlightenment discourses arise, one neoconservative the other anarchistic. The neoconservative discourse of the *posthistoire* accepts the crystallised and unswayable functional societal structures established by modernity, but renders cultural modernity in itself obsolete as the processes of modernisation accelerate; the anarchistic discourse, on the other hand, rejects the validity of both societal modernity and cultural modernity, unmasking reason as the will to instrumental mastery which becomes objectified in the so-called 'iron cage' of societal modernity, and when exposed is dispelled as 'primordial anarchism takes over.

Although de Man also eschews the paradigm of consciousness, he is from the beginning sceptical about getting beyond Hegel. He sees Hegelianism in all historicising strategies, whether they are organic or genetic. In 'Sign and Symbol in Hegel's *Aesthetics*' de Man declares that '...whether we know it, or like it, or not, most of us are Hegelians and quite orthodox ones at that.'[18] He indicates the investment literary practitioners have in equating aesthetics with poetics, or literary experience with literary theory, which he interprets in Hegelian terms as the equating of art with the symbolic. Hegel's *Aesthetics* stands out as the key text that both appears to theorise the accomplishment of this equation; on the other hand, the text asserts this 'concrete interpenetration of meaning and of form' at the very moment that he declares the end of art. De Man points to the irony of a literary history that would finish art 'at the very moment that a new modernity was about to discover and to refine the power of the symbol beyond anything that Hegel's somewhat philistine taste could ever have imagined?'[19] Aesthetic theory that follows grapples with this complication in Hegel, only to dismiss him as naïve or useless for understanding the art and literature that follows him. But de Man reads in this peculiar irony a far more complicated condition. On de Man's reading Hegel's philosophy, like all philosophies that strive to contain the experiential in the theories of history, is an 'allegory of the disjunction between philosophy and history, between literature and aesthetic...between literary experience and literary theory'.[20]

De Man is also extremely sceptical about the possibility of disentangling literary from philosophical discourse, though he is always careful to respect the so-called intentional structure of all texts. He is wary indeed of the possibility of an aesthetic critique of philosophy. In his early work he shows how every text can be given two antithetical, mutually contradictory readings and how it is often impossible to prioritise one over the other based on some notion of intentional structure. His later readings show how this impossibility is further exacerbated at every moment in the reading of a text as the figural and the literal are always inescapably present. The choice of one or the other at every moment radically influences the production of meaning. In short, he shows how John Locke's fear that the unnatural association of ideas might lead to the production of monsters is justified, as it is the inevitable outcome of reading. From this perspective, reading can only be viewed as an allegory, every one inevitably made redundant on every subsequent repetition of the process.

This insight is carried forward in his late work when he reads philosophical texts. In the essays on Locke, Kant, Pascal, Hegel, Schiller and Kierkegaard, he shows how propositional structures inevitably struggle with figuration and how the movement of philosophical texts is determined by the necessary but impossible task of controlling figuration. Ultimately, this control is facilitated by using figures to mask or paper over aporias or contradictions in the argument. Under these conditions theorising discourses (in particular aesthetics) lose their critical functions and begin to collaborate with any regime of knowledge. Theory is thus never fully successful in achieving the status of critique: it is inevitably made complicit with ideology.

The value of de Man's deconstructive critique has been undermined since the 1988 emergence of his wartime journalism. This was particularly true in Britain and in America where his work seemed to threaten the very foundations of the literary canon. His work was associated with a pernicious form of Nietzscheanism, which was no doubt linked to his collaboration with Nazism: romantic critics who had grown up with the lessons of Paul de Man had to then clarify the relationships they had drawn between Nietzsche and such writers as Shelley, Keats and Blake - distancing their readings from the influence of de Manian deconstruction. Hence it was possible to condemn his suspicious motivations, meanwhile keeping on board a distorted version of his work. On the one hand, for some critics de Manian Nietzscheanism was pernicious precisely because it was 'postmetaphysical': it not only appropriated Nietzsche's critique of Kantian metaphysics - his questioning of the value of 'the will to truth', his notion of untruth as a condition of life; his critique of *a priori* categories of mind which guarantee a transcendental realm of true knowledge; his claim that truth is one interpretation based on a pragmatic need for stability; his critique of the picture theory of language - but it also adopted a 'death of the author' stance, flouting Nietzsche's clear advocacy of unlimited expressivity in the 'will to power'. In retrieving the importance of expressivity in Nietzsche's philosophy, it was then possible to draw parallels between Nietzsche and romantic writers - to talk, for example, about Shelley's sceptical idealism.

On the other hand, de Manian Nietzscheanism was pernicious not so much because it was pluralist - many critics were happy to read many voices in the operation of romantic texts - but because it annihilated the vocabulary upon which the historical notion of self-fashioning could claim to exist. These critics were happy to concede to a pluralism of perfected liberal democracy - 'the end of history' in Francis Fukuyama's[21] sense - but they were unwilling to read romantic writers as the first 'modern' writer's to perceive the 'nothingness of being'. Ironically, then, in this critique of de Manianism where what becomes the most important issue is how the reading of these romantic writers will be institutionalised, de Man's strongest insight is confirmed.

Habermas himself has been accused of a certain short-sightedness in his Universal Pragmatics - Edward Said points out that for all his talk about 'discourse ethics' he does not address racist theory, anti-imperialist resistance or oppositional practice in the empire. And on this charge Habermas admits to Eurocentrism, saying that he has nothing to say about 'anti-capitalist, anti-imperialist struggles in the Third World. De Man's thinking, on the other hand, is oriented toward resistance, the inevitability of resistance to theory. In other words, while de Man's thinking finds the resistance in all forms of representation, Habermas's thinking refuses to represent resistance.

It is precisely resistance that de Man reads in romantic aesthetics, a 'paradoxical dialectic' that is eliminated in the institutionalisation of the term 'romanticism'. In a recent book called *The Meaning of Literature*, Timothy Weiss makes the claim that all of literature itself is a romantic institution. By this he means that the terms that serve to circumscribe canons - genius, image, symbol - all take their bearings from eighteenth century debates. De Man was early to point this out: but he also noted how the modern was understood in relation to the institutionalised romantic Anglo-American criticism of the early 1960's. Earl Wasserman and M.H. Abrams, for example, viewed a pre-romantic aesthetic as having failed because it was painfully impotent, unable to move beyond analogy to 'internalise the external and integrate the spiritual and the phenomenal'. From this perspective the romantics were seen as able to participate in history making - in true Hegelian fashion - insofar as they succeed in overcoming the crisis of poetic failure of their pre-romantic predecessors, and hence move aesthetics on to a more totalising plane of epistemology. In this the romantic period is seen as characterised by romantic writers who self-consciously address (and indeed solve) the problem of 'healing' the mind/body dualism that opens with Descartes. What is overcome in this periodising, historicising strategy, then, is a very anti-historical enlightenment logic in which the struggle between 'reason' and 'unreason' is consciously resolved with reason, via the imagination, winning out.

For de Man this periodising technique depends on the conflation of the phenomenal with the material. It has a counterpart in the work of Georg Lukács where changing modes of production are posited, rather than consciousness, as the means by which reason necessarily works through history. As Lukács puts it,

> the reasonableness of human progress develops ever-increasingly out of the inner conflict of social forces in history itself...history itself is the bearer and realiser of human progress.[22]

In the first instance, progress amounts to the objectification of rational structures, where the polarities rational/irrational, analytical/existential, consciousness/faith underwrite the differences between philosophy and literature, and where literature is cancelled out with the predominance of philosophy. In the second instance these binarisms invite a synthesis, the form of which is determined nevertheless by philosophy: the narrative of this synthesis consists of the aggregate of historical periods. But conflating the philosophical and the literary - as these techniques do - eliminates or distorts the problem of the history, reducing it to an antithesis between 'positions of extreme positivism or equally extreme subjective primitivism'.[23] Both of these positions make the *concept* of modernity merely the process of modernisation, an evolutionary process the effect of which is to not only contribute to the discourse of 'postmodernity' (after modernisation, *posthistoire*), but also, more importantly as Habermas notes, it

> dissociates 'modernity' from its modern European origins and stylise(s) it into a spatio-temporally neutral model for processes of social development in general. Furthermore, it breaks the internal connections between modernity and the historical context of Western rationalism, so that processes of modernisation can no longer be conceived of as rationalisation, as the historical objectification of rational structures.[24]

De Man too rejects what he calls the 'misconceived' formulation of modernism, which posits absolute changes that nevertheless accrue in evolutionary terms as progress. This understanding of modernism leads to ways of reading in which early works are overcome at a higher level in later works. This happens with critical evaluations of Georg Lukács's work, for example. Often (especially in the American context) Lukács's works are divided into pre and post Marxist phases whereby the early pre-Marxist period is simplistically rejected for political reasons. In these cases the theoretical/political interest motivates methodological procedures. By contrast, de Man reads continuity in his oeuvre, which must be understood in terms of philosophical strengths and weaknesses in relation to the nineteenth and twentieth century intellectual heritage of European romanticism and idealism.[25] This philosophical context constitutes for de Man what Habermas calls the 'conceptual horizon of Western rationalism in which modernity arose'.[26] Habermas, like de Man, is not concerned with evaluating modernism as an aesthetic affect as is Lukács (suggested at least by a reading of one strand of his work). In aestheticising modernism, Lukács reads it as psychopathology, a wholesale and summary rejection of reality which is purely subjective and lacking both content and direction. Like Freud's psychoanalysis, it is an empty gesture: it expresses nausea, longing or discomfort. It represents an ideological problem related to the dogma of the solitariness of man, to the glorification of the abnormal and to an undisguised anti-humanism. The portrayal of reality, in other words, is distorted and distortion becomes an inseparable part of the portrayal of reality.

Interestingly, this dichotomy between modernism and realism both links Lukács's thinking with Habermas's, and severs it definitively from de Man's. De Man's reading of Lukács's *Theory of the Novel*, for example, subordinates the content of his argument (the story-stuff, or what Victor Sklovskij called 'motivation' - 'the elements comprising the material it uses'[27]) to the terminological, rhetorical, systemic and perspectival elements of its construction. Generally, these include 'a pre-Hegelian terminology, but a post Nietzschean rhetoric, with a deliberate tendency to substitute general and abstract systems for concrete examples' and the perspective of 'a mind that claims to have reached such an advanced degree of generality that it can speak, as it were, for the novelistic consciousness itself.'[28] These elements of construction are caught in an interaction which rests precisely on the relationship between philosophy and literature. De Man draws a chiasmic philosophical/literary comparison between Lukács and Hegel: on the one hand, the philosophical and literary conjoin at the level of *fabula* as Lukács's novel and Hegel's Spirit relate the histories of their own respective journey's. However, this conflation of the literary and the philosophical is overturned at the level of the *sujet* as Hegel's Spirit acquires unquestionable authority in attaining 'a full understanding of its own being', while Lukács's novelistic consciousness is never so certain: '...being caught in its own contingency, it remains a mere phenomenon without regulative power.'[29]

The value of Lukács's thinking is in not succumbing so easily to what de Man calls the 'urge for totality': his theory of the novel retains the dual themes of estranged reality and the totality of inwardness, articulating them structurally as irony. De Man seizes on how irony as a structural category conflicts with, but is nevertheless made to represent the imitation of reality. Although Lukács registers the dangers of 'inwardness for its own sake' - since parts and wholes are brought together conceptually rather than organically, in an 'ever-suspended' relationship - he does not develop a 'genuine hermeneutic of the novel'. In fact he does quite the opposite, which is to reject out of hand a hermeneutic theory of language based on inwardness (such as, for example, phenomenology which pits a right-wing epistemology against a left-wing ethics). Nevertheless, as de Man points out, Lukács's rejection of all aspects of organicism is not consistent: if homogeneous unity is impossible at the level of inwardness, it is recovered in time conceived as a unifying *duree* capable of reconciling ironic discontinuities. Thus Lukács's earlier advance on Hegel is clawed back as this theory of time, which is also a theory of history, is conceived of at the level of *fabula*: all of the structural complexities apparent at the level of the *sujet* when the issue was the question of the modern self, become reified to the very extent that tense structures are ignored as temporality is reduced to a simple flow. Consequently, it is in the early Lukács that the 'urge for totality' - which in Lukács's case will become his theory of realism - can first be discerned.

What this analysis misses is, again, a very 'paradoxical dialectic' found in romantic poetics in which the qualitatively different realms of the phenomenal and the material are brought together in a so-called synthesis. This happens with historical discourses which generalise by articulating together entirely incompatible entities such as 'modern' and 'literature': a notion of historical time as a single, coherent, causal and evolutionary process moving progressively from one stage to another is combined with existential time understood as a form of spontaneity.[30] This spontaneous existential time is cancelled or contradicted in different ways, but never capable of being drawn into synthetic union with the forms of its representation in literature, or by such forms of historical representation as would seek to understand it as part of a process of developing spirit based on the trope of reflection or, on the other hand, as an unfolding of a history of ideas. For de Man, these devices create the *illusion* of a parasitic relationship between theory and practice (an inevitable and unavoidable error). Whenever the term 'modernity' is employed as a value in itself, rather than as designating the particular contents of the contemporary, it is a ploy, but one that has the value of partly restoring the link between literary theory and literary praxis.

Because the character of modernity is complicated by the diverse means and manners of representation, any conceptual definition will necessarily negate the concept, not in a Hegelian sense where there is a negation of negation that still somehow leaves you in the conceptual realm, or as a negative dialectic in Adorno's sense. This sort of negation is paradoxical, the self-contradiction of the concept, or 'the manner in which it discovers the impossibility of being modern.'[31] This *discovery* occurs as a consequence of the structure of the concept: its temporality makes the process of referring it to a fixed single linguistic event very difficult.

De Man turns to Nietzsche in order to analyse what happens when, as he says, 'a genuine impulse toward modernity collides with the demands of a historical consciousness or a culture based on the disciplines of history'. Nietzsche's text 'Of the Use and Misuse of History for Life' starts precisely by criticising the conjoining of the terms 'modernity' and 'history' in the German academic discourse of his time, a conjoining that makes modernity a way of describing a *state* of mind rather than, as it should be, a temporal term linked with 'life' and the ability to forget all that precedes the present. Rather than modernity consisting of a culmination and solidification of the past in the present, it is a rejection of the past born out of a desire for pure presence which precipitates a new beginning through an authentic throwing (of oneself) into action:

> Thus defined, modernity and history are diametrically opposed to each other in Nietzsche's text. Nor is there any doubt as to his commitment to modernity, the only way to reach the meta-historical realm in which the rhythm of one's existence coincides with that of the eternal return.[32]

This radical differentiating of modernity from history is certainly the surface desire of Nietzsche's text: however, on de Man's reading, it never really succeeds in disentangling itself from a sense of historical causality. To temporalise modernity as 'life' must include the 'temporal experience of human mutability', which in Nietzsche's is presented as a kind of 'pessimistic wisdom', the deeply historical experience of passing that is neither forgettable nor separable from the present. Hence it is that the existential time with which he seeks to cancel or forget history can only operate dialectically on itself: however adamant Nietzsche's denial of history, 'the text leads him irrevocably' to the discovery that 'the rejection of the past is not so much an act of forgetting as a critical judgement directed against himself'.[33] Nietzsche advocates that the student have the strength to indict, condemn and severe himself from the past for its injustices: this act of judgement would certainly be a parricide of sorts, though not the type of sacrificial killing that would engender a totemic sense of community as it does with Freud. Nietzsche's text advocates disregarding what he calls 'established pieties' and the activity of brutally attacking and rooting out the past in order to allow the present to live. The process is one of forgetting and then an active unforgetting which elicits the clarity needed for insight into the violence and weakness historically conditioning human affairs. This paradoxical forgetting and unforgetting and the violent destruction of the past is necessary for two reasons: because it is impossible to entirely extricate oneself from the past, and because there is an imperative to create a new past.

There is a determinism in Nietzsche's typically modern gesture insofar as forgetting the past and recreating a past implicates modernism in the motion of history. More than this, modernism becomes the *engendering* force of history and so part of 'a generative scheme that extends far back into the past.' In this, history and life cannot be extricated from each other: history depends on modernism's radical renewal for its continuance, but this dependence puts history in a situation of infinite regression, infinitely conquered by the radical condition of its own renewal. When Nietzsche confronts the paradox of his call for the 'truly new, powerful, life-giving, and original', that is that even his own text is part of this regressive historical process, he delegates the responsibility for renewal to 'youth' who, like himself, will not be able to achieve a renewal through self-forgetting. For de Man it is this aporetic predicament that constitutes modern modernity: 'Modernity and history' he says, 'seem condemned to being linked together in a self-destroying union that threatens the survival of both.'[34]

De Man links this analysis of modern modernity with the specificity of literature, which, for him is always modern. Writer's of literature - unlike writer's of history who remain remote from their object - depend on the past but are always actively engaged with the 'new' which destroys anything that interferes with its performativity. However, although literature is possessed with a desire for 'pure immediacy', something in the structure of this assertion seems to introduce rhetorical devices that specifically put the possibility of being modern into question. How is it, de Man asks,

> that a specific and important feature of a literary consciousness, its desire for modernity, seems to lead outside literature into something that no longer shares this specificity, thus forcing the writer to undermine his own assertions in order to remain faithful to his vocation?[35]

Although for de Man, literary consciousness is inherently modern insofar as its specificity is constituted through its desire for newness, to embrace the 'modern' as a descriptive term (especially in relation to the ancients), not only indicates a lack of literary sensibility on the part of the critic, but carries the critic into a discourse that is not literary: evaluations of modern literature which are detached (as with Fontenelle objective, scientific, historical *perfectibilité*) or committed (such as Perrault's 'technological man') are couched in discourses that 'lead away from literary understanding'.[36]

This uncritical fascination with the present seems to be characteristic of most modern writers. Baudelaire's work, like Nietzsche's, suppresses memory of anteriority, with imagery that evokes new beginnings, the *tabula rasa* of pure perceptual immediacy, meanwhile cancelling this pure presence in the mode of its representation. Severing the present from a pernicious and threatening past nevertheless preserves the form of extended time. For de Man Baudelaire's description of Constantin Guys, as a man of action and an observer and recorder of events, is a case in point. Baudelaire's analysis of Guy's work is characteristic of the so-called modern. The improvisational style is a conscious attempt to repeatedly capture the instantaneous present, to postpone the final closure of the form so as to 'outrun time, to achieve a swiftness that would transcend the latent opposition between action and form.[37]

What is effectively at stake here is the status of the modern as the so-called ability of literature to 'move outside art', and to inhabit the present as the absolute facticity of the new. In de Man's reading, this nostalgia for the present, and equally the ability to forget or repress the knowledge of the ephemeral and phantom character of the self manifests as literature's nostalgia for a specificity, a specificity which involves it in a movement away from itself, and a second movement that returns it to itself. In other words, what characterises the modern is literature's insatiable desire to move away from its centre, a desire that inevitably fails: the desire for the purely new of presence inevitably involves a return to itself, but this cannot be understood in a temporal frame. Both the movement away and the return occur simultaneously. As Walter Benjamin says, '...ambiguity is the law of the dialectic brought to a standstill'.

Habermas's counter to de Man would be that the discourses of *posthistoire* cannot be reduced to aesthetics. In fact, as stated earlier, there are two forms: the first is motivated by this neoconservative evolutionary social-scientific functionalist model of modernisation which posits the so-called 'dissolution of the internal links between the concept of modernity and the self understanding of modernity gained within the horizon of Western reason'.[38] The theoretical problem in this version is that ignoring this conceptual horizon means that research into modernisation is directed toward 'the husk of self-understanding that appears to be overtaken' rather than toward the 'unchecked dynamism of societal modernisation'.[39] The second version emerges in the area of aesthetics and conflates the distinctive domains of culture and society: here the distinctiveness of the emergence of Occidental rationalism that Weber first observes is explained away as merely the 'will to instrumental mastery'. In other words, this version does not make a distinction between the secularisation of Western *culture* (in which cultural spheres of value - empirical sciences, autonomous arts, theories of morality and law - take shape within independent learning processes driven by their respective inner logic) and the development of new structures of *society* in accordance with the institutionalisation of 'purposive-rational economic and administrative action' (the coupling of capitalist enterprise and bureaucratic state apparatuses which operate in tandem).[40] For Habermas, the critical force of this exposure of reason as the mere will to power is that it 'shakes the iron cage in which the spirit of modernity has been objectified in societal form';[41] however, such 'primordial anarchism', and the mortification of narratives of reason-governed social progress which issue from it, make it logically impossible to attend to actual social progress.

In this very useful description of the social-scientific functionalist and philosophical aesthetic 'postmodernisms', Habermas clearly distinguishes between two theories of the 'end of history' which seemingly work in tandem, blindly ignoring the conceptual horizon within which 'the self understanding of European modernity' has been formed. However, the claim I want to make here is that Habermas too easily conflates the social scientific critique and the philosophical aesthetic anarchistic critique together under the rubric 'postmodern'. De Man's thinking, for example, which might on a superficial reading be grouped within the 'primordial anarchism' of aesthetically driven critiques, has not ignored the conceptual horizon in which the self understanding of European modernity was formed. Indeed, the very significance that he gives to so-called Romantic writers is an indication that he takes this conceptual horizon very seriously indeed. In fact, the critique of 'romanticism' as an institutionalised historical concept that reacts to rationalisation processes forms a great deal of de Man's thinking. As his work of the 50's and 60's clearly indicates, reading these writers at the level of procedures, rather than motivation, reveals an alternative agenda to that of reconciling mind and nature, and in Habermas's terms returning European thought to what he calls a form of traditionalism. This agenda suggests not counter-Enlightenment thinking, but a struggle with the nature of consciousness itself. This struggle inevitably leads to poetic speculation on the relationship between mind and language, and how the necessities of language thwart the intentions of consciousness as freedom.

So both Habermas and de Man single out aesthetic theorising on modernity as a source of much wrong thinking. For Habermas, Baudelaire wrongly fuses aesthetic and historical experience of modernity: the experience of modern involves the problem of grounding in an acute way. With the breakdown of the realm of everyday life, subjectivity becomes decentred, which changes the horizon of temporal experience, reducing it to the temporal horizon of the decentred subject. Hence the modern work of art occurs at the intersection of the actual and the eternal. This actuality, however, is self-consuming as it can no longer put itself in opposition to history as a shape. In this experience, confirmation is found as the aesthetic past of a future present. Hence the temporality of the modern manifests as a flash - its appearance and its collapse appear simultaneously. And herein is the link between modernity and fashion or mode: the concept of beauty exists in the interface between mode and eternal meaning. It is in this way that the authentic work of art is radically bound to the moment of its emergence. The flash stops the flow of trivialities as the eternal and the actual come into conflict - eternal beauty comes about only in the mode of the contemporary. The function of the dandy is to look for modernity, to cause surprise by using the extraordinary to expose the extraordinary, 'to distil eternal from the transitory'.

So, for de Man modernity is not to be understood as merely an accumulation of background influences, as occurs in conservative versions of literary history. Nor is it simply the will to instrumental mastery, as advocates of the mortification of the grand narrative would have it.[42]

The 'modern' exists in absolute antithesis to 'tradition'. As de Man says, the true antithesis is between this theory of history and those modern writers and philosophers who

> ...have made human consciousness the centre of their concern and language the medium of their exploration.[43]

In other words, the problematics of consciousness and language supersede the possible synthesis of phenomenal and material domains.

De Man's turn to *aesthesis* refocuses the problem of reality vs. appearances (arguably the organising principle of Western philosophy since Plato), first as the ironic polarity of inner consciousness vs. language,[44] and then, in his later work, with the polarity of mode vs. meaning in the realm of linguistics. On this reading, dialectic is not prohibited, as it is with the two versions of the *posthistoire* outlined by Habermas; however, the parameters of its felicity are strictly delimited by sphere. In line with Habermas's own thinking, de Man reads two different spheres of concern, but rather than these being culture and society, they are those of form and content. Form involves issues such as the 'how' of representation: they include intentionality, arc pragmatic, assume a subjective freedom; content involves the 'what' of representation, is concerned with reference, oriented toward the hermeneutics of understanding. Although the problematics of representation involve the overlapping of spheres of form and content, they do so independently: form and content are not antitheses, they are contradictory, different in kind. Hence dialogue can occur in the domain of mode (form) and in the domain of meaning (content), but it cannot occur between mode and meaning. Equally, these mutually exclusive spheres exist *necessarily* together.

This clarity with regard to the conditions for dialectic *potentially* provides a clearing for a doubled domain - one that includes *both* moral norms and ethical identities; however, the political potential in this diremptive ethics is inevitably undermined by an aesthetic ideology directed toward (perhaps necessarily) communicative felicity. Viewed from this perspective, the conflicting either/or opposition between a relativising pure historicism and the absolutism of transcendentalism which Habermas sees as organising the failures of modernity ('the one side carries the burden of self-referential, pragmatic contradictions and paradoxes that violate our need for consistency; the other side is burdened with a foundationalism that conflicts with our consciousness of the fallibility of human knowledge'), is not an either/or opposition, but an unavoidable ontological crisis. Whereas this 'unavoidable experience' of crisis is, for Habermas, definitive of modernity, linked with the life world and marking the opportunity for exploring 'a third path' to overcoming,[45] the trajectory of de Man's thinking makes this ontological dilemma, ultimately, a linguistic condition, a condition upon which the very possibility of criticism rests.

NOTES AND REFERENCES

1. Hans Robert Jauss, *Toward an Aesthetic of Reception*, trans. Timothy Bahti, Brighten, The Harvester Press Ltd., 1982, p. 5.
2. David Hoy, 'Splitting the Difference: Habermas's Critique of Derrida' in *Habermas and the Unfinished Project of Modernity*, ed. by Passerin d'Entreves and Benhabib, Oxford: Blackwell's 1996, p. 124.
3. Karl Marx, 'The Destiny of Capitalism' from *Capital*, in *Marxism: Essential Writings*, ed. David Mclellan, Oxford: Oxford University Press, pp. 49-51.
4. Matei Calinescu, *Five Faces of Modernity*, Durham: Duke University Press, 1987, p. 13.
5. Peter Osbourne, *The Politics of Time: Modernity and Avant-Garde*, London: Verso, 1995, p. 9.
6. Christopher Norris, *Against Relativism: Philosophy of Science, Deconstruction, and Critical Theory*, Manchester: Manchester University Press, 1997, pp. 70- 81.
7. Jurgen Habermas, *The Philosophical Discourse of Modernity*, trans. by Frederick Lawrence, Oxford: Blackwell, 1987, p. 7.
8. Paul de Man, 'The Resistance to Theory' in *Yale French Studies*, 63 (1982), p. 363.
9. Jonathan Swift, *The Battle of the Books*, ed. by Angus Ross and David Woolley, Oxford: Oxford University Press, 1984, pp. 1-22.
10. Jauss makes the point that previous to the Enlightenment two views of art history prevailed - one which singularly traced the transformation of style in relation to political changes and the other of which proposed plural historical paradigms based on determining contextual factors ascertained from 'sources of sources' worked through the lives of authors (Jauss, 1982, 47-48).
11. Jacques Derrida, *Of Grammatology*, trans. Gayatri Chakravorty Spivak, John Hopkins University Press, 1976, p. 107.
12. Jurgen Habermas, *The Philosophical Discourse of Modernity*, trans. Frederick Lawrence, Oxford: Blackwell, 1987, p. 192.
13. 'Resistance to Theory' in *Yale French Studies*, 63, (1982), pp. 355-371.
14. *Ibid.*, p. 365.
15. In *The Positivity of the Christian Religion* (1795-6), Hegel claims that Christian Orthodoxy became positive despite Jesus' opposition to the positivity of Judaism for two reasons: first, because of the need to compromise for the purposes of ingratiating itself with and assimilating

itself to Judaism; secondly, the citizens of Greece and the Roman Republic were made self-seeking individuals susceptible to authoritarian rule by the Roman Empire.

16. *Ibid.*, p. 75.
17. Jürgen Habermas, *The Philosophical Discourse of Modernity*,
18. de Man, 'Sign and Symbol in Hegel's Aesthetics' in *Aesthetic Ideology*, Minneapolis: University of Minnesota Press, 1996.
19. *Ibid.*, Paul de Man, 1996, p. 94.
20. *Ibid.*, Paul de Man, 1996, p. 104
21. Francis Fukuyama, 'The End of History?' The National Interest 16 (Summer 1989), 3-18.
22. George, Lukács, *The Historical Novel*, Merlin Press Ltd., 1962.
23. *Op. cit.* p. 143.
24. Jürgen Habermas, *The Philosophical Discourse of Modernity*, Oxford: Blackwell, 1987, p. 2.
25. Paul de Man, 'Georg Lukács's "Theory of the Novel"' in *Blindness and Insight*, Minneapolis: University of Minnesota Press, 1971, p. 52.
26. *Ibid.*, p. 3.
27. Boris Eichenbaum, 'Introduction to the Formal Method' in *Literary Theory: An Anthology*, ed. by Julie Rivkin and Michael Ryan, Oxford: Blackwell, 1998, p. 12.
28. *Op. cit.*, de Man, 1971, p. 52.
29. *Op. cit.*, de Man, 1971, p. 53.
30. Paul de Man, *Blindness and Insight*, p. 142.
31. Paul de Man, 'Literary History and Literary Modernity' in *Blindness and Insight*, Minneapolis: University of Minnesota Press, 1971, p.?
32. *Ibid.*, p. 148.
33. *Ibid.*, p. 150.
34. Paul de Man, *op. cit.*, p. 151.
35. *Ibid.*
36. *Ibid.*, p. 156.
37. *Ibid.*, p. 158.
38. *Op. cit.*, Habermas, 1985, p. 3. Habermas cites Arnold Gehlen and Gottfried Benn as among those who advocate the 'counting up of supplies' because modern culture has 'crystallised', bringing the history of ideas to a conclusion. He also notes that H.E. Holthusen suggests that Gehlen may have borrowed the term posthistoire from his intellectual ally Henrik de Man, Paul de Man's uncle and mentor. The inclusion of this speculation suggests that Habermas thinks the connection is important. However accurate this link might be, in what follows I will clearly distinguish Paul de Man's thinking from the circle of influences that is here being drawn.
39. *Ibid.*, pp. 3-4.
40. *Ibid.*, p. 4.
41. *Ibid.*, p. 4.

42. In many ways Ronald Bush's essay 'Paul de Man, Modernist' is provocative but it means nothing in de Man's own terms. *Theoretical Issues in Literary History*, ed. by David Perkins, Cambridge Mass. and London: Harvard University Press, 1991.
43. *Op. cit.*, p. 143.
44. Paul de Man's reading of this polarity in Rousseau is crucial here.
45. Jurgen, Habermas, 'Questions and Counterquestions' in *Critical Theory: A Reader*, ed. by Douglas Tallack, Hemel Hempstaed: Harvester, 1995, pp. 388-389.

CONTRIBUTORS

Abhai Maurya, Department of Slavonic and Finno-Ugrian Studies, University of Delhi.

Claudia Wenner, formerly Visiting Lecturer in German, Department of Germanic and Romance Studies, University of Delhi.

Dilip Loundo, holds the Brazilian Chair, Goa University, Goa.

Dominique de Gasquet, formerly Visiting Lecturer in French, Department of Germanic and Romance Studies, University of Delhi.

Kathleen Kerr, School of Humanities and Social Sciences, English Division, University of Sunderland, Sunderland.

Kavita Bhatia, Centre of German Studies, Jawaharlal Nehru University, New Delhi.

Krishnan Unni P., Department of English, Deshbandhu College, University of Delhi.

Lalita Subbu, Department of English, Hindu College, University of Delhi.

Margit Köves, General Fellow, Indian Council of Philosophical Research, New Delhi.

Namwar Singh, literary critic, former Professor of Hindi, Centre of Indian Languages, Jawaharlal Nehru University, New Delhi.

Rekha Basu, Department of Philosophy, Hindu College, University of Delhi.

Sharmistha Lahiri, Department of Germanic and Romance Studies, University of Delhi.

Shaswati Mazumdar, Department of Germanic and Romance Studies, University of Delhi.

Tapan Basu, Department of English, Hindu College, University of Delhi.

Virginia Nieto-Sandoval Millán, Research Scholar working on Indian art, Indian Council of Social Science Research, New Delhi.